The Cheap Video Cookbook

by

Don Lancaster

Howard W. Sams & Co., Inc.
4300 WEST 62ND ST. INDIANAPOLIS, INDIANA 46268 USA

Indianapolis, Indiana 46268

FIRST EDITION
FOURTH PRINTING—1982

International Standard Book Number: 0-672-21524-1
Library of Congress Catalog Card Number: 78-51584

Printed in the United States of America.

Preface

The word "breakthrough" is often abused, especially in the field of hobby computer electronics. But what else could you call a new video display technique that so dramatically slashes the cost of getting words, op-code, and graphics out of a microcomputer and into a television set that it is bound to displace most of the traditional methods of video display?

With the ideas in this book, you can replace a $200 video board or much of a $500 to $1500 terminal with a single sided pc board that can cost as little as $20 and contain only seven integrated circuits. And those are real exotic ICs to boot—mostly things like hex inverters and baby PROMs.

At the same time you realize such a ludicrous hardware reduction, you gain incredible flexibility, thanks to total software control of just about everything in this new cheap video world. And all this with surprisingly few words of software coding. Your same hardware does alphanumeric and graphics displays in virtually any format.

These new cheap video methods also uniquely solve the traditional problems of getting a microprocessor to go fast enough to time a video display and getting the display bandwidth needs low enough that a relatively unmodified tv set can handle the output attractively. While the book leans heavily toward the 6500 and 6800 microprocessor systems, you can go outside these families and apply cheap video ideas to many other microcomputers.

Above all, cheap video does not mean poor video. Things like a 24-line by 80-character display with a full scrolling Cursor, complete interlace, double stuffing, and memory repacking is easily done, and can be made totally transparent while still keeping a lot of time and space for other programs to run simultaneously. Things like color graphics displays, high-resolution black and white graphics, full interlace, and so on, are all easily done with these new cheap video methods.

The first chapter begins with the basics to determine what is really needed for alphanumeric and graphics video display systems. We look at the design principles of cheap video and then check into commercial examples of ready-to-go circuits and kits. From there, we go into the secrets behind cheap video, particularly the all-important *upstream tap* and the *Scan microinstruction.*

The second chapter shows you how to design cheap video software. Software for Scan microinstructions. Software for alphanumeric programs of virtually any format. Software for color and black-and-white high-resolution graphics displays. Software for editors and full-performance scrolling Cursors. And software for graphics loaders. Important new software designs you will find are hardware-free interlace, character density improving *double stuffing* and *memory repacking* methods for efficient use of 80-character line lengths.

Hardware is presented in Chapter 3. Here the interface circuitry you will need between your computer and tv set is introduced on a block-by-block basis. We start with the decoding and Scan microinstruction controlling PROMs and work through the data-to-video conversion, high-frequency timing, sync and positioning circuits, video-enhancement (bandwidth reduction) techniques, and output circuitry. After this, you will find the detailed interfacing of a KIM-1 microcomputer, followed by complete details of adding a new video input to your conventional tv set.

The nuts-and-bolts construction and debug details on the TVT 6⅝ follow in Chapter 4, along with complete details of four modules that program your TVT 6⅝ for upper- and lower-case alphanumerics and high-resolution and color graphics. Full size printed-circuit layouts and everything you need to build, debug, and modify your own cheap video system is included.

Chapter 5 covers *transparency,* or ways to compute and display simultaneously. One of the real surprises is the high throughput you can have and still be transparent. For instance, you can do a 12×80 display and transparently save almost two thirds of the available computer time to run BASIC or some other high-level language. Most useful display formats can save well over half the computer time for other uses.

The appendix gives you IC pinouts, ASCII coding, number conversion chart, and duplicates of all pc patterns.

DON LANCASTER

Cheap video pc boards, kits, assembled units, and program tapes are available commercially from:

PAIA Electronics
1020 West Wilshire Blvd.
Box 14359
Oklahoma City, OK 73114
(405) 842-5480

A catalog and price list will be sent on request. Dealer inquiries are invited.

This book is dedicated to the Yeahbut.

Contents

CHAPTER 5

CHAPTER **1**

Some Basics

A *microprocessor-based video display* can be any scheme to get words or pictures out of a microcomputer and onto a tv screen or other video display. If they happen to be working with a microprocessor or microcomputer, any of the traditional video terminals "glass teletypes," or tv typewriters (tvt's) are all microprocessor-based video displays.

But, our interests here will be in something newer, far cheaper, and far simpler than these traditional approaches to video display. This new *cheap video* approach to microprocessor-based video display gets you from your microcomputer to a plain old tv set with practically no hassle, cost, or complexity. The method combines an absolute minimum of dedicated hardware with some operating software commands, and two new concepts called an *upstream tap* and a *Scan microinstruction.* The final result of this new architectural approach to cheap video display gives us incredible flexibility and potential at very low cost.

For instance, the methods we will be looking at in detail will let you display over 2000 upper and lower case ASCII characters on a largely or totally unmodified tv set *with stock video bandwidth,* at a cost of around $20, and using only seven integrated circuits worth of dedicated hardware on a small *single-sided* pc card. You can use almost the same circuit to build a 256 × 256 graphics display instead, totally controlled by your microcomputer. Full-color graphics of somewhat lower resolution is equally easy to do.

If you are into word processing, the cheap video ideas of this book give you extreme flexibility. Double and triple Cursor systems; adding and removing words, lines, and paragraphs; rearrangement; justification and hyphenation; and so on, are easy to provide because cheap video gives the display memory to the microcomputer at any time for any reason.

The methods we will show you solve the dilemma of how to get a microprocessor with an execution time of several microseconds per instruction to *directly* provide all of the timing signals needed for a tv display. This eliminates completely the need for complex stand-alone dedicated-system timing and cursor-control circuits. The cheap video methods also drastically reduce the bandwidth needs of a video display. This lets you stuff 64 or even 80 high-resolution characters per line through an ordinary rf modulator or a tv set with a normal video bandwidth. Full interlace is inherent in our methods and the ability to *double-stuff* characters is easy to pick up.

Cheap video is easily used for stand-alone terminal applications, where a single dedicated microprocessor and a few integrated circuits replace the dozens to hundreds previously used. But, our cheap video displays really shine when you simply tack cheap video onto a computer system that is already doing something else. For instance, a small plug-in card lets you display the contents of a KIM-1 microcomputer directly on your tv set, with an absolute minimum of modifications to either.

Change one small PROM memory and the same card can be used on most any 6500- or 6800-based computer system. Cheap video works with many other microprocessors but works best if you have at least 12 always-there and fully decoded address lines and can advance the program counter at a 1-microsecond (μs) rate.

Thanks to a plug-in module approach, you can make the *same* hardware work for graphics or alphanumerics or a combination of the two. You can add *transparency* techniques that let you run other programs and your display at the same time—without any apparent interruption to either. For instance, you can run a 12×80 character display and an Extended BASIC program together—with a continuous display and still keeping around two thirds of the normal computer time for the BASIC. The same transparency ideas work well for game displays and their move computation, or for the Cursor, character entry, and keyboard scanning involved in word-processing systems.

With a *memory repacking* scheme that is almost free, you can stash 40- and 80-character lines into your display memory with just about the same efficiency as binary line lengths. And, while not shown here, it is an easy matter to pick up HEX/ASCII conversion for op-code displays, end-of-line bell ringers, color modulators, gentle (crawling) Cursors, and loads of other add-ons for your own use, once you understand cheap video and what it can do for you.

THE RULES OF THE GAME

We have five *first principles* to cheap video:

1. Leave the existing microcomputer system nearly as you find it, making only a bare minimum of minor changes.
2. Use a plain old tv set, also leaving it nearly as you found it, again making only a bare minimum of minor changes.
3. Put some hardware between the microcomputer and the tv set that lets them talk to each other. Keep the hardware as simple and flexible as possible. Use PROMs as needed to give flexibility from μP system to system.
4. Add two key elements to the microprocessor architecture. One of these is a *Scan microinstruction* that sequentially addresses a block of memory under control of a PROM in the interface hardware. The second is an *upstream tap* that lets a block of memory output to the interface hardware, even, and particularly when that memory does NOT have control of the μP's data bus.
5. Use software and firmware sequences to control what the interface hardware is going to do.

What we really want to do is to eliminate anything at all between the microprocessor and the tv set. Since this is not quite possible, we reduce the size, cost, and the "dedicatedness" of our interface as much as we possibly can. Typically, an alphanumeric interface can end up with three hex inverters, two baby PROMs, a shift register, and a character generator.

SOME ARCHITECTURE

Fig. 1-1 shows the three key parts of a microprocessor-based video display. These parts are the *microprocessor* or microcomputer; a card of dedicated *interface hardware;* and the *tv set* or video monitor.

Characters or graphics to be displayed are usually stored in a portion of the *memory* of the microprocessor. Often, we will use one 8-bit word for a standard ASCII alphanumeric character and its possible Cursor. In a graphics display, the same 8-bit word may be used in any of several formats, with each stored bit representing one resolvable element on the display. The memory needs a simple modification before it can be used for video display. A new set of connections, called an *upstream tap,* must be added so the memory can output characters or symbols to the interface hardware even if it does NOT have data bus access to the microcomputer.

A MICROCOMPUTER HAS . . .

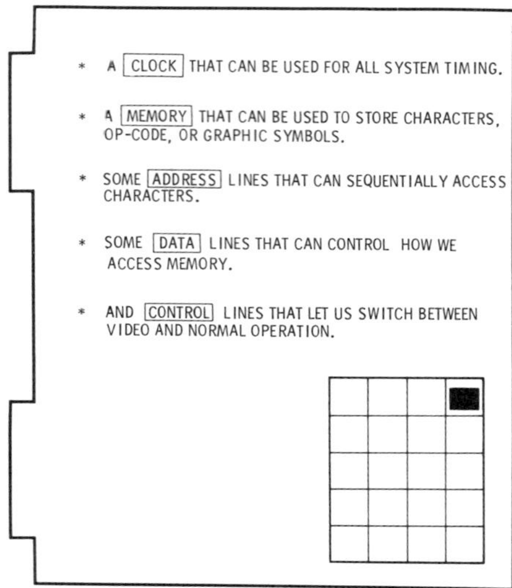

(A) Microprocessor-based video displays get us from here . . .

A TV SET NEEDS . . .

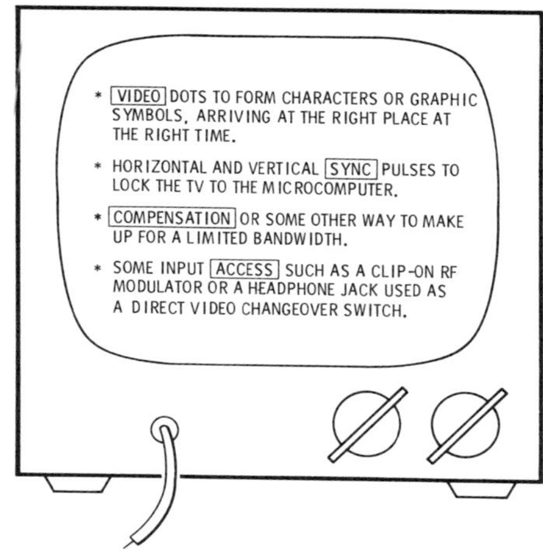

(B) . . . to here, with . . .

Fig. 1-1. Three key parts of a

Our interface hardware does two important jobs for us. On the computer side, it causes the microcomputer to access its display memory in just the right way so we receive characters in the right sequence and at the right time. On the tv side, the interface hardware delivers *composite video* that contains both bandwidth-enhanced characters and properly positioned horizontal- and vertical-synchronizing pulses.

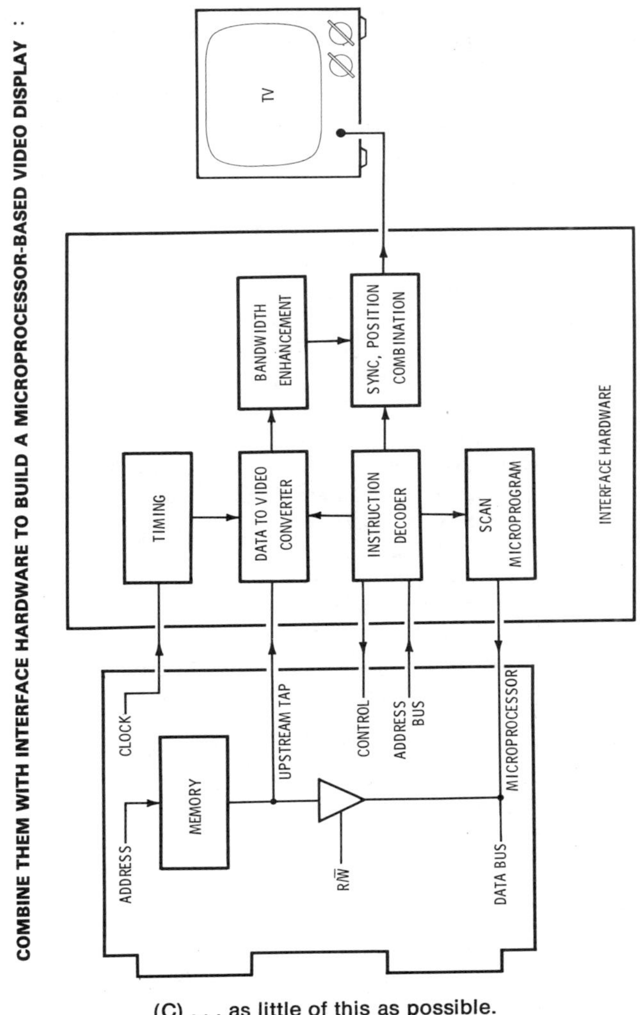

COMBINE THEM WITH INTERFACE HARDWARE TO BUILD A MICROPROCESSOR-BASED VIDEO DISPLAY :

(C) . . . as little of this as possible.

microprocessor-based video display.

To get the system to work, we load some *Scan software* into our microcomputer and run it. The Scan software causes the microcomputer and the interface hardware to talk to each other, Simpler versions of Scan software take up thirty to a hundred words of machine-language code. This is easily stored in memory or externally on cassette tape. The initial design of Scan software is extra tricky since you have to control exactly both what the computer is doing and precisely how long it is going to take to do it as well. Further, very limited times are available for some of the things the software has to do. We will be looking at software design in detail in the next chapter. Once designed and debugged, the Scan software is as simple and easy to use as any other short program would be.

The central controller of our interface hardware is called an *instruction decoder*. The instruction decoder decides what is to happen next. The instruction decoder is usually a small read only memory or PROM, and is customized to work with the particular microprocessor and address locations selected for your system. The decoder can activate a *Scan microprogram* that is a second small read only memory. The Scan microprogram in turn can cause the computer to sequentially address a block of memory words, typically spending one microsecond on each word. This results in a string of characters or graphics data being sent to the interface hardware, timed just as we need it for a horizontal character line or a horizontal line of graphic elements.

The Scan microprogram makes the microcomputer block-access memory on a 1-microsecond-per-character basis. The character words accessed go out our upstream tap and reach the interface hardware where they enter a box we call a *data-to-video converter*. For alphanumerics, the data-to-video converter is usually a dot-matrix character generator, combined with an external- or internal-serial video-shift register. For graphics, the data-to-video converter can be nothing more than a video-shift register, or it can combine a blanking gate or a data selector and a shift register for other graphics formats. The *raw video* output of the data-to-video converter in turn goes to a *bandwidth enhancer* that predistorts the video to anticipate how the tv set is going to try and mess it up with its limited bandwidth. One simple form of bandwidth enhancer widens the white portions of the display. The amount of widening is selected to produce the best compromise between sharpness, brightness, and uniformity.

Our instruction decoder has other tasks besides controlling the Scan microprogram. In an alphanumeric system, it tells the character generator which row of dots to work on. In graphics systems, it does the formatting and blanking for us. It also decides when horizontal or vertical-sync pulses are needed. These are used to lock the tv scan to the computer. Output-sync commands are routed to a positioning delay circuit and then to a *video combiner* where they are mixed with enhanced video to form a *composite-video* output. The composite video may be used as is for a monitor, can be internally offset for simple tv interface, or can drive an rf modulator or Class 1 tv device for clip-on rf entry.

We will be looking at much of the details of hardware design and television interface in Chapter 3.

In the simplest of video-display systems, the microcomputer takes turns computing and displaying, just like a keyboard monitor may take turns running and monitoring. In more elegant cheap video-display systems, you can gain partial to complete *transparency*, in which the computer can do other things at the same time that it is displaying. Transparency techniques are important enough that we will use all of Chapter 5 for them.

Our Scan program only causes words *already in memory* to appear on the screen. The Scan program does not care how the words got there in the first place. You put the characters or graphics into the memory with ordinary software any way you like. Your computer has total access to the display memory at any time for any reason. The only difference between the display memory and any other memory in your computer is the upstream tap; this the rest of the computer does not know about and need not use. Some very important advantages of immediate memory access are that you can load and dump the screen at incredible baud rates; you can easily edit and rearrange the contents of the screen; you can remove things from the screen, work on them, and replace them, often without needing additional storage; and you can rapidly update things like a real-time clock or a complex game quickly, easily, and without the "memory busy" access hassles of more traditional circuits.

A COMMERCIAL EXAMPLE

Before we check into the benefits and limitations of this exciting new display technique and investigate the key "secrets" behind it, let's take a quick look at a commercial system already available.

The TVT 6⅝ (Fig. 1-2) is a *Synergetics* design available commercially through PAIA Electronics, 1020 West Whilshire Boulevard, Oklahoma City, OK 73114, and several retail computer stores. You will find complete construction, design, and debug details on the TVT 6⅝ in Chapter 4.

This is a six integrated-circuit interface-hardware card. Its block diagram appears in Fig 1-3. A plug-in module of one or two additional ICs programs the TVT 6⅝ for its alphanumeric, graphics, or combined modes of operation. Four available modules include an

Fig. 1-2. TVT 6 5/8 Cheap Video System attached to KIM-1 Microcomputer. Cable at top delivers video to tv display.

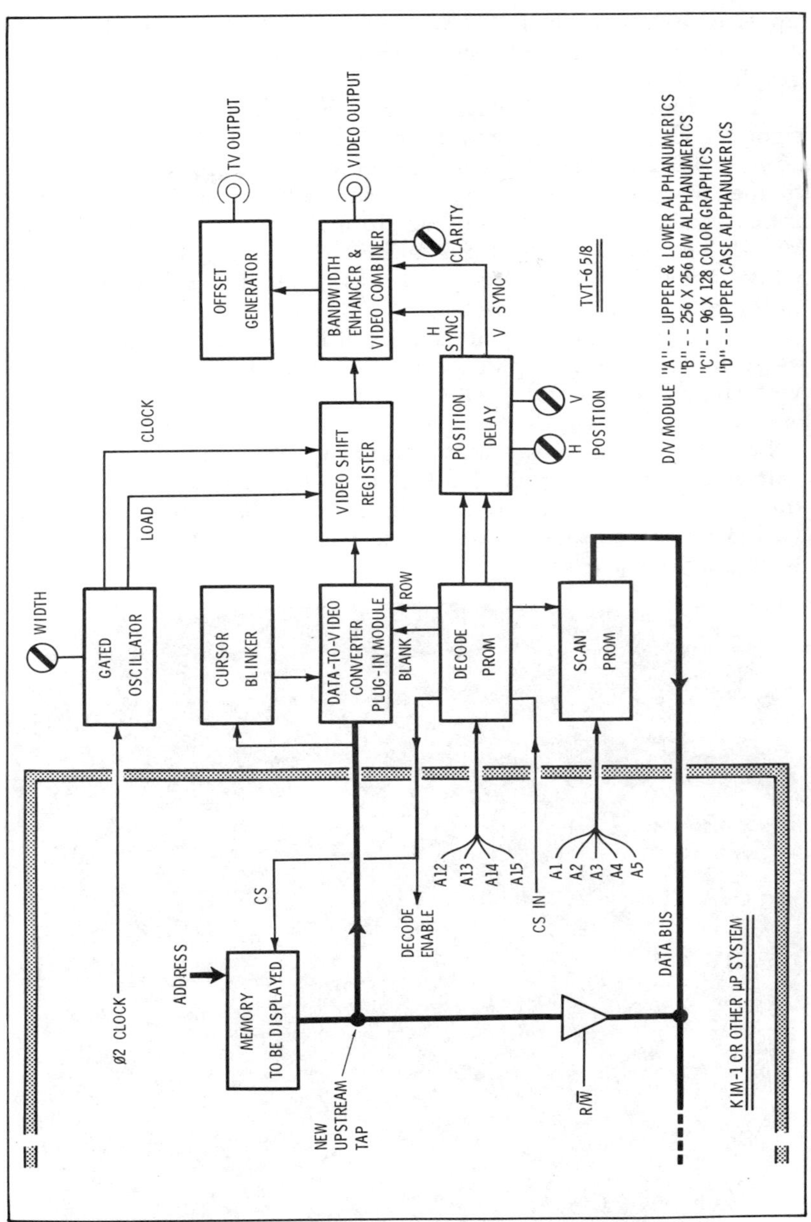

Fig. 1-3. TVT 6 5/8 uses plug-in submodules to select graphic or alphanumeric modes. Typical system uses seven ICs, can be built for as little as $20.

upper-case-only alphanumeric, combined upper- and lower-case alphanumeric, high resolution black and white graphics, and color graphics versions.

The alphanumeric-display formats that already have fully designed and debugged software include 1 × 40, 16 × 32, 16 × 40, 16 × 64, 32 × 64, 12 × 80, and 24 × 80 character groupings. Thanks to the total programmability, you can make virtually any display format you want. The graphics formats now available include 96 × 128 color, 128 × 128 black and white, and 256 × 256 black and white. Once again, there is practically no limit on format, thanks to the total software control.

On-card switches give you a choice of line length,Cursor visibility, video polarity, and graphics-response speed. Four controls set the vertical and horizontal positioning, the output enhancing clarity, and the graphics width.

Besides the Scan programs, software support includes full scrolling Cursor programs, graphics loaders, and others. Since almost everything is under software control, there are no hardware changes involved for extreme Cursor or editing complexity—all you do is add words to your programs.

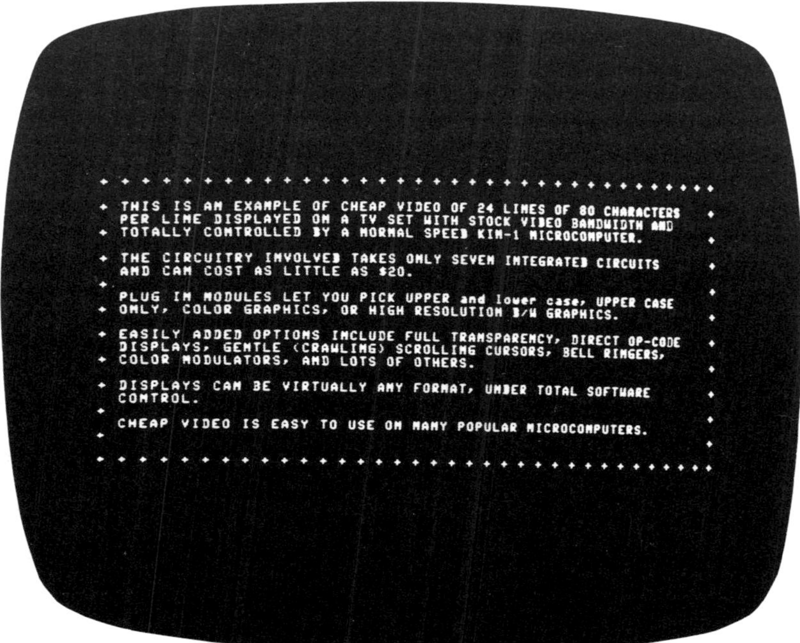

Fig. 1-4. Typical alphanumeric cheap video display.

Three typical display examples using the TVT 6$\frac{5}{8}$ are shown in Figs. 1-4 through 1-6.

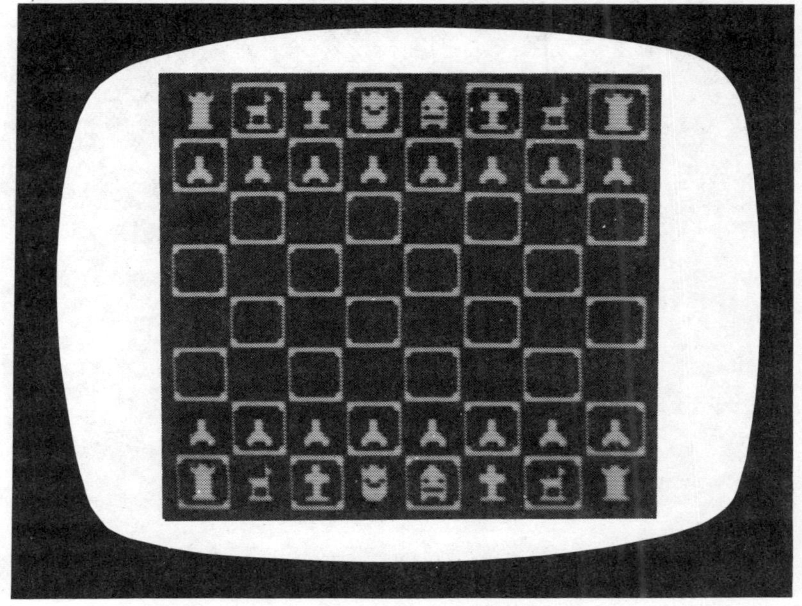

Fig. 1-5. Chess display using color graphics cheap video.

SOME SECRET FORMULAS

Much of what has been said so far sounds like we are speeding up a microprocessor more than is possible, or that we are stuffing too many characters into far too small a bandwidth, or perhaps we are forgetting that the sync signals a tv set needs must be very exactly specified and provided for, particularly for a stable and fully interlaced display.

To get around these obvious problems that have made earlier tvt and video display systems expensive and complicated, we have to pull some sneaky tricks. We can call these tricks the *secret formulas* behind our new cheap video displays. The details of how, why, and where we use these secrets appear later in the book. For now, let's take a quick look at some key secrets to our new cheap video techniques.

The Scan Microinstruction

Basically, you add a new instruction to the instruction set of your microcomputer called Scan. When you tell the microprocessor to

Fig. 1-6. High resolution black and white graphics display used for typography. Note full justification of characters.

scan, it goes to where you tell it to start and then causes the μP's internal *program counter* to appear on the address lines for a selected number of *sequential* clock cycles. For instance, if we are doing a 64-character line, our Scan instruction causes the address lines to start at some value and count up 64 counts by ones, binary-counter style. If we are using a 6500 or 6800 system with a 1-megahertz (MHz) clock, the Scan instruction advances us one count per microsecond for a total of 64 μs.

Fig. 1-7A shows the typical variation of a short portion of a 6502's address lines during a traditional program run. In general, the address line values advance. Sometimes the address lines advance once per microsecond, such as when the microcomputer is carrying out a two word immediate instruction such as "Load the Y register with the value AO." Sometimes the address lines advance only once each 2 μs. This happens with a one word immediate instruction such as "Clear the Carry bit" or "No Operation." Sometimes our address lines back up and repeat as the short loop in the middle shows; this is often the result of a relative branch causing a loop. And, sometimes, the address lines go out of range to pick up a page zero

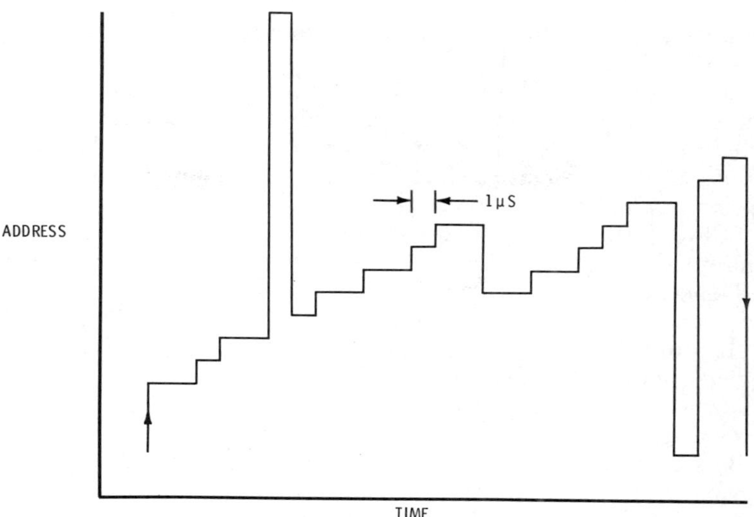

(A) Typical behavior of 6502 address bus during normal program.

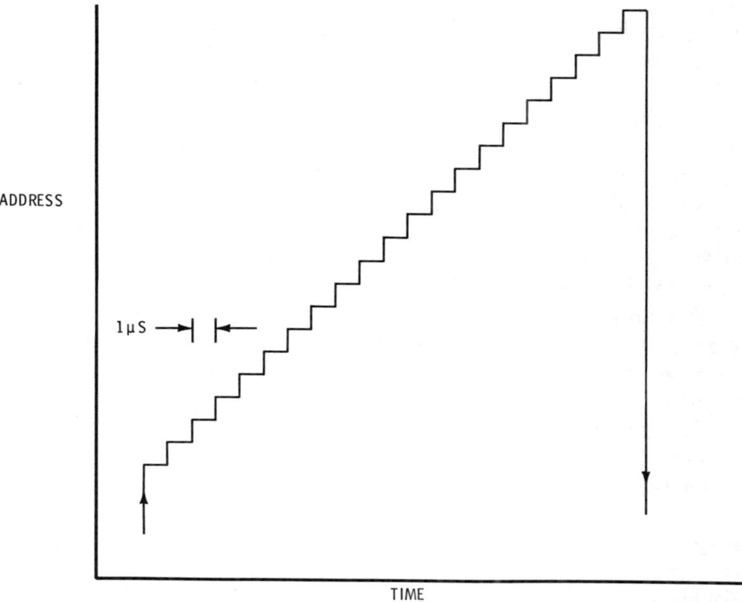

(B) Scan microinstruction forces the 6502 to advance addresses uniformly once each microsecond from starting address.

Fig. 1-7. Scan microinstruction is used to sequentially access rows of characters stored in memory.

address on the bottom or a higher page address during a memory read or write instruction.

In general, the address lines are an apparently random jumble of values. But note that sometimes the address lines advance at a 1-μs rate, even though our fastest usual instructions take 2 μs to execute. *Note also that the address lines are connected to all memory in the system at all times.*

In Fig. 1-7B, we have forced the microprocessor into a Scan mode, simply by using an external microprogram, counter, or interrupt sequence. This makes the address line start at some computed address and advance exactly a selected 64 counts, spending 1 μs on each count. For instance, we can give the command "Load the Y register with the value AO" repeating 31 times, followed by a "Return from Subroutine" command to get the 64 sequential counts as needed.

Be sure to note that this Scan instruction is *portable* in that we can move it around and use it almost anywhere we like. This lets us pick up different blocks of characters or lets us tell a character generator to work on a different row of dots for a particular character line. Usually we will *call* our Scan instruction by requesting a Jump to Subroutine that goes to an address that activates the instruction decoder and Scan microprogram in the interface hardware. The length of our Scan instruction is programmable, but the hardware and software must agree on the maximum possible Scan length. When the Scan instruction is completed, the return from subroutine jumps us back to wherever we happened to be in the main program.

During a Scan microinstruction, many strange and wondrous things might happen inside the microprocessor. We might, for instance, load an otherwise unused Y register with the op-code for "load Y," and repeat the operation for a total of 31 times. This admittedly makes absolutely sure that we have the Y register loaded before we do not use it. Here, at long last is a perfectly legal and major use for a write only memory. The key point is this—*No matter how strange or ridiculous the coding—IF IT WORKS, USE IT.* All we want to do during a Scan is advance the address line a selected number of characters at a one-per-microsecond rate starting with a computed address, nothing more. We do try to keep anything ridiculous that is going on during a Scan from wiping out anything we might need later, such as flags, the accumulator, pointers, the stack, or otherwise used registers.

Note particularly that we have used normal speed memories and normal operating frequencies during the Scan mode. While it may seem externally that the microprocessor is running at double speed, nothing the microprocessor needs or uses responds to this speed doubling. In fact, the Scan instruction actually takes many times *longer* than a normal instruction to execute. But the neat and handy thing is that during the entire long execution time, we have tricked the address bus into advancing at the right once-per-microsecond rate.

Even neater is the fact that our Scan microinstruction causes ALL memory in the machine to be addressed at the one-word-per-microsecond rate. While only the Scan Microprogram generator has *data*-bus access, every other memory in the machine is addressed the same way, with individual memory chip selects or enables preventing data-bus interference.

The Upstream Tap

An *Upstream Tap* is a new set of connections that go *directly* from the memory used for character storage to the interface hardware. It is of crucial importance that the display memory can output to the interface hardware when it does NOT have access to the data bus of the microcomputer.

Fig. 1-8 shows how a typical upstream tap is added. We have to have external and noninverting bus drivers present between the memory output and the "true" data bus. This is needed even if the memory chips used have common input/output data pins. These drivers may be already available on your system; if not, you can add them using a 74LS640 or something similar.

We also add some simple logic to provide either the usual chip select to the display memory or a new select called Scan Enable that is derived in the interface hardware. This lets your memory behave normally during usual computer operation and also enables it for *character output only* during a Scan. This logic can be a single AND gate which behaves in the circuit as a *negative logic* OR gate. It may also be included in the instruction decoder in the interface hardware. If your upstream tap goes directly to a MOS memory output pin, it should be kept physically short to minimize any capacitive loading. Long cables would slow down your memory. Upstream taps connected to bipolar or TTL outputs are not nearly as critical and can be longer.

Fetch-But-Do-Not-Execute Operation

A normal microprocessor instruction has two parts—the *fetch* where needed information is gathered, and the *execution* where the intended operation is carried out. *During a Scan microinstruction, we continuously fetch and never execute.* This lets us output characters at a rate that seems to be twice as fast as usual.

Fig. 1-9 shows how the Scan microinstruction and the upstream tap gang up to do this fetch-but-do-not-execute maneuver. The

Scan program makes the Scan microinstruction advance the microprocessor at a one-character-per-microsecond rate. The character memory sends characters out the upstream tap to the interface hardware for conversion to serial video. At no time does the microprocessor wait for an "answer" from the memory. The memory knows it is supposed to output characters to the interface and the interface

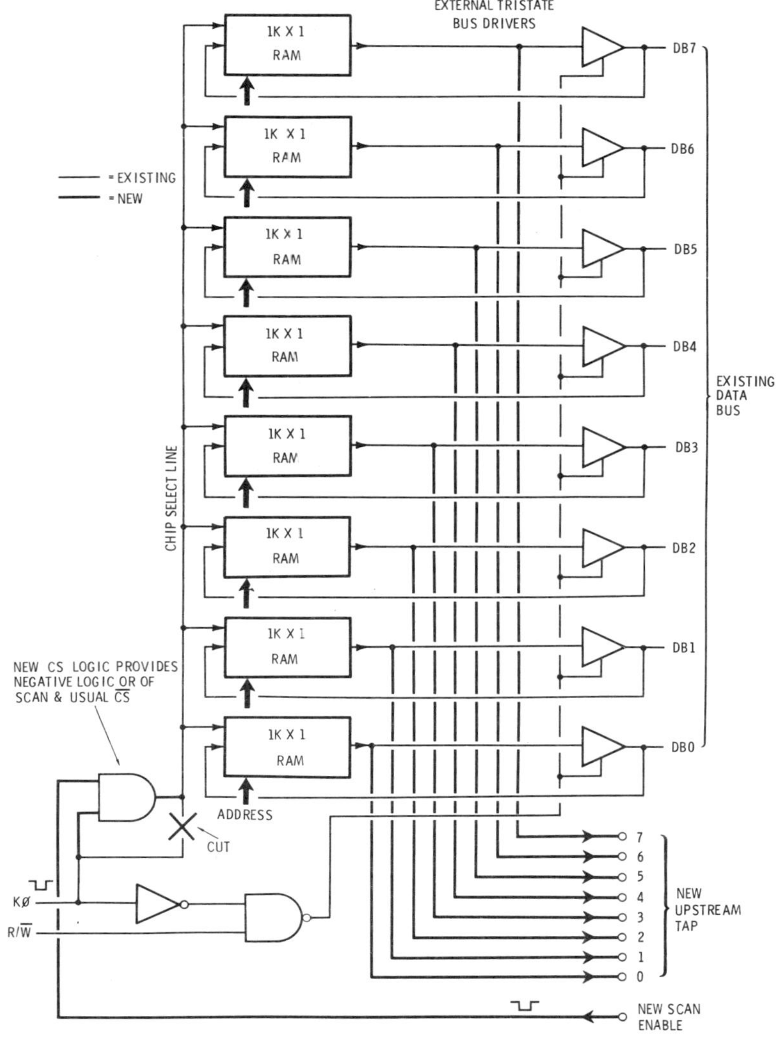

Fig. 1-8. Adding upstream tap to existing microprocessor memory.

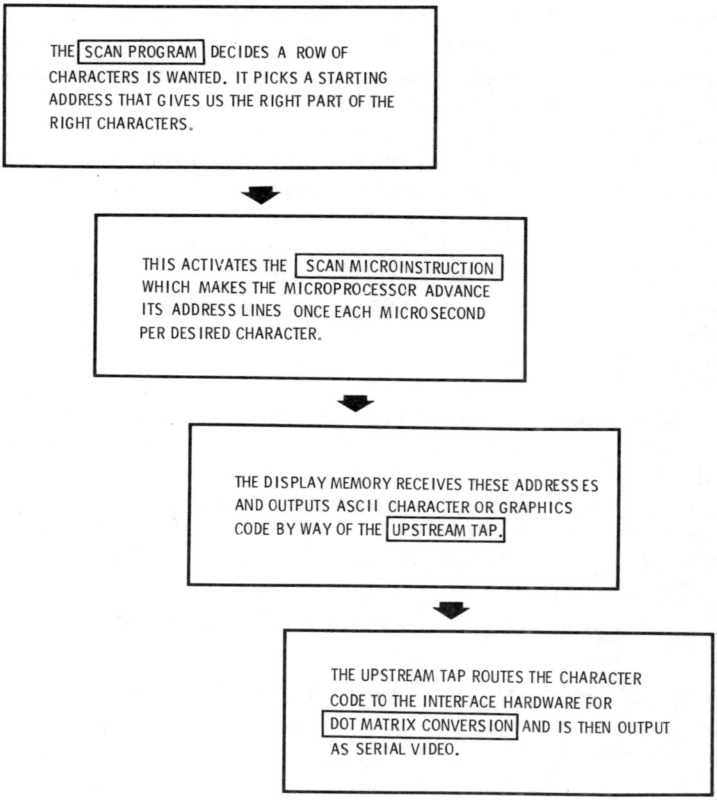

THE SCAN PROGRAM DECIDES A ROW OF CHARACTERS IS WANTED. IT PICKS A STARTING ADDRESS THAT GIVES US THE RIGHT PART OF THE RIGHT CHARACTERS.

↓

THIS ACTIVATES THE SCAN MICROINSTRUCTION WHICH MAKES THE MICROPROCESSOR ADVANCE ITS ADDRESS LINES ONCE EACH MICROSECOND PER DESIRED CHARACTER.

↓

THE DISPLAY MEMORY RECEIVES THESE ADDRESSES AND OUTPUTS ASCII CHARACTER OR GRAPHICS CODE BY WAY OF THE UPSTREAM TAP.

↓

THE UPSTREAM TAP ROUTES THE CHARACTER CODE TO THE INTERFACE HARDWARE FOR DOT MATRIX CONVERSION AND IS THEN OUTPUT AS SERIAL VIDEO.

Fig. 1-9. Scan microprogram and upstream tap work together to convert code in memory to video dots on tv screen.

knows it is to receive characters and knows what to do with them. The CPU, though, is ignorant of both and could not care less. It thinks it is busy loading its Y register with worthless data while all this is happening.

Constant One-Microsecond Character Times

All characters and graphics are chunks usually gotten at a one-per-microsecond rate. This happens regardless of how many characters are on a horizontal line. This gives us a minimum video bandwidth. It lets us stay within the usual bandwidth restrictions of an ordinary tv set or a clip-on rf modulator. It also gives us enough time to let the computer directly work on characters. Besides making the key scan microinstruction possible, this opens all sorts of new software and control possibilities. Our "raw" bandwidth needed ranges from 1.5 MHz for color graphics through 3 MHz for a 5 × 7 character to a maximum of 4 MHz for high resolution graphics. These values are further minimized with the bandwidth-enhancement circuit in the interface hardware.

One result of this once-each-microsecond constant time is that very long character lines may have to run with a reduced horizontal frequency. Up to 40 characters or its equivalent graphics are easily displayed at normal horizontal speeds. Longer character lines may mean a reduced horizontal frequency which takes simple hold and width modifications to the set in use. Thus, the 64- or 80-character lines may not be suitable for video titling, superposition, or for color display.

Double Stuffing

Double stuffing is a technique that crams twice as many characters vertically than is usual. Fig. 1-10 compares ordinary noninterlaced characters with interlaced and double-stuffed, interlaced characters. With no interlace, all character fields are identical, giving us a normal height character with stripes in it. With interlace, the even and odd field characters are offset one line from each other; this fills in the stripes and greatly improves appearance.

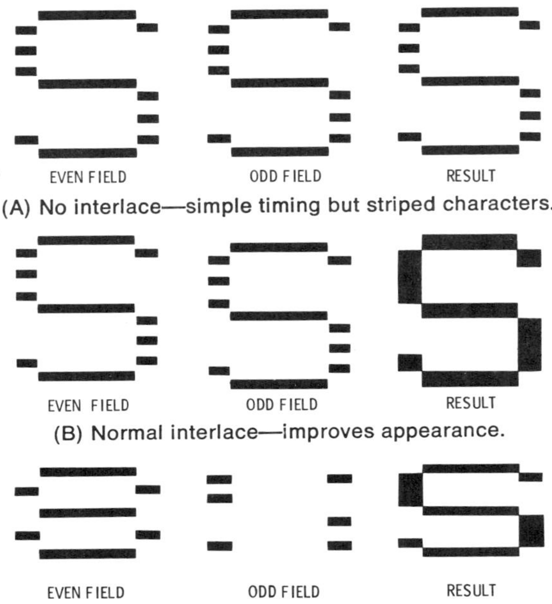

Fig. 1-10. How double stuffing puts more characters on tv screen.

With double stuffing, we put down half the dots (lines 0,2,4,6) on one field, and the other half (lines 1,3,5,7) on the other field. Double stuffing lets us put twice as many characters on the screen as usual. Double stuffing can also greatly increase throughput of a transparently operating program. In theory, we could get as many as 64 lines of characters vertically, but 24- to 32-character rows is a more practical limit for pleasing and legible results, particularly if transparent operation and high throughput is needed.

Double stuffing does introduce slight flicker to the normal video display. This can become downright annoying if the contrast, brightness, and room lighting is set wrong, particularly on random full-screen displays that contain lots of dashes. With the proper settings and reasonable program material the flicker is not objectionable. No flicker is present on reverse video (black characters on white background) double-stuffed displays.

A second double stuffing possibility lets you put characters down on one field and graphics on the second. This is handy for games, pc layouts and schematics, and similar uses.

SOME GOOD THINGS ABOUT CHEAP VIDEO DISPLAYS

Let's briefly sum up the advantages and disadvantages of this new cheap video display approach. We will start with the good things:

1. *LOW COST*—The methods typically cost one tenth of what traditional approaches did. High-performance alphanumeric circuits can cost less than $20 in singles; graphics even less.
2. *SIMPLE*—The method usually takes only seven or eight ordinary integrated circuits on a small, *single-sided* pc card. It needs only +5-volt supply power.
3. *LOW BANDWIDTH*—Long character lines and high-resolution graphics are easily and attractively put on a tv set with normal video bandwidth, with or without routing through a conventional rf modulator.
4. *FAST*—Characters can be put on and off the screen at incredible baud rates. The microprocessor can real-time interact with the display memory, and can easily retrieve information already on screen.
5. *VERSATILE*—The same hardware gives you many display formats simply by changing software. Cheap video works with many different microprocessor systems with a few minor modifications. Since almost everything is done with software, there

is practically no limit to how fancy your cursor or editing system gets.

6. *MINIMUM MEMORY*—The need for a separate and specialized display memory is gone. The computer can use the area set aside for display memory at any time for any reason.

AND THE BAD STUFF . . .

On the debit side, we have:

1. *TRANSPARENCY*—In simpler systems, we alternate compute and display modes. Extra transparency takes more effort. Details on this and solutions to the total transparency problem appear in Chapter 5.
2. *REDUCED HORIZONTAL RATE*—Long line lengths may run at a reduced horizontal rate. This may take width and hold modifications and can cause a poorly chosen tv set to sing objectionably.
3. *USING EXISTING HARDWARE CAN BE TRICKY*—An upstream tap must be provided. Extra tricks are needed if the microprocessor cannot directly change its address lines once each microsecond. Bus oriented systems require that the display memory and the tvt interface hardware work together as a single module. Latches may be needed.
4. *DOUBLE STUFFING FLICKERS SLIGHTLY*—A wrong choice of program material or control settings can cause an objectionable display if double stuffing is used. This is eliminated by using a reverse video (black on white) display.

WHICH MICROPROCESSOR?

Its simply not reasonable to expect any interactive software technique to work with any available microprocessor. There are obvious architectural and language differences that are bound to cause troubles. Which microprocessors can we use and how much hassle is involved?

We will almost always assume that a microprocessor is already available and in use, and that your main goal is to add cheap video to an existing design. All the cheap video systems of this book were designed and debugged around the *MOS Technology* 6502 microprocessor and the KIM-1 and KIM-2 microcomputers. Because of the strong positive feedback involved between developing something and the thing it is being developed on, these displays work elegantly, cheaply, and simply on a KIM-based system. We will use 6500 software, both as theory and design examples.

What we are going to show you would very simply extend to any other 6500-based system. Conversion to a 6800 series system is usually a matter of software reworking and changing the code in a single integrated circuit. Early 8080 systems will be somewhat more difficult to use since the address outputs are not continuous and since it takes extra effort to convince the display memory to output characters at a one-per-microsecond rate. These problems are eased on the Z-80 systems if they are running fast enough in their normal modes. So, the techniques of this book should be reasonably applicable to the three mainstream microprocessor technologies in use today, although the 6500 and 6800 will be much easier to use than the 8080 or Z-80.

Going further afield, microprocessors with only eight address lines or with multiplexed data and address buses or very slow microprocessors or those with limited drive will introduce serious problems that will take a lot of creative effort of your own to resolve.

Chart 1-1 sums up the key needs of a microprocessor-based cheap

Chart 1-1. Picking a Microprocessor—6502 Often Best Choice for Methods of This Book

Microprocessor-Based Video Displays Work Best With . . .	We Can Live With . . .	Your Microprocessor??
16 always there & fully decoded address lines	12 fully decoded address lines, latched to eliminate any "holes"	
A program counter that can be tricked into advancing the address bus once each microsecond	Circuitry at the display memory that creates the illusion of a once-per-microsecond program counter advance	
A display memory that has noninverting tristate buffers between its output and the true data bus	A display memory to which you can reasonably add noninverting tristate buffers between its output and the true data bus	
Excess drive of at least one LS load on all address and data buses	Add-on buffers or drivers	
A single +5-volt supply with 200 mA excess capacity	Multiple supplies	

video display system. We would like to see 16 address lines there all the time, with no holes or dropouts in each cycle but we can live with 12. We have to have a program counter that can advance an address bus once each microsecond, or at least be capable of humming a few bars and faking it. We must have a way to add an upstream tap to the display memory that outputs when it does NOT have data-bus access. And, we have to have enough drive available for one more LS load on all address and data lines, along with 200 MA, or so, of excess + 5-volt supply power.

If you are new to learning about and building these cheap video display techniques, be sure to separate completely understanding cheap video from using it on an odd-ball microprocessor system. Always start with the debugged software and hardware of this book on a KIM-1 system; then go on to others, if you must.

A DESIGN PLAN

We have now seen what these new cheap video ideas can do for us, along with their key design concepts, advantages, and limitations. The rest of the book will show you how to design and build your own cheap video systems. Software and hardware design theory will show up in the next two chapters. This is followed by the nuts-and-bolts construction and debug details of the TVT 6⅝ in Chapter 4. The all-important transparency techniques are saved for Chapter 5.

Some background textbooks and materials that you will want are listed in Chart 1-2. You should have these on hand and fully understand them before you start anything with cheap video.

Chart 1-2. Texts to Have on Hand When Working With Cheap Video Displays

* **For Video Displays in General:**
  - *TV Typewriter Cookbook* (Sams 21313)
* **For Machine Language Programming and μP Selection:**
  - *An Introduction to Microcomputers I* (Osborne 2001)
  - *An Introduction to Microcomputers II* (Osborne 3001)
* **For Software, Hardware, and System Design:**
  - *6500 Programming Manual* (MOS Technology)
  - *6500 Hardware Manual*
  - *KIM-1 Users Manual*
  - *KIM-2 Users Manual*
  - *MCS650X Instruction Set Summary*
  - —Plus comparable manuals for your system.

Now, on to that software design . . . .

CHAPTER 2

Software Design

Microprocessor-based, cheap video uses software and hardware working together to get us from code in a memory to dots on a screen. The software of this chapter has to work hand in hand with the hardware of the next. Neither hardware nor software can stand alone in the cheap video world. They have to continuously interact with each other, especially during your system design.

In this chapter, we will be using the *MOS Technology* 6502 microprocessor and the KIM-1 system architecture. This system has a 16-bit–wide address bus and a separate 8-bit–wide data bus and normally runs with a 1-MHz crystal clock rate. Instruction times are usually 2 μs or more.

You can easily adapt this software to 6800-based systems. While cheap video will work with other microprocessor families, you will be pretty much on your own if you stray too far from the 6502 or 6800.

These are our main software problems:

* How do we assign our *address and data-bus definitions* for display use?
* How do we build a *Scan microinstruction* that gives us a line of character code that outputs at a 1-MHz rate?
* How do we combine just enough of the Scan microinstructions in the right place and at the right time to build a complete *Scan program* that meets the exact timing needs of a tv set?
* How do we build a *Cursor controller* or its *graphics loader* equivalent so we can enter and remove characters and provide the usual Cursor motions?

The answers to these questions are all found in this chapter. You will be seeing fully tested and debugged TVT 6⅝ alphanumeric

Chart 2-1. Alphanumeric and Graphics Cheap Video Can Use Same Instruction Decoder. Here Is How Display Instructions Are Decoded

Address A15	A14	A13	A12	Alphanumeric	Graphics
0	0	0	0	Normal Computer Use	Normal Computer Use
0	0	0	1	Normal Computer Use	Normal Computer Use
0	0	1	0	Normal Computer Use	Normal Computer Use
0	0	1	1	Normal Computer Use	Normal Computer Use
0	1	0	0	Normal Computer Use	Normal Computer Use
0	1	0	1	Normal Computer Use	Normal Computer Use
0	1	1	0	Output Blank Video Line	Output Blank Video Line
0	1	1	1	Output 1st Row of Character	Output Blank Video Line
1	0	0	0	Output 2nd Row of Character	Output Live Video Line A
1	0	0	1	Output 3rd Row of Character	Output Live Video Line A
1	0	1	0	Output 4th Row of Character	Output Blank Video Line
1	0	1	1	Output 5th Row of Character	Output Blank Video Line
1	1	0	0	Output 6th Row of Character	Output Live Video Line B
1	1	0	1	Output 7th Row of Character	Output Live Video Line B
1	1	1	0	Output Vertical-Sync Pulse	Output Vertical-Sync Pulse
1	1	1	1	Normal Computer Use	Normal Computer Use

software for 1 × 40, 16 × 32, 16 × 40, 16 × 64, 32 × 64, 12 × 80 and 24 × 80 character lines, along with graphics software for black and white formats of 128 × 128 and 256 × 256; as well as a four-color format of 96 × 128.

We will save some software details for later, such as techniques for full transparency, integrated Scan and Cursor programs, and so on, after we have picked up the software fundamentals here.

This is a very heavy chapter, and you will find lots of things done in either strange or subtle ways. You are urged to have the background material of Chart 1-2 both mastered and on hand before continuing. Fortunately, if you are using a TVT 6⅝ on a KIM, all you will need are the *results* of this chapter without having to go too far into the gory details of where the results came from.

BUS DEFINITIONS

The starting point of any software design is to define what each bus line in the microcomputer system is going to do and how it is going to be used. In 6502 systems, we have a 16-bit-wide *address bus* and an 8-bit-wide *data bus.*

Address Lines

Some workable definitions for our address bus appear in Fig. 2-1. We assign the lowest address lines to the horizontal character posi-

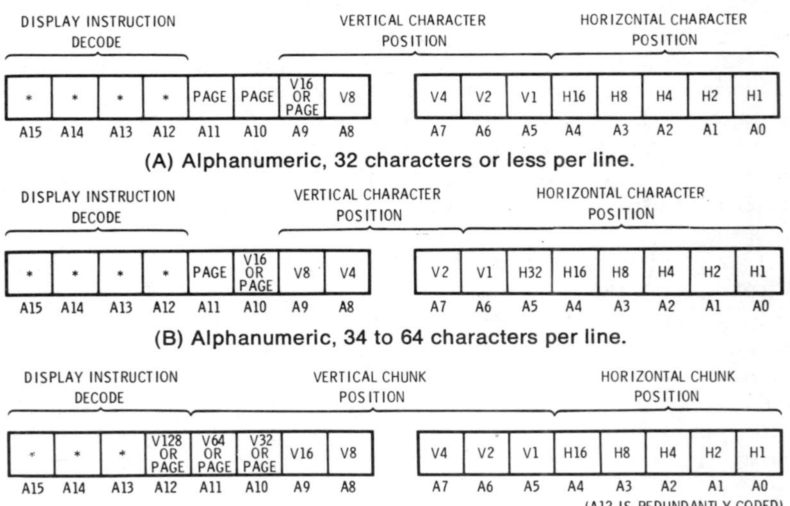

Fig. 2-1. Address bus assignments.

tions, followed by the vertical character positions. Higher lines still are used to define the page of characters (usually 256 words) that is being output. Our highest available address lines are routed to a special *display instruction decoder* circuit which decides whether normal or display operation is to be provided.

For instance, in Fig. 2-1A, for a 16 × 32 alphanumeric display, we use five bits for the horizontal character locations, and four more bits for the vertical character locations. The next three bits select the location of the display memory. The top four bits serve as our instruction decoder.

Note that a one count change of the address bus moves you one character to the right, and that 32 sequential address bus advances will output a continuous horizontal line of 32 characters. Thus by simply letting the program counter of the microprocessor advance once each microsecond, the code for a line of characters will be output automatically.

The coding of Fig. 2-1B gives us a 64-character horizontal line by adding a most significant horizontal bit and bumping everything else up a notch to make room. Normally, you would use the code in Fig. 2-1A for lines of 32 characters or less and the code in Fig. 2-1B for 34 to 64 characters.

If we try to use these formats on nonbinary line lengths, there will be unused locations in the display memory. These unused locations are often too small and too dangerous to use for any other program, so they end up wasted. Running the 64-character code at 32 characters or less per line would give us a *memory packing* or efficiency of 50% or less. Even with memory at a cost of 0.1 cent a bit and 4 cents a word, this is often an intolerable waste.

Later in the chapter, we will look at some sneaky ways to *repack* the lower eight address lines so we can put 40- or 80-character lines into our display memory with just about the same memory packing efficiency as we used for the binary 32- and 64-character line lengths.

Our graphics formats might follow Fig. 2-1C. In an alphanumeric display, each word normally stands for a character. In a graphics display, each word relates to a piece of the display we can call a *chunk*. The chunk might be one line of eight dots, four dots on top of four dots, or three dots on top of three along with four possible color values for the entire chunk. Because graphics decoding is often simpler, we can use address A12 redundantly, as both part of instruction decoder space and display memory addressing.

Instruction Decoding

Chart 2-1 shows how we decide whether to use the computer normally or in its display mode. We route the top four address lines to a circuit that acts as an *address decoder*. A programmable read only memory or PROM is one way to do this decoding, as we will see in the next chapter.

The same decoder can be used for graphics or alphanumerics. In the TVT 6⅝, we switch between the two by changing a small plug-in hardware module and selecting the proper Scan software. On our decoder, combinations 0000, 0001, 0010, 0011, 0100, 0101, and 1111 are reserved for normal computer operation. This final "upper-core" decoding is particularly important on the 6502 for proper use of the reset, interrupt, and mask vectors in the operating system.

Intermediate decodings turn the control of the computer over to the TVT 6⅝ so that characters or sync can be output. Decoding 1110 will output only a vertical-sync pulse, while the remaining decodings will decide which line of alphanumeric dots to output for a particular pass on a dot matrix character generator. For instance, decoding 0110 gives us a blank line, while decoding 0111 gives us the top row of dots on an alphanumeric character.

The TVT 6⅝ uses a character generator that supplies a 5 × 7 alphanumeric dot format. A top line is usually all blanks, so this means a total of eight horizontal passes is needed for a row of dot matrix characters. Should we really want a row of characters, we increment the instruction decoder each Scan to pick up the right row of dots. If we only want a blank line, we simply output the top (blank) row over and over again as often as needed.

While fancy 7 × 9 character generators are available, they are expensive and take extra video bandwidth. They also use address space very inefficiently, limit the number of character rows you can get on the screen, and cut heavily into throughput during transparent operation.

A graphics display does not need all those different passes for a row of characters. All it needs is a *blanking* output line and an optional A/B chunk select line that picks the upper or lower half of a display chunk. But, there is no reason why we cannot use the *same* instruction decoder for alphanumerics and graphics, simply by relabeling some of the outputs on our decoder.

In fact, there is a subtle and neat trick you can pull using *redundant* decoding for your graphics. You can now make address line A12 into a "don't care" decoding during a Scan which lets you address a larger block of graphics display memory. Thus decodings 1000 OR 1001 can be used for a live "A" graphics Scan, and decoding 1100 OR 1101 can be used for a live "B" graphics Scan. During these times, we are free to have A12 a zero OR a one, letting us address the 8K block of memory we need for a 256 × 256 graphics display.

The display mode *memory* map of Fig. 2-2 gives a different way to look at what the instruction decoder does. The bottom 24K of the computer is free for any use. Our display memory should be located somewhere in this bottom 24K. The "middle" 36K of memory space is reserved for control of our cheap video display. The top 4K is available for computer use, particularly operating systems and vector storage.

Any address in your computer called between 6000 and EFFF will activate the display instruction decoder. This turns out to be the key to deciding what part of what character is to be output when.

On a KIM-1, we will avoid using page 00 for display memory since it has the operating system storage slots on it and since it is very useful for standard programs. We will also stay off page 01 since this page has the stack on it. On a bare bones KIM-1, we can use pages 03 and 04 for a 512-character 16 × 32 display of 16 lines of 32 characters each. On an expanded (more RAM) KIM, we might use pages 04-0A for a 24 × 80 character display.

We will note in passing that the KIM has a nice little unused RAM sitting between 1780 and 17E6. This is a dandy place to stuff a Scan program, and gives us a strong reason to keep all Scan programs under a hundred words or so long.

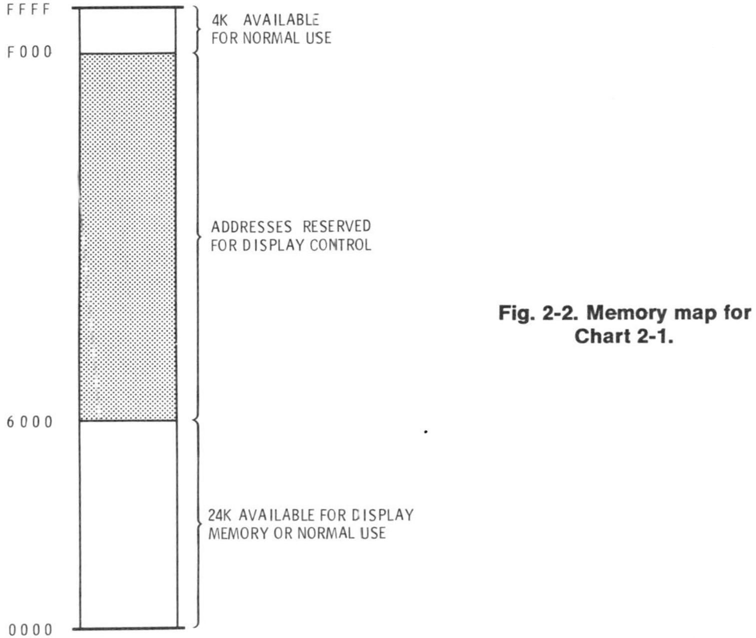

Fig. 2-2. Memory map for Chart 2-1.

It looks like we are using a large number of addresses simply to run our cheap video display. But these addresses are not used anyway in many systems. And the addresses left over are more than adequate for, say, running Extended BASIC and a transparent display simultaneously. No attempt was made to further restrict the cheap video address space, although this is easily done with extra gating. Obvious routes to gaining even more "use the computer normally" space are to use a display enable that deactivates the tvt during nondisplay times, to use an alternate way to pick up vertical sync, to use more complete instruction decodings (enabling the tvt only during valid display memory *addresses*), and to use I/O instructions if they are available.

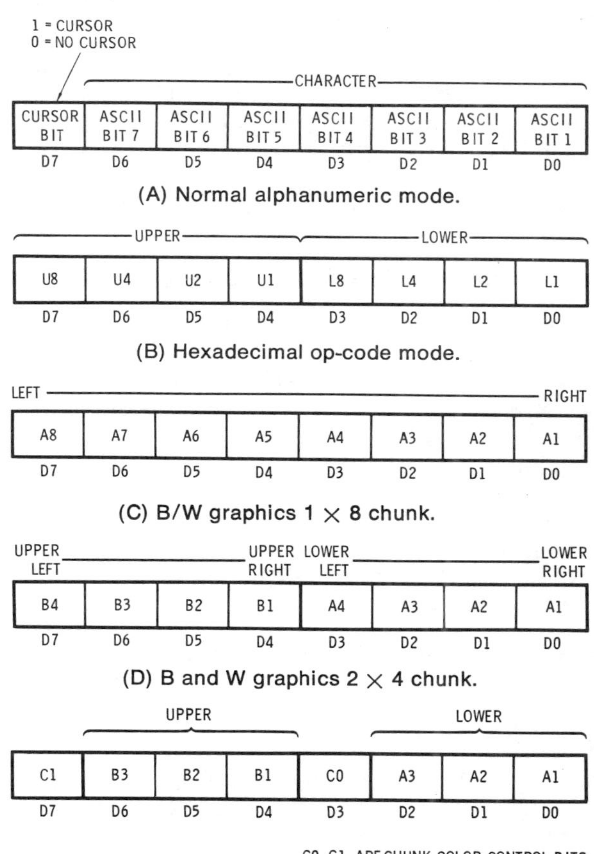

Fig. 2-3. Data bus assignments.

The Data Bus

Our data bus definitions are shown in Fig. 2-3. They are more obvious than the address definitions. For normal alphanumerics, the usual 7-bit ASCII code goes on the bottom seven bits. The eighth bit is reserved as an optional cursor. A one provides a possible Cursor and a zero withholds it. If we go to a special hex op-code mode and use an add-on Hex-ASCII converter, we can slowly *alternate* displaying the upper hex character, the lower hex character, and a "start of new character" blank *in the same screen position.* For this, we use the format of Fig. 2-3B, where numbers 0 through 9 and the letters A through F are displayed in response to a one-of-sixteen hex code.

The three graphics data-bus assignments change as we change what we call a chunk. For one line of eight dots, the data bus looks just like the screen, with white normally a "1" and black a "0." The chunk with four dots on top of four dots puts the left half up and the right half down. Our color format does the same thing, but shortens everything to three on three, leaving us with two color-control bits left over in bus positions D3 and D7.

THE SCAN MICROINSTRUCTION

The two essential keys to a microprocessor-based cheap video display are the software *Scan microinstruction* and the hardware *upstream tap*. In order for us to get a row of character code out of the microcomputer rapidly, we have to add a new instruction called SCAN. Since SCAN is not available internally to the CPU chip, we have to add it on the outside through a technique called *microprogramming*. Microprogramming can combine a string of several available and existing instructions into a new, longer, instruction that does what we want it to.

In the case of our Scan microinstruction, we want the microprogramming to do the following:

To start at a computed address and then cause the program counter to appear on the address bus, and then advance at a one microsecond per count rate for N counts. N is often 32, 40, 64, or 80.

The trick is to find some combination of existing instructions that can be put together in a string to get this result. For openers, we will get to our microinstruction with a Jump to Subroutine (JSR) command in whatever program that needs the Scan microinstruction. We will end the microinstruction with a Return from Subroutine (RTS) to get back out of the microinstruction.

This use of a subroutine for our Scan microinstruction is the key to making the microinstruction *portable*. This lets it be called from any of the shaded memory areas of Fig. 2-2. Portability lets us move the instruction around nearly anywhere we want to pick up the right part of the right line of character code stored in display memory.

But, what coding can we use to force the needed once-per-microsecond advance? A quick look at the obvious No-Operation (NOP) instruction is discouraging, because a NOP takes *two* microseconds to execute. It advances the address bus only once each *two* microseconds. Thus, the obvious route of

NOP NOP NOP . . . NOP RTS

works beautifully as a Scan microinstruction—except it is slow by a factor of two.

Instead, we will have to look at other instructions in the machine that will advance the program counter on the address bus once per microsecond. Available instructions are listed in Chart 2-2 for the

Chart 2-2. Some 6502 Instructions That Will Advance Address Bus One Count per Microsecond for 2 μs

Instruction		Op-Code	What Else Is Affected?
ADC	Add Immediate	69	Accumulator, N,Z,C,V Flags
AND	And Immediate	29	Accumulator, N,Z Flags
BCC	Branch on Carry Clear	90	Carry must be set first
BCS	Branch on Carry Set	80	Carry must be clear first
BEQ	Branch on Equal	F0	Zero Flag must be 0 first
BMI	Branch on Negative	30	Negative Flag must be 0 first
BNE	Branch on Not Equal	d0	Zero Flag must be 1 first
BPL	Branch on Positive	10	Negative Flag must be 1 first
BVC	Branch on Overflow Clear	50	Overflow must be set first
BVS	Branch on Overflow Set	70	Overflow must be clear first
CMP	Compare Accumulator	C9	N,Z,C Flags
CPX	Compare X Register	E0	N,Z,C Flags
CPY	Compare Y Register	C0	N,Z,C Flags
EOR	Exclusive Or Immediate	49	Accumulator, N,Z Flags
LDA	Load Accumulator	A9	Accumulator, N,Z Flags
LDX	Load X Register	A2	X Register Value
LDY	Load Y Register	A0	Y Register Value
ORA	OR Immediate	09	Accumulator, N,Z Flags
SBC	Subtract Immediate	E9	Accumulator, N,Z,X,V Flags

Note:
NOP or "No Operation" is missing from the list since it is too slow.
Of instructions listed, the Command LDY does the least damage to existing programs, flags, and registers.

6502. There are 19 of them. Any of these instructions could be used end-on-end as often as needed to give a microinstruction.

But, our Scan microinstruction cannot stand alone. It has to lie inside a larger *Scan program.* All of these 19 instructions change or damage something in the machine when they are used. The trick is to minimize the damage to anything needed by an existing program. This means we want an absolute minimum of changes in flag status, the accumulator, and the index registers.

We might get sneaky and do something like AND the accumulator immediately with FF; ORA it immediately with 00; or EOR it immediately with 00. And these most often will give us no damage to anything. They usually will leave everything just as it was before, except for our desired two-count advance of the program counter on the address bus. But, as we will see in just a moment, there is an even sneakier trick we can pull to cut in half the PROM storage needed for our microinstruction—and these three dodges of AND, ORA, and EOR for no change will not go along with the memory savings.

Instead, we reserve the Y register for use as a write only memory during a Scan. We simply use LDY (AO) as our element in a Scan microinstruction. Each time we load the Y register, the program counter advances once per microsecond for 2 μs. No flags are changed; the accumulator is unchanged; and the X register is unchanged. We even have partial use of the Y register, as long as we do not have to hold a value through a single Scan microinstruction.

So, we simply stack up enough load-the-Y-register LDY commands as needed for the microinstruction. It looks like this:

LDY LDY LDY . . . LDY RTS

Chart 2-3. The 6502 Scan Microinstruction Coding for 32-Character, One-Microsecond-per-Character Scan

XX00	LDY	A0	A0	
XX02	LDY	A0	A0	
XX04	LDY	A0	A0	
XX06	LDY	A0	A0	
XX08	LDY	A0	A0	
XX0A	LDY	A0	A0	
XX0C	LDY	A0	A0	
XX0E	LDY	A0	A0	Note:
XX10	LDY	A0	A0	"XX" is any high address that
XX12	LDY	A0	A0	activates the Scan instruction
XX14	LDY	A0	A0	decoder.
XX16	LDY	A0	A0	
XX18	LDY	A0	A0	Coding shown repeats for XX20
XX1A	LDY	A0	A0	through XXFF, a total of eight
XX1C	LDY	A0	A0	times.
XX1E	**RTS**	**60**	**60**	

Chart 2-3 shows the Scan microinstruction coding for a 32-character, 1-μs-per-character Scan. We simply load Y with something fifteen times, followed by an RTS or a Return to Subroutine. Each LDY advances us two counts, one on the first microsecond, and one on the second. Our RTS instruction does all sorts of strange things to the address bus during its 6 μs execution—*but the first 2 μs advance the program counter on the address line just exactly like the LDY instruction does.* And, after the first 2 μs, RTS has put us back in the main Scan program and out of the Scan microinstruction.

Fig. 2-4 shows one possible way to generate our microprogram. We use a Programmable Read Only Memory of the next chapter. When the instruction decoder activates the Scan PROM, its tristate

Chart 2-4. The 6502 Scan Microinstruction Coding for 64-Character, One-Microsecond-per-Character Scan

XX00	LDY	A0	A0
XX02	LDY	A0	A0
XX04	LDY	A0	A0
XX06	LDY	A0	A0
XX08	LDY	A0	A0
XX0A	LDY	A0	A0
XX0C	LDY	A0	A0
XX0E	LDY	A0	A0
XX10	LDY	A0	A0
XX12	LDY	A0	A0
XX14	LDY	A0	A0
XX16	LDY	A0	A0
XX18	LDY	A0	A0
XX1A	LDY	A0	A0
XX1C	LDY	A0	A0
XX1E	LDY	A0	A0
XX20	LDY	A0	A0
XX22	LDY	A0	A0
XX24	LDY	A0	A0
XX26	LDY	A0	A0
XX28	LDY	A0	A0
XX2A	LDY	A0	A0
XX2C	LDY	A0	A0
XX2E	LDY	A0	A0
XX30	LDY	A0	A0
XX32	LDY	A0	A0
XX34	LDY	A0	A0
XX36	LDY	A0	A0
XX38	LDY	A0	A0
XX3A	LDY	A0	A0
XX3C	LDY	A0	A0
XX3E	**RTS**	**60**	**60**

Note:

"XX" is any high address that activates the Scan instruction decoder.

Coding shown repeats for XX40 through XXFF, a total of four times.

outputs are activated, and the Scan microinstruction takes command of the data bus of the microcomputer and forces a Scan microinstruction. At the same time, a disappearing *Decode Enable* command prevents anything else in the system from grabbing the data bus.

A quick glance at Chart 2-4 seems to suggest that we need a 64 × 8 PROM. But, since it does not matter with what we load Y and since the code following an RTS instruction does not matter, *we can make both columns of Charts 2-3 and 2-4 identical.* This means that we load the Y register with the command code for load Y, or A0, and that we follow the RTS (60) with another RTS (60) code.

Now, since both columns are identical, we can use one column and call it half as often. To do this, we simply ignore the least significant address line. And this slashes our PROM down to the baby 32 × 8, two-dollar size.

So, once again we have doubled something. This time it is how much code we can get out of a 32-word PROM. As a further refinement, we add a switch to the most significant address line going to the PROM. With this switch connected to address bus line A5, we generate the 64-character microinstruction of Chart 2-4. With the switch connecting the PROM to the positive supply and force feeding a "1," we generate the 32-character microinstruction of Chart 2-3 instead. Note that both Scans are generated with a 100% packing density.

Our Scan microinstruction usually has to start at some address that is an even multiple of the Scan length. For instance, valid start-

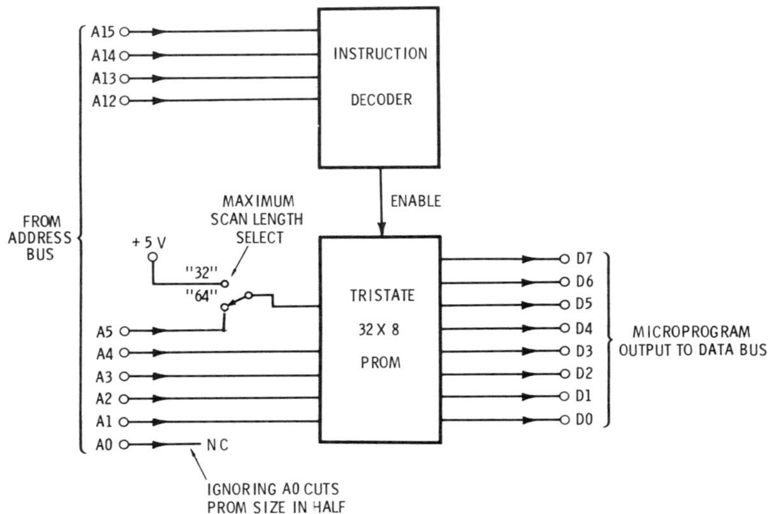

Fig. 2-4. PROM method of Scan microprogram generation used in TVT 6 5/8.

ing addresses for the 64-character lines are XX00, XX40, XX80, or XXC0. The 32-character lines can use these starting locations, as well as new addresses XX20, XX60, XXA0, and XXEO.

By "X", we mean any address that activates the instruction decoder. It turns out that the rightmost X lets us pick the page of display memory being converted to dots. The leftmost X will give us a blank line if X is hexadecimal "6." An X of "7" gives us the top row of dots. An X of "8" gives us the second row of dots, and so on to an X of "D," which gives us the bottom row of dots. Leftmost X values of 0,1,2,3,4,5,E, and F will *not* activate the Scan microinstruction. Values of 0 through 5, or F allow normal computer operation, while an X value of E outputs a vertical-sync pulse only.

Making It Portable

By changing the starting address of the JSR instruction that gets us into the Scan, we change which characters are going to be output, and which portions of them are going to appear as dots on the screen. Several examples in Chart 2-5 should make this clear. An instruction of JSR 20 C0 94 will output the third row of dots on the fourth line of 64 characters, and so on.

In this example, the subroutine starts at address 94C0 and scans 94C0 through 94FF. The "9" says to do a Scan and work on the third row of dots. The "4" says to use page 04 of the computer, on which

Chart 2-5. Examples of How We Call Our Portable Scan Microinstruction

Assume we have a 16 × 64 display format per Fig. 2-1B and that our display memory is on pages 04 through 07.

JSR	20	00	60	Outputs a 64-μs blank video line.
JSR	20	20	84	Outputs the second row of dots on the second line of 64 characters.
JSR	20	20	94	Outputs the third row of dots on the second line of 64 characters.
JSR	20	C0	94	Outputs the third row of dots on the fourth line of 64 characters.
JSR	20	40	C5	Outputs the sixth row of dots on the seventh line of 64 characters.
LDY	A0	00	d0	Outputs only a vertical-sync pulse.
JSR	20	1A	30	Calls some other subroutine in the computer; out of range of the Scan decoder.
JSR	20	02	60	Outputs a blank video line that lasts only 62 μs instead of 64.
JSR	20	0A	60	Outputs a blank video line that lasts only 54 μs instead of 64.

the lower rows of characters for the display are stashed. The "C0" says start on the fourth line of characters that go on the screen.

Why the fourth line? Check back to Fig. 2-1B. C0 decodes as 1100-0000. So we start with all horizontal bits at zero, and the lower-most vertical bits at 11. The top of our verticle line is 00. The next one down is line 01. The next vertical line is coded 10, and our fourth line down is coded 11, or V1 = 1 and V2 = 1.

Note that page 04 has not been enabled to run the data bus, since the Scan microinstruction has control of the data bus. But page 04 has been activated enough to output characters out the upstream tap to the interface hardware.

Be sure to go through all the examples of Chart 2-5 so you understand exactly how we move the Scan microinstruction around to get the right string of characters outputting the right row of dots. Note that we do *not* use a JSR to get a vertical-sync pulse. A simple Load Y or anything similar is used instead. Also note that if we call a JSR that is out of the instruction decoder range, the decoder assumes this is a normal subroutine that is part of an ordinary computer program, and that a Scan is NOT wanted.

We also have the option of jumping into the middle of a Scan microinstruction. This gives us a short line. Short lines are handy during a blank line to make room for extra computation time. This turns out particularly important when we are doing an interlaced sync, for nearly an entire line is needed to compute the proper position of the vertical sync pulse. Short lines also give us a compatible but inefficient way to do 40- and 80-character lines, as well as other line lengths. Note that **the Scan microinstructions can be any length so long as they all END a constant time apart.** The constant distance from falling edge to falling edge of sequential Scan microinstructions sets the horizontal line time and is the edge from which our horizontal-sync pulses will be derived.

Timing Overhead

Fig. 2-5 shows us the *timing overhead* needed to call and recover from a Scan microinstruction. A total of ten microseconds is needed

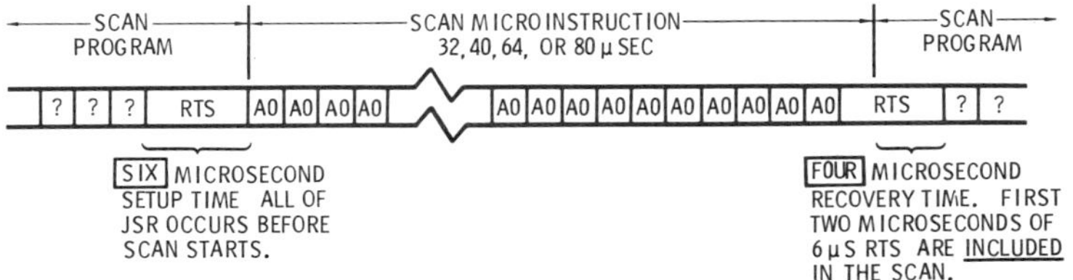

Fig. 2-5. Timing overhead for a Scan microinstruction using 6502 coding. A total of 10 μs is needed to get into and back out of a Scan.

for a 6502 on a 1-MHz clock. Six of these microseconds happen *before* the Scan microinstruction starts; these are used up by the JSR command calling the Scan. Four of the microseconds occur *after* the Scan microinstruction ends as the RTS command is completed.

Note that the RTS command normally takes 6 μs. *Two of the six microseconds are spent inside the Scan microinstruction acting as the final two 1-μs advances of the program counter on the address bus.* The remaining four microseconds are taken out of the regular program that is calling the Scan microinstruction.

SCAN PROGRAMS

Our Scan microinstruction gives us a convenient way to output a group of characters in a one-character-per-microsecond burst. If we simply fed one of these to a tv set, the tv would not have the slightest idea what to do with it. All we would get is a disorganized and apparently random brief flash of dots.

A tv set normally has a *Raster Scan* in which a video-controlled spot moves rapidly to the right and slowly down the screen. One trip down the screen is called a *field*. This may be all we need, but more often, two interleaved fields are combined to produce an *interlaced frame*. During an interlaced raster Scan, there are usually 60 fields per second, resulting in 30 interlaced frames per second.

To make our Scan microinstruction burst into recognizable characters, we have to repeat them over and over again. This is called *refreshing* a raster, and a complete refresh is needed 60 times a second. Our output video can only turn the spot on and off. It does not normally determine the spot position. To tell where we are, we have to lock the video to the raster with horizontal and vertical *synchronizing* pulses.

It is the job of our *Scan program* to provide sync pulses and refresh as needed for a continuous and stable display. A Scan program is ordinary software. It has the ability to call a Scan microinstruction any time it needs one. The design of a Scan program is rather tricky, since you have to be extra careful not only to have the program run, but also the program has to take exactly the right number of microseconds to do everything. And there is often too few microseconds there to do what you want to do in the available time.

Chart 2-6 summarizes what the tv set needs in the way of video and sync signals. Our vertical-sync pulse frequency has to be very close to 60 Hz. If it misses by .06 Hz or more, you will get a hum bar that will go waltzing through your display at a 10-second-or-faster rate. The hum bar is caused by a tv with poor shielding and power-supply regulation. It may be absent in a quality video monitor. This is particularly annoying on the smaller double-stuffed 64- and 80-character lines. For an ideal display, we should either lock

Chart 2-6. Some Ground Rules for Scan Software Design

VERTICAL-SYNC PULSES are needed 60 times a second and last for three horizontal line times, typically 200 μs.

Frequencies above 60.06 Hz or below 59.94 Hz will cause a hum bar that crosses the screen faster than once each 10 seconds. Ideally, the system timing should be line locked, but crystal control is adequate if it is within range.

A few microseconds of pulse-to-pulse vertical-sync jitter is tolerable during interlaced operation, but its value should be minimized.

HORIZONTAL-SYNC PULSES are needed once each horizontal line and last 5 μs.

Horizontal frequencies are usually 15,750 Hz for black and white and 15,735 Hz for color. When video titling or superimposing existing program material, these values must be externally locked.

Horizontal frequencies as low as 10 kHz may be used if the set is properly modified for reduced width and extended hold range. Only smaller screen portables should be used with extremely low horizontal frequencies.

Twice the horizontal frequency must be an exact and *even* multiple of the vertical rate for no interlace. For full interlace, twice the horizontal frequency must be an exact and *odd* multiple of the vertical rate.

Each horizontal line must be identical in length. Horizontal-sync pulses are derived from the FALLING EDGE of the Scan microinstruction. The time from falling edge to falling edge must be constant and identical for ALL horizontal lines.

BLANKING AND RETRACE At least 20 horizontal lines should be reserved for vertical blanking and retrace. Horizontal-sync pulses may be omitted during the vertical-sync pulse time if at least ten blank horizontal lines follow the vertical-sync pulse before characters or graphics are presented.

On a stock tv set, at least 17 μs per horizontal line should be reserved for blanking, overscan, and spot defocusing toward the edge of the screen.

Horizontal- and vertical-positioning controls should be provided.

DOT MATRIX CHARACTERS take several sequential lines for their presentation. Usually, the uppermost character line is coded as all blanks.

A 5 × 7 dot matrix can be presented in eight lines but ten are more attractive. A 7 × 11 (including descenders) dot matrix can be presented in 12 lines, but 14 are more attractive.

Characters should not be output faster than one per microsecond if a tv with stock video bandwidth or an rf modulator is being used. A graphics rate of eight dots per microsecond is a comparable upper limit.

to the power line or else get as close to a stationary hum bar as we possibly can.

Our horizontal-scan frequency is much more tolerant of deviations from its normal value, but it also has two critical restrictions. Twice the horizontal frequency must be an exact even multiple of the vertical-sync pulse for no interlace and an exact odd multiple of the vertical sync pulse for full 2:1 interlace. In addition, *we require that the spacing from horizontal-sync pulse to horizontal-sync pulse is held absolutely constant.*

This means that every loop and every branch in the Scan program has to take *exactly* the same number of microseconds to execute. The time from *falling edge* to *falling edge* of any Scan microinstruction sets the time between horizontal-sync pulses.

If we are superimposing video on existing programs for titling or annotation, we have to lock to the external program material, matching the usual 15,750-Hz black and white or 15,735-Hz color frequencies. If we have a stand-alone display, anything near this will work well.

At a 1-microsecond-per-character output rate, character lines of 32 characters and 40 characters can be run at normal horizontal frequencies, may be used on a color set, or may be locked to an external program. This is also true of any graphics display of 256 × 256 or fewer resolvable elements.

The longer character lines of 64 and 80 characters usually need a reduced horizontal frequency. This in turn takes the simple hold and width modifications to the tv set detailed in Chapter 3. We are pretty much limited in our choice of display to small screen, transformer-operated, black and white portables for these longer line lengths. Once again, this reduced horizontal rate for long lines lets us get by with unmodified video bandwidth and lets us shove long line lengths through an ordinary rf modulator, besides making all of the direct microprocessor control possible in the first place.

Some Magic Numbers

If at all possible, we would normally like to use the already existing 1.0-MHz or other crystal in the microprocessor for all system timing. We also have to end up with a reasonable horizontal frequency that is an exact multiple of the vertical-sync rate. The vertical-sync rate, in turn, has to be very close to 60 Hz. Only certain combinations of clock frequency, microseconds per horizontal line, number of horizontal lines, and vertical-sync rates are possible. Fig. 2-6 shows some magic-number choices for us that are useful for Scan programs.

One of the first sets of magic numbers we will be using combines the stock 1.0-MHz crystal with a 63-μs horizontal line and a 265-

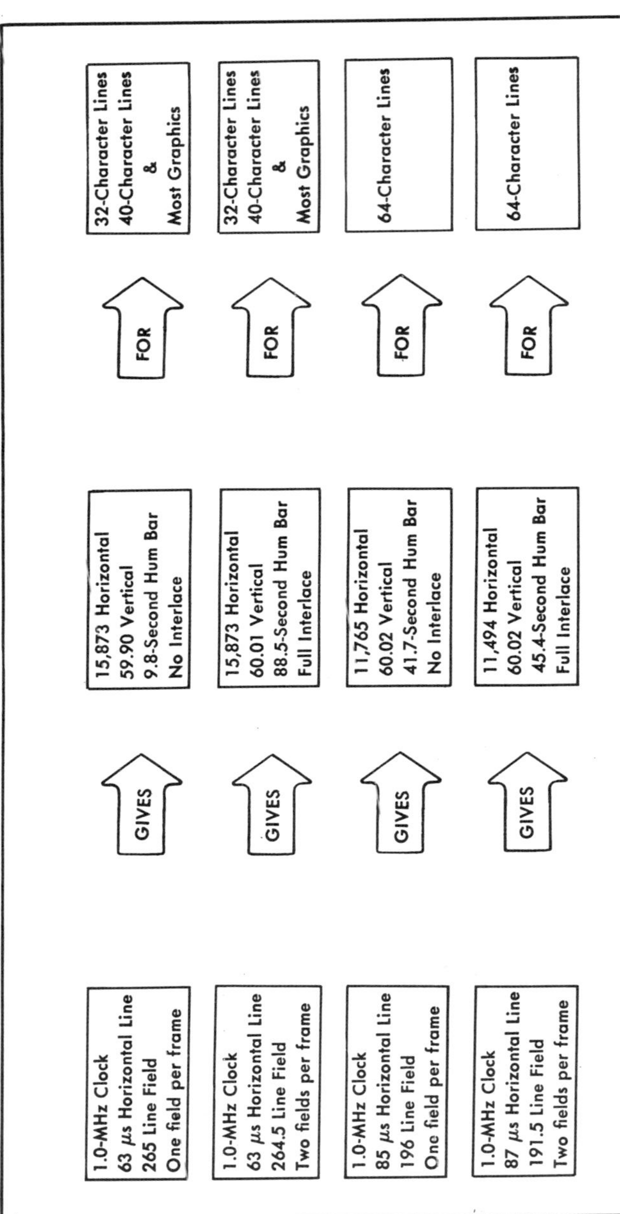

Fig. 2-6. Some magic numbers for

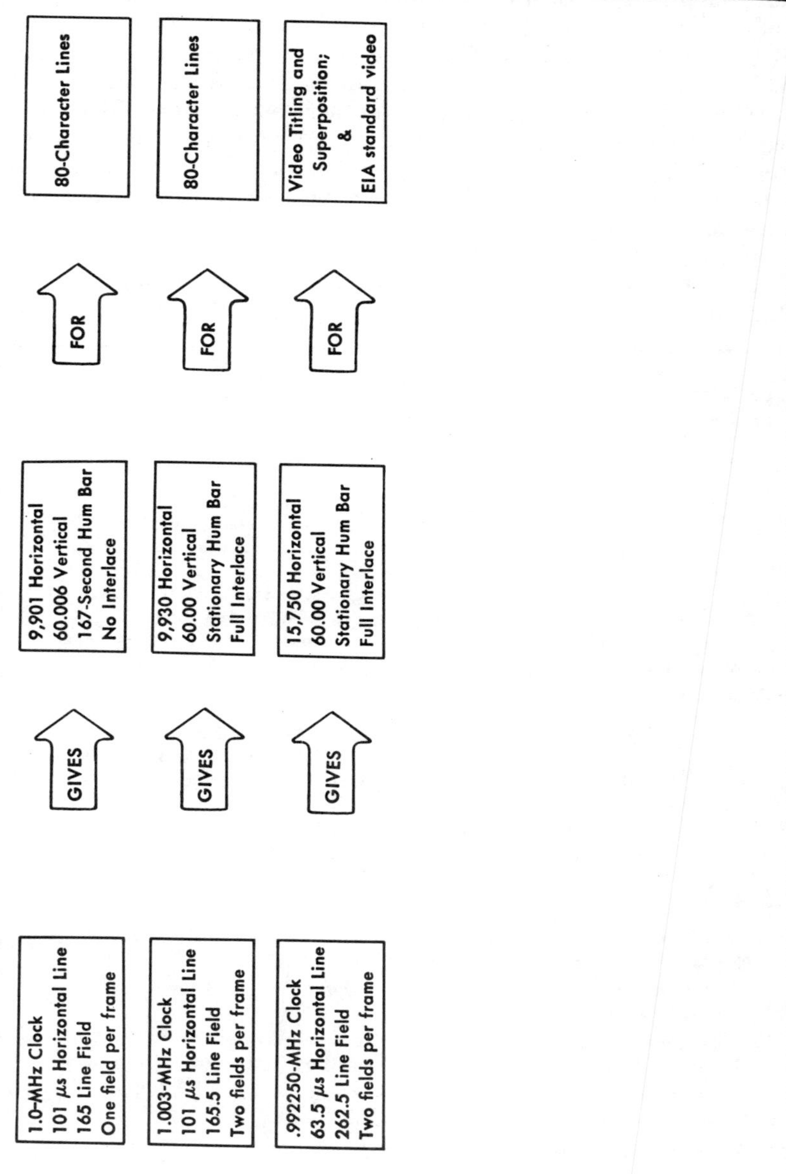

Scan software design.

line noninterlaced frame. This combination gives us a near standard horizontal and a just tolerable hum bar slightly faster than 10 seconds. It may be used for very simple Scans of 32 or 40 characters, as well as most graphics. The other sets of magic numbers can be picked up from Fig. 2-6 for video titling and superposition, interlace, 64- and 80-character lines, and other combinations. Ideally, we would like to be able to trim the crystal slightly or do an actual line lock, but this often is not needed, particularly with large characters on shorter lines. Line lock is simple enough to add once your application is in its final form.

As our first Scan program, let's put one line of 40 characters on the screen, without interlace. Besides giving us something simple to start on, this 1 × 40 display might be used on a point-of-sale terminal

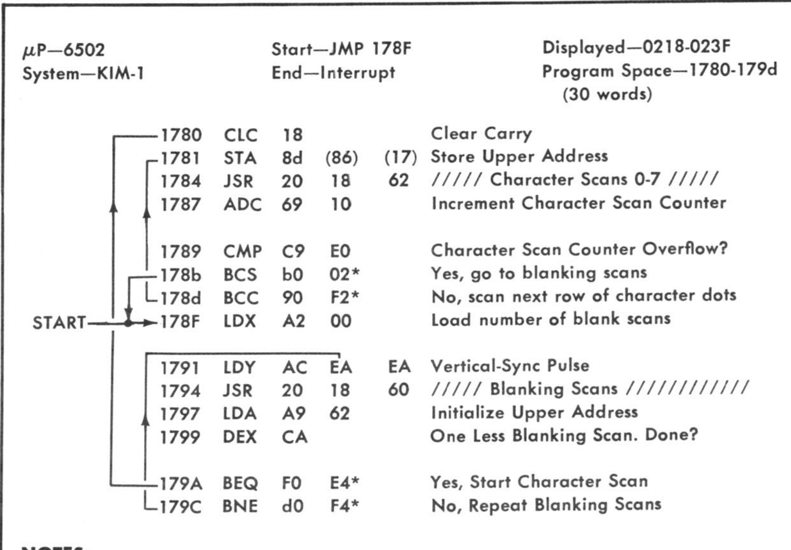

```
μP—6502                Start—JMP 178F        Displayed—0218-023F
System—KIM-1           End—Interrupt         Program Space—1780-179d
                                               (30 words)

         1780  CLC  18                    Clear Carry
         1781  STA  8d  (86)  (17)        Store Upper Address
         1784  JSR  20  18    62          ///// Character Scans 0-7 /////
         1787  ADC  69  10                Increment Character Scan Counter

         1789  CMP  C9  E0                Character Scan Counter Overflow?
         178b  BCS  b0  02*               Yes, go to blanking scans
         178d  BCC  90  F2*               No, scan next row of character dots
START——→ 178F  LDX  A2  00                Load number of blank scans

         1791  LDY  AC  EA    EA          Vertical-Sync Pulse
         1794  JSR  20  18    60          ///// Blanking Scans ////////////
         1797  LDA  A9  62                Initialize Upper Address
         1799  DEX  CA                    One Less Blanking Scan. Done?

         179A  BEQ  F0  E4*               Yes, Start Character Scan
         179C  BNE  d0  F4*               No, Repeat Blanking Scans
```

NOTES:

TVT 6 5/8 must be connected and both the Scan 658-KS64 and Decode 658-KD8 PROMs must be in circuit for program to run.

Step 1784 goes to where the upper address stored in 1786 tells it to. This value changes throughout the program.

Horizontal Frequency 15,873 Hz with 1.0-MHz clock. Vertical frequency 60.125 Hz with 8-second hum bar. No interlace. 256 blanking lines; 8 active scan lines.

TVT 6 5/8 switch must be in the "64" position.

( ) Denotes an absolute address that is program location sensitive.

* Denotes a relative branch that is program length sensitive.

Fig. 2-7. Program for a 1-line, 40-character

or somewhere else where you only have a bare minimum of RAM available, or else have very little information to present. We will need 40 characters of display memory storage and 30 locations of Scan program storage, for a total of 70 words. The program is shown in Fig. 2-7.

Our characters are stored in locations 0218 through 023F, with

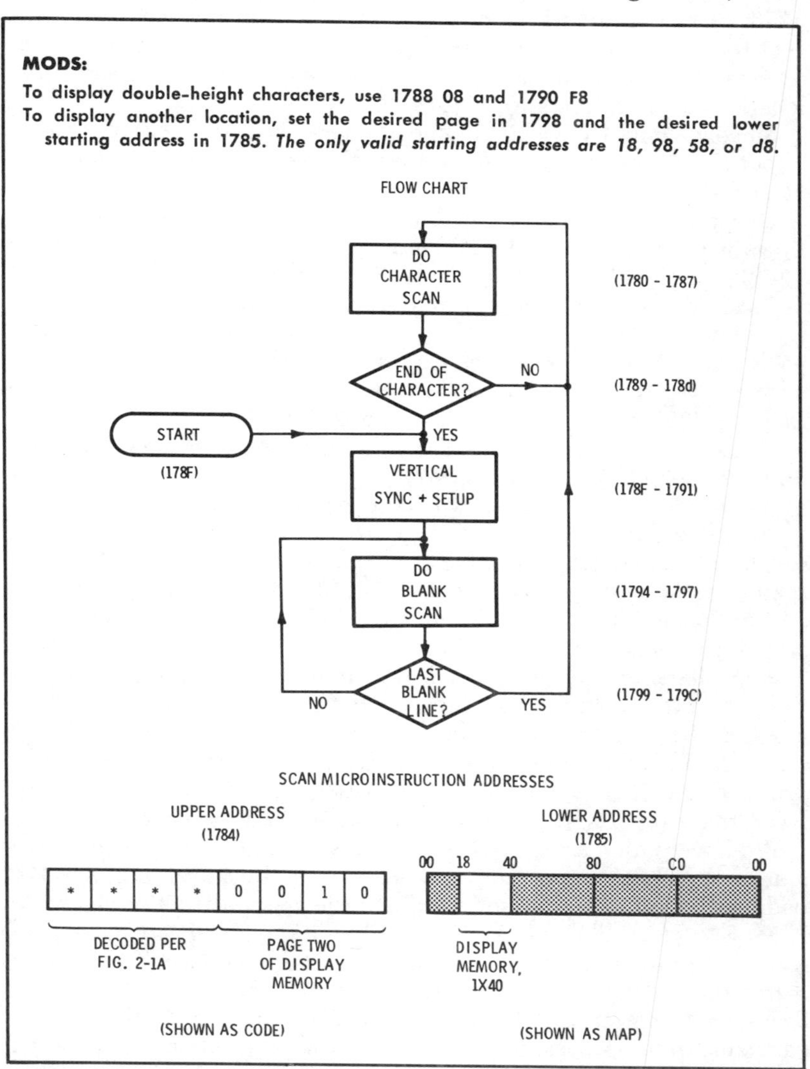

no-interlace TVT 6 5/8 Raster Scan.

0238 being the leftmost character. The Scan program is stored in 1780 through 179d.

The key to picking a new row of character dots each time is to jump to a Scan microinstruction at a *computed* location. A jump to subroutine JSR then activates the Scan microinstruction and outputs a row of character code for us. Locations 1785 (lower address) and 1786 (upper address) store our computed starting location. Note that these addresses have to be RAM, since you first store the values you want the Scan to start with in them, and then use the same two locations as an address for a JSR.

Since we only have a single line of characters, we need only worry about computing a new high address; the low address stays constant at hex 18.

Our program starts by loading the right number of blank Scan lines in the X register (178F) and producing a vertical-sync pulse (1791). Incidentally, it is always a good idea to load X *before* the vertical-sync pulse. This will help our transparency as we will see in Chapter 5. This is followed by our first blank Scan at 1794. After each blank Scan, X is reduced by one (1799), and tested. As long as the X register has some value other than zero in it, the program loops to 1792 and repeats another blank Scan.

When all the blank Scans are finished, the X register hits zero and the Branch on Equal (179A) loops us to the part of the program that is going to put down the character dot rows.

Step 1784 next puts down the top row of character dots for us as it calls a Scan miscroinstruction at a computed address. While this is going on, the upper address value is held in the accumulator. After a row of dots is scanned, we increment our character Scan "counter" in step 1787 and test it for the final character line in 1789. If another row of character dots is needed, the program loops to 1781, stores the computed new upper address, and then scans that row of dots.

After the last line of character dots is complete, we go on to once again load the number of blank lines wanted for the next frame, produce a vertical-sync pulse and then go on to the blank Scans. Everything repeats at the noninterlaced 60-Hz frame rate.

We have pulled a sneaky trick in steps 1792 and 1793 to save two words. A vertical-sync pulse can be gotten by any LDY XX EX coding. Since the X's do not matter to the sync instruction, let's use LDY EA EA. But EA is also a No-Operation (NOP) or a way to use up 2 μs without doing anything. So, we have two "free" no-op words buried in our existing code. These are used to make the blank Scans long enough to take the needed 63-μs microseconds. If your particular microprocessor will not allow this stunt, just add 4 μs of NOP or some other "wheel spinning" between 179A and 179C, and then branch directly to 1794.

Loop Timing

Note particularly the timing of each loop. Our active Scan microinstruction takes 40 μs. The overhead to get into and out of the Scan microinstruction takes another 10 μs. *Thirteen* microseconds are spent in the program in every loop in every direction, over and above the microinstruction call. The Scan plus overhead plus the program equals $40 + 10 + 13 = 63$ μs, the time of one horizontal line.

Let's double check to prove that each loop does, in fact, take exactly 13 μs to execute:

Between blank Scans:

1797	LDA	2 μs
1799	DEX	2 μs
179A	BEQ (not taken)	2 μs
179C	BNE (taken)	3 μs
1791	NOP	2 μs
1792	NOP	2 μs
	TOTAL	13 μs

From the last blank Scan to the first dot row:

1797	LDA	2 μs
1799	DEX	2 μs
179A	BEQ (taken)	3 μs
1780	CLC	2 μs
1781	STA	4 μs
	TOTAL	13 μs

From a character dot row to the next character dot row:

1787	ADC	2 μs
1789	CMP	2 μs
178b	BCS (not taken)	2 μs
178d	BCC (taken)	3 μs
1781	STA	4 μs
	TOTAL	13 μs

From the last character dot row to the first blank Scan:

1787	ADC	2 μs
1789	CMP	2 μs
178b	BCS (taken)	3 μs
178F	LDX	2 μs
1791	LDY	4 μs
	TOTAL	13 μs

If any one of these loops takes longer than the others, our Scan ends up in deep trouble. We will get a torn or otherwise unstable display. *Any differences in loop times from falling edge to falling edge of the Scan microinstruction will ruin the display.*

Some Finer Points

An odd number of microseconds for each horizontal line time seems to be a good initial choice for the 6502 systems. A branch is almost always involved in the loops, and branches taken use up 3 μs, compared to the 2 or 4 μs of most common instructions. We can sometimes convert an odd line time into an even one or vice versa by taking a branch that goes nowhere, such as BCC 90 00 with the carry cleared. But this wastes two words and, worse still, wastes 3 μs of critical loop time.

We can call any "wheel spinning" times in the loops *equalization.* The combination PHA PLA gives us 7 μs of delay in only two code words. NOP gives us 2 μs of equalization in one code word. Going to a subroutine and immediately returning uses up 12 μs in four code words. And the combination of loading the Y register, decrementing it, and branching if not equal can give us 6 + 5Y μs of delay in five code words. Delay values of 6, 11, 16, 21, 26, 31, . . . microseconds are available simply by picking larger values for Y.

The trick is to do useful things at the same time you are equalizing, for otherwise, there simply is not enough time both to make things come out even and to do the needed calculations as well. *Make all your loops the same length, but minimize any equalization-only steps in doing so.*

Any addition done in a program (such as 1787) has to be preceded by a known state of the carry flag. We come out of the blanking loop with the carry set, so we have to clear it in 1780. But the carry is already cleared, coming out of the BCC from the character dot row loop, so it is ready to go without wasting any time reclearing it. Note that for immediate additions, we have the option of always having the carry *set* and adding *one less* than normal. Either way, *always be certain that the carry is known before any addition is done.*

Is step 178b and 178C wasted? Can we save two words here? Leave the BCS off, and loop the character-scan counter to 1780 instead of 1781, and this loop still takes 13 μs. But the loop from the final character Scan to the first blanking run would now take only 12, instead of 13 μs, and there is no free and obvious way to equalize 1 μs. In this particular instance, there are lots of blank lines following the 1-μs error, so we can get away with this simplification. In general, you must keep all loops identical in execution time.

> *Your Turn:*
>
> Design and debug a 1 × 40, TVT 6 5/8 noninterlaced Scan program needing 28 or fewer words of storage. Modify it for double-height characters.

Note the asterisks and parentheses in the program. These will help you move the program around. An asterisk is a relative branch; these values change if you lengthen or shorten the program; they usually do not change if you simply move the program somewhere else. The parentheses are absolute locations. They will always change if the program is moved somewhere else, but may or may not change if the program length changes.

Two modifications of our 1 × 40 program are also shown in Fig. 2-7. We get double-height characters by adding only half enough each time at 1787. We relocate the display memory anywhere below 0FFF we like by putting the desired page in 1798 and the desired starting address in 1785. Note that the only valid starting addresses are 18, 58, 98, and d8. Why is this?

16 × 40, No Interlace

So far, we have been lucky. All the loops worked out just right, without making them longer or shorter than needed. But, what can we do when we have to compute the location of a new row of characters, or the exact position of a vertical-sync pulse?

There are two things than can help us. First, we can shorten any blank line by any even amount we need to gain compute time. In the case of a 40-character line, we can go as low as two blanks, leaving us an extra 38 μs of compute time on top of the 13 μs we already had available. If you are careful, you can do a lot of things in 51 μs. And even more time is available in slower 64- and 80-character Scans.

A second approach is called *pipelining*. If there is not enough time between Scan microinstructions to do something, you set up and prepare for as much of it as you can as early as you can, *before* an intervening blank or live Scan. This will be very handy later in our graphics software where blank lines do not exist between chunks.

The obvious extension of our 1 × 40 program is to make it into the 16 × 40 no-interlace Scan program of Fig. 2-8.

We have kept pretty much the same setup and vertical blanking Scans (17A0-17Ad), and the same sequence to put down a complete set of character dots for one line of characters (1780-178b). In order to change the character lines, we add a blank line between each row of characters. We make the Scan portion of this blank line short, and then use the extra time available to compute the

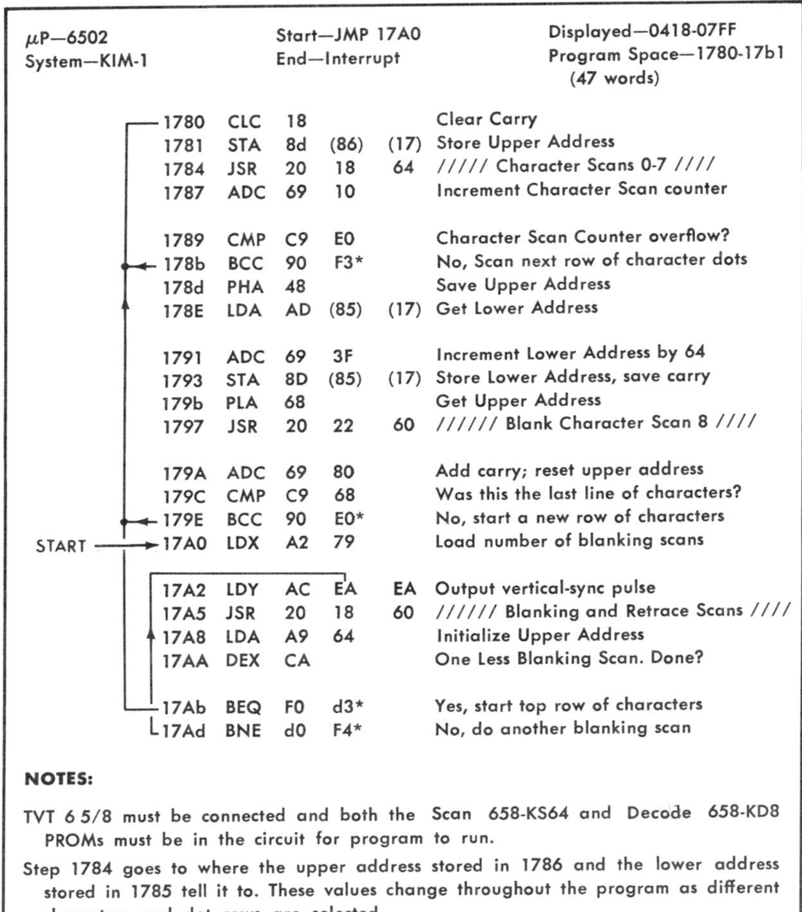

μP—6502
System—KIM-1

Start—JMP 17A0
End—Interrupt

Displayed—0418-07FF
Program Space—1780-17b1
(47 words)

```
        1780  CLC  18                 Clear Carry
        1781  STA  8d  (86)  (17)     Store Upper Address
        1784  JSR  20  18    64       ///// Character Scans 0-7 ////
        1787  ADC  69  10             Increment Character Scan counter

        1789  CMP  C9  E0             Character Scan Counter overflow?
        178b  BCC  90  F3*            No, Scan next row of character dots
        178d  PHA  48                 Save Upper Address
        178E  LDA  AD  (85)  (17)     Get Lower Address

        1791  ADC  69  3F             Increment Lower Address by 64
        1793  STA  8D  (85)  (17)     Store Lower Address, save carry
        179b  PLA  68                 Get Upper Address
        1797  JSR  20  22    60       ////// Blank Character Scan 8 ////

        179A  ADC  69  80             Add carry; reset upper address
        179C  CMP  C9  68             Was this the last line of characters?
        179E  BCC  90  E0*            No, start a new row of characters
START → 17A0  LDX  A2  79             Load number of blanking scans

        17A2  LDY  AC  EA    EA       Output vertical-sync pulse
        17A5  JSR  20  18    60       ////// Blanking and Retrace Scans ////
        17A8  LDA  A9  64             Initialize Upper Address
        17AA  DEX  CA                 One Less Blanking Scan. Done?

        17Ab  BEQ  F0  d3*            Yes, start top row of characters
        17Ad  BNE  d0  F4*            No, do another blanking scan
```

NOTES:

TVT 6 5/8 must be connected and both the Scan 658-KS64 and Decode 658-KD8 PROMs must be in the circuit for program to run.

Step 1784 goes to where the upper address stored in 1786 and the lower address stored in 1785 tell it to. These values change throughout the program as different characters and dot rows are selected.

Horizontal Frequency is 15,873 Hz with 1.0-MHz clock. Vertical frequency is 59.90 Hz with 9.8-second hum bar. No Interlace. 144 active lines, 121 blank, 265 total.

( ) Denotes an absolute address that is program location sensitive.

* Denotes a relative branch that is program length sensitive

Fig. 2-8. Program for a 16-line, 40-character-per-line,

MODS:

To Change the Number of Display Lines or the Height of the Characters, Use:

Lines	Height	179d	1788	17A1
16	Normal	68	10	79
12	Normal	67	10	9d
8	Normal	66	10	C1
8	Double†	66	08	81
4	Normal	65	10	E5
4	Double†	65	08	C5

† Only works if upstream tap and chip select is across 1K or less of display memory.

FLOW CHART

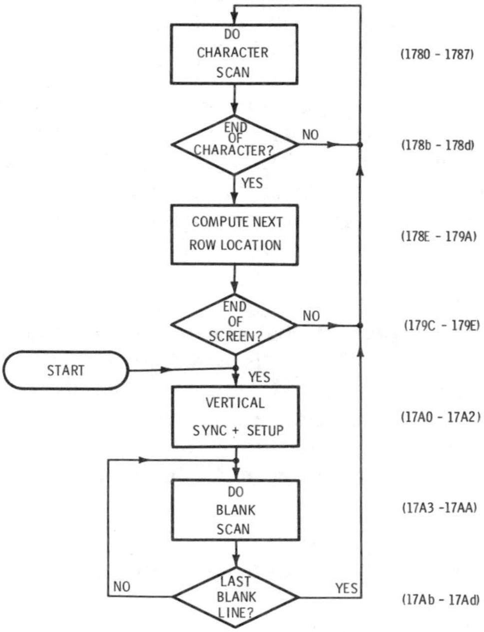

SCAN MICROINSTRUCTION ADDRESSES

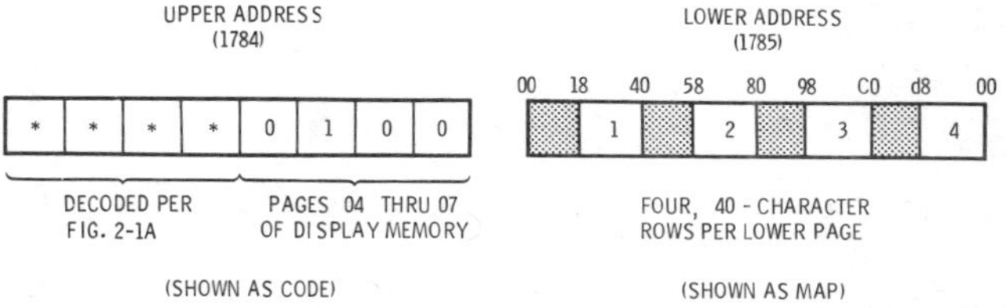

no-interlace TVT 6 5/8 Raster Scan.

starting address for the next row of characters. We do this in steps 178d through 179b.

Remember that our accumulator held the upper address for us during the active Scans. We stash this upper address temporarily on the stack (178d) and then get the lower address for modification. We add 64 counts to the lower address in 1791 by adding hex 3F plus a carry. Our new lower address is then restored in 1793.

Our carry gets set every time there is a lower address page overflow. This happens once every *four* character rows. When an overflow occurs, we have to suitably modify our upper address as well. But carry or no carry, our upper address is wrong anyway, since its one past the bottom of the character and should be set to the top of a new character row. So there are two things we have to do to our upper address: We have to *reset* it to the top line; and, if a page overflow happened on the lower address, we have to add one to the page select.

We correct the upper address by getting it back out of the stack in 179b, take time out for a blank Scan microinstruction (this is an example of pipelining), and then correct the upper address in 179A. We then check for the last line on the screen, and in 179E, either repeat a new character row, or else go on to the blanking Scans.

Timing Details

It is extremely important that the blank line that computes the next row of characters for us is *exactly* the same length as the character row times. If it is not, you get a bunch of teeth that tear up the display, bandsaw style. Let's check to make sure we have taken exactly enough time to move to the next character row, by comparing this time against one of the other loops in the Scan program:

From a dot row to the next on the same character:

1787	ADC	2 μsec.
1789	CMP	2 μsec.
178b	BCC (taken)	3 μsec.
1780	CLC (equalization)	2 μsec.
1781	STA	4 μsec.
plus		
	Scan Overhead	10 μsec.
plus		
	Scan Microinstruction	40 μsec.
	TOTAL	63 μsec.

From the last dot row on one character to the top (blank) dot row on the next row of characters:

1787	ADC	2 μsec.
1789	CMP	2 μsec.
178b	BCC (not taken)	2 μsec.
178d	PHA	3 μsec.
178E	LDA	4 μsec.
1791	ADC	2 μsec.
1793	STA	4 μsec.
179b	PLA	4 μsec.
plus		
	Scan Overhead	10 μsec.
plus		
	Short Blank Scan	30 μsec.
	TOTAL	63 μsec.

Thus, by making the calculation part of the loop longer by 10 μs, and shortening the blank Scan by 10 μs, we come out even with a 63-μs line.

We have cheated a bit once again by 1 μs on the first blanking loop. But, in this program, there is enough blank Scan time during retrace for recovery. Where is this loop? How can you fix it with more code?

> *Your Turn:*
>
> Design a Scan program for a 16-line, 64-character-per-line, no interlace TVT 6 5/8 raster Scan. Use an 85-μs horizontal line time. Be sure to initialize the lower address once each frame.

Our 16 × 40 Scan looks great at first glance. We get lots of characters on the screen, a stock horizontal frequency, and we are doing all this with only 47 words of Scan program. But, there are many things wrong with this program, and we have shown it to you only as a stepping stone to the good stuff that follows.

Some of the problems we are about to fix are:

* The Scan will not run on a bare bones KIM-1 since the display memory is too big to fit on pages 02 and 03.
* We actively work on the lower address (1785) but never re-

initialize it. This is dangerous and limits us to multiples of four character rows per raster.

* There is no interlace. Interlace makes much more attractive characters, particularly on long line lengths. Interlace is also essential for titling and superposition of existing video.
* There is no double stuffing possible since we do not have interlace. This severely limits how many character rows we can put on the screen.
* Only 40 of each 64 words of display memory are used. The rest are wasted, a total loss of 384 locations.

Let's attack these problems one by one. They are all solvable with some simple mods and a few more words of code.

Adding Interlace

In an *interlaced* Scan, two $\frac{1}{60}$th second fields are interwoven in order to form a single $\frac{1}{30}$th second frame. On the first pass, the scan starts in the upper left corner and ends at the bottom middle of the screen, moving rapidly to the right and slowly downward and generating *one half* of the needed horizontal Scan lines. On the second trip, the Scan starts in the upper middle and ends at the bottom right, putting down the remaining horizontal Scan lines. If 525 Scan lines are used, there are 262½ spent on each field. Interlace always takes an *odd* number of total Scan lines.

Interlace does lots of good things for us. It lets us lock our Scan to existing interlaced-program material for titling and superposition. It gives us much more attractive characters since it eliminates the ugly stripes common to most noninterlaced Scans (Fig. 1-10A). This is extra important on long character lines and characters whose width is narrow compared to their height. Finally, interlaced Scans seem to be essential for the *double-stuffing* techniques that let you double or nearly double the number of characters on the screen.

Our microprocessor-based cheap video displays use a very simple software interlace, *There are no hardware differences at all.* To pick up interlace, you simply add a few words (around 25) to your Scan program. Because of the simplicity and the tremendous advantages of interlace, *you should use interlace for practically all video displays.*

Fig. 2-9 shows how to add interlace. We reserve the first blank Scan line to calculate our interlace activity for that field. On the first field, we put down N scan lines and deliver a vertical-sync pulse *early* during the first blank Scan. On the second field, we put down N + 1 Scan lines and deliver a vertical-sync pulse *late* during the first blank Scan. The net result is 2N + 1 horizontal Scan and two equally spaced vertical-sync pulses per field. This is identical to the traditional and more complicated hardware ways of doing the same thing.

There usually will be a very slight jitter between even and odd vertical-sync pulses. Typically, you can reduce this to 1 μs. But, even if the jitter is 10 or 12 μs, there seems to be no visual effect on the screen. All jitter does to us is slightly *uncenter* the spacing between sequential per-frame raster lines, a negligible effect. Nevertheless, if you are a programming purist, you will probably want to adjust your early- and late-sync times to be as close to exactly one-half the horizontal line time as you can get.

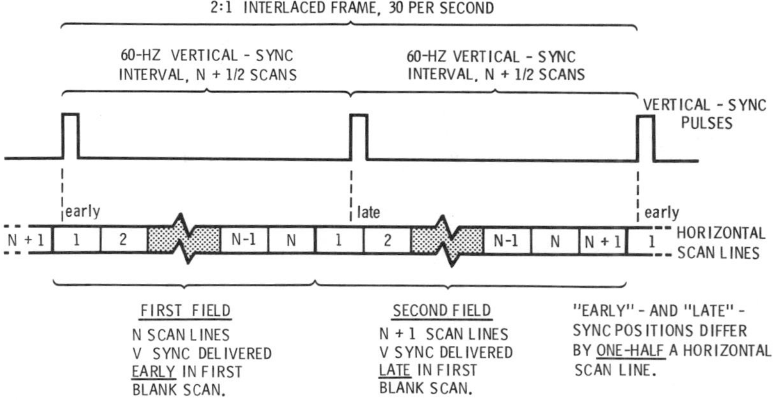

Fig. 2-9. Adding interlace is essentially free; requires just a few extra words in the Scan program.

Our software interlace generator is usually followed by a hardware vertical-position control. Once the sync pulses are generated, it is a simple matter to delay them.

16 × 32 Interlaced Scan

This will be our first Interlaced-Scan program and it is shown in Fig. 2-10. The program gives you sixteen lines of 32 characters each and will fit nicely and densely on pages 02 and 03 of a bare bones KIM-1. A standard horizontal frequency is used and the magic numbers give us an almost stationary hum bar. *This is an ideal short display, and should be the starting point for everything you do with cheap video displays.*

Except for interlace, the program uses the same ideas we used on the 16 × 40 program. All but our first blank Scan line are generated in 17C2 through 17d3. The characters are generated in 1780 through 178F. Note the 10 μs of equalization in 1785 and 1786 needed to lengthen the Scan lines, since we only have a live character time of

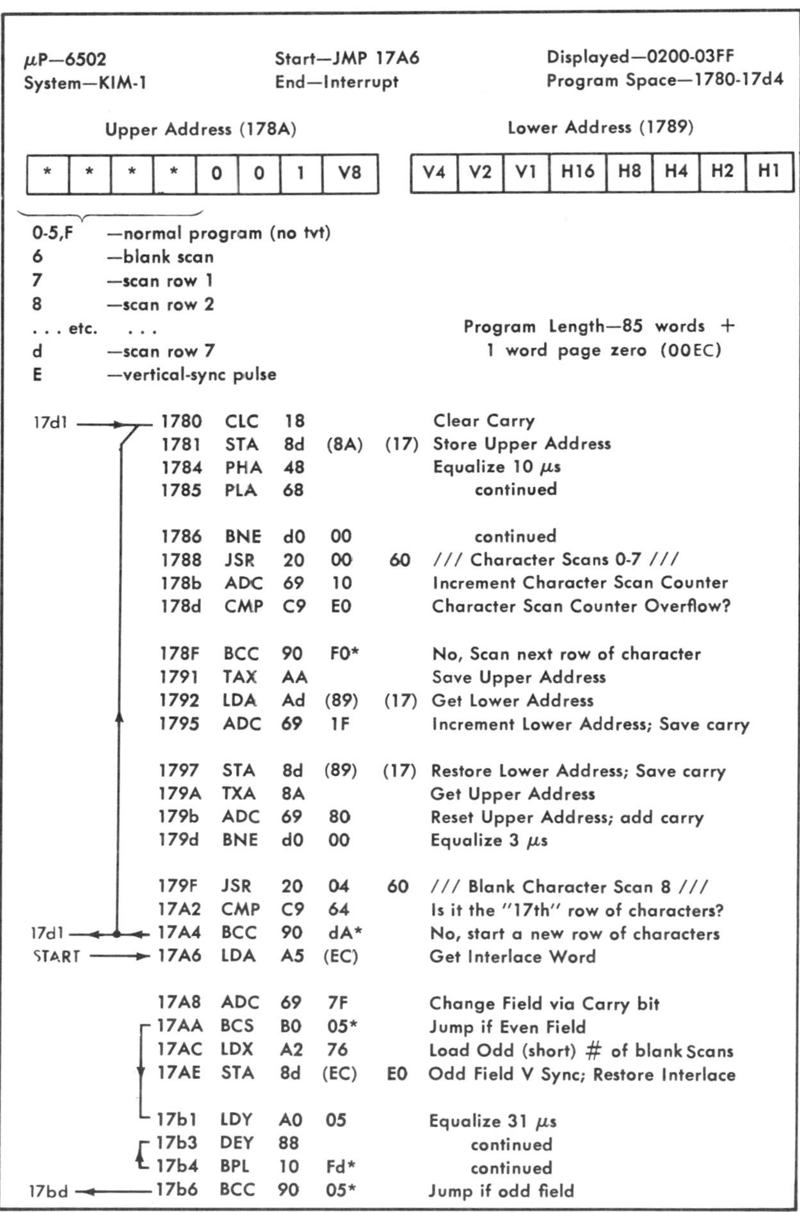

μP—6502
System—KIM-1

Start—JMP 17A6
End—Interrupt

Displayed—0200-03FF
Program Space—1780-17d4

Upper Address (178A)

*	*	*	*	0	0	1	V8

Lower Address (1789)

V4	V2	V1	H16	H8	H4	H2	H1

0-5,F —normal program (no tvt)
6 —blank scan
7 —scan row 1
8 —scan row 2
. . . etc. . . .
d —scan row 7
E —vertical-sync pulse

Program Length—85 words +
1 word page zero (00EC)

	Address	Op	Code			Comment
17d1 →	1780	CLC	18			Clear Carry
	1781	STA	8d	(8A)	(17)	Store Upper Address
	1784	PHA	48			Equalize 10 μs
	1785	PLA	68			continued
	1786	BNE	d0	00		continued
	1788	JSR	20	00	60	/// Character Scans 0-7 ///
	178b	ADC	69	10		Increment Character Scan Counter
	178d	CMP	C9	E0		Character Scan Counter Overflow?
	178F	BCC	90	F0*		No, Scan next row of character
	1791	TAX	AA			Save Upper Address
	1792	LDA	Ad	(89)	(17)	Get Lower Address
	1795	ADC	69	1F		Increment Lower Address; Save carry
	1797	STA	8d	(89)	(17)	Restore Lower Address; Save carry
	179A	TXA	8A			Get Upper Address
	179b	ADC	69	80		Reset Upper Address; add carry
	179d	BNE	d0	00		Equalize 3 μs
	179F	JSR	20	04	60	/// Blank Character Scan 8 ///
	17A2	CMP	C9	64		Is it the "17th" row of characters?
17d1 ←	17A4	BCC	90	dA*		No, start a new row of characters
START →	17A6	LDA	A5	(EC)		Get Interlace Word
	17A8	ADC	69	7F		Change Field via Carry bit
	17AA	BCS	B0	05*		Jump if Even Field
	17AC	LDX	A2	76		Load Odd (short) # of blank Scans
	17AE	STA	8d	(EC)	E0	Odd Field V Sync; Restore Interlace
	17b1	LDY	A0	05		Equalize 31 μs
	17b3	DEY	88			continued
	17b4	BPL	10	Fd*		continued
17bd ←	17b6	BCC	90	05*		Jump if odd field

Fig. 2-10. Program for a 16-line, 32-character-per-line,

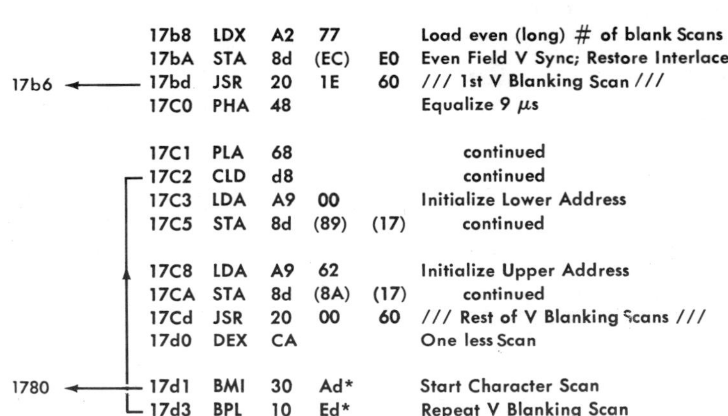

```
                17b8  LDX  A2  77          Load even (long) # of blank Scans
                17bA  STA  8d  (EC)   E0   Even Field V Sync; Restore Interlace
17b6 <-------   17bd  JSR  20  1E     60   /// 1st V Blanking Scan ///
                17C0  PHA  48              Equalize 9 µs

                17C1  PLA  68                 continued
              ┌ 17C2  CLD  d8                 continued
              │ 17C3  LDA  A9  00          Initialize Lower Address
              │ 17C5  STA  8d  (89)   (17)    continued
              │
              ^ 17C8  LDA  A9  62          Initialize Upper Address
              │ 17CA  STA  8d  (8A)   (17)    continued
              │ 17Cd  JSR  20  00     60   /// Rest of V Blanking Scans ///
              │ 17d0  DEX  CA              One less Scan
              │
1780 <--------┼ 17d1  BMI  30  Ad*         Start Character Scan
              └ 17d3  BPL  10  Ed*         Repeat V Blanking Scan
```

NOTES:

TVT 6 5/8 must be connected and both the Scan (658-KS8) and Decode (658-KD64) PROMs must be in circuit for program to run.

Both 17AE and 17bA require that page 00 be enabled when page E0 is addressed. This is done automatically in the KIM-1 decode circuitry.

Location 00EC on page zero is reserved as an interlace storage bit.

Step 1788 goes to where the upper address stored in 178A and the lower address stored in 1789 tells it to. Values in these slots continuously change throughout the program.

For a 525-line system, use 17Ad 54 and 17b9 55 and a KIM-1 crystal of 992.250 kHz. This is ONLY needed for a video superposition or titling applications; the stock 1-MHz crystal is used for ALL OTHER uses.

Normal program horizontal frequency is 15,873.015 Hz; Vertical 60.0114 Hz. 63 µs per line, 264.5 lines per field; 2 fields per frame, 529 lines total.

TVT 6 5/8 switch must be in the "32" position.

( ) Denotes an absolute address that is program location sensitive.

* Denotes a relative branch that is program length sensitive.

Continued on next page.

interlaced TVT 6 5/8 Raster Scan.

To display other pages, use:

Pages Displayed	17A3	17C9	TVT Connection
0000-01FF	62	60	KIM-1
0200-03FF	64	62	KIM-1
0400-05FF	66	64	KIM-2
0600-07FF	68	66	KIM-2
0800-09FF	6A	68	KIM-2
0A00-0bFF	6C	6A	KIM-2
0C00-0dFF	6E	6C	KIM-2
0E00-0FFF	70	6E	KIM-2

For higher pages, move contents to 0200-03FF or 0400-05FF.

FLOW CHART

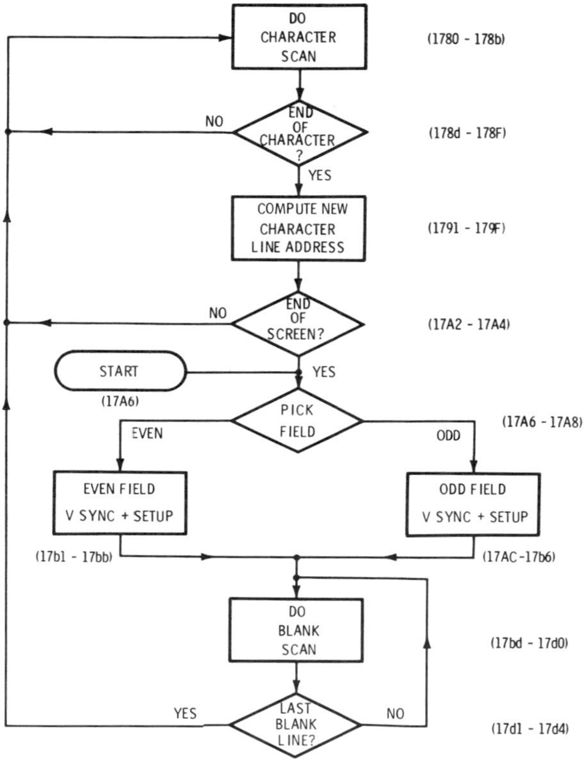

Fig. 2-10 *Continued.* Program for a 16-line, 32-character-per-line, interlaced TVT 6 5/8 Raster Scan.

32 μs. Our sequential rows of characters are calculated as before in steps 1791 through 17A4.

Our interlace calculation is done on the first blank Scan line. We have to do two things. First, we have to decide *how many* blank Scans we want on the field we just started; and secondly, we have to pick an early or late vertical-sync pulse and deliver it during the first blank Scan. Always pick the number of blank lines *first;* this will help transparency later.

We store an *interlace* word "ILCE" on page zero at location 00EC. It does not matter what the value is that this word starts out as. In each field, we retrieve ILCE, add hex 80 to it, and replace it. This will *set* the carry on one field and *clear* it on the next field. We will use the resultant carry bit to *steer* us either to an early sync pulse and N blank lines or a late sync pulse N + 1 blank lines.

On the early sync field, we load the X register for N blank scans in 17AC. We next produce a vertical-sync pulse and restore the new interlace word in 17AE. This is followed by 31 μs worth of wheel-spinning equalization, after which we go on to the rest of the blank Scans.

On the late sync field, we first wheel spin for 31 μs in 17b1 through 17b4 and then load the X register with N + 1 blank Scans in 17b9. This is followed by the vertical-sync pulse and interlace word restoration in 17bA. After this, we go on to the rest of the blank Scans.

Note particularly the steering action of the carry bit. If carry is cleared, we do the early sync program followed by the equalization. If carry is set, we do the equalization first, followed by the late sync program.

We run this Scan program by jumping to the starting address at 17A6. This program will only run when your TVT 6⅝ is connected to your KIM-1. The hardware length switch on the TVT 6⅝ must be in the "32" position.

We stop our display by interrupting, either to return to a main program, a Cursor controller, or the computer operating system.

Your Turn:

> Design a 16 × 40 interlaced TVT 6 5/8 program running on a normal horizontal frequency. Modify it to an 8 × 40 double-height character program that uses pages 02 and 03 for display memory.

Fig. 2-10 also shows us how to move the display memory around as needed for other system uses. Remember that your upstream tap has to be available at the chosen locations when we do this. If you move your 16 × 32 program to KIM-1 pages 00 and 01 and add a Hex-ASCII converter, the stack and all operating system values can be displayed at once.

We can convert our 16 × 32 interlaced Scan into exact EIA magic numbers of 15,750 Hz horizontal and 60 Hz vertical by using a crystal of 992.250 KHz and changing the number of blank lines as shown in the program. This is *only* needed for video superposition and titling. All other applications can run with the stock 1-MHz crystal.

Should you want to eliminate interlace for a comparison, just load 17A9 FF. Note how the stripes appear in the characters. To return to full interlace, load 17A9 7F.

More Characters

There are many ways we can get more characters on the screen. We have already picked a 5 × 7 character generator to minimize video bandwidth and the number of vertical lines per character. You can add lines by shortening the number of blank Scans, so long as twenty or so blank Scan lines remain. You can also skip the top blank line of each character row, but this tends to put the characters too close together.

Another way to put more characters on the screen is to put two characters in the same slot, alternating them at a slow rate. This is the key to hex op-code displays, but is a very special route to go.

We might be tempted to spend less time computing and more time displaying, still staying within the normal horizontal line time. At the computer end, we could use "brute force" software that would simply call one Scan microinstruction after another. This could get us down to a nonscan time of 10 μs, leaving us with a limit of 53 characters or so per line.

> *Your Turn:*
>
> Write a "brute force" Scan program that calls, rather than computes, all live scans needed for a 1 × 53 display. Are you able to attractively display this many characters?

Unfortunately, there is trouble on the tv end that usually prevents this. Between the normal time needed for horizontal retrace, the extreme overscan of many stock tv sets, and fairly bad spot defocusing toward the screen edges, you will find it very difficult to attractively display more than 42 characters per horizontal line if you stick to a one-microsecond-per-character rate and standard horizontal frequency and width on a stock tv set.

So, what does this leave us? How else can we increase the character density on the screen? Here are three good ways to go:

* By *double stuffing* characters, we can double or nearly double the number of characters vertically on the screen. Double stuffing only needs Scan program changes and is "free" in the same sense that interlace was free with a few extra software words.
* By going to a *reduced horizontal rate,* we can put 64- or 80-character lines on the screen, yet still stay within the normal video bandwidths of unmodified tv sets and rf modulators. A reduced horizontal rate does take hold and width modifications to the set, but these are easily and safely done on small-screen black and white sets.
* By using *memory repacking* techniques, we can store 40- and 80-character lines in a display memory in pretty much the same space that we can store binary 32 or 64 length lines. This raises the number of characters on the screen for a given number of available display memory words or, alternately, reduces the per-character storage cost. Memory repacking tends to make the Scan and Cursor software more complex, but this usually takes only a few extra words.

These three techniques of double stuffing, reduced horizontal, and memory repacking can be used in any combination. How much of this you want to do depends on your application.

For minimum memory and simple operation, the 16 × 32 interlaced Scan is a good choice and should *always* be your starting point for anything fancier. Double stuffing can bring this up to 32 × 32 or 32 × 40 with a stock horizontal frequency and width.

The 64-character line is a good choice for general use and text editing, and results in very simple Scan programs and Cursor hardware. But, much of the software already written for microcomputer use assumes an 80-character teletypewriter line. For compatibility, we might like to use an 80-character line with reduced horizontal operation, or else we can use *two* 40-character lines per teletypewriter line, staying within the normal horizontal range. Lines 80 characters long also let us put two separate 40-character lines side by side for source and object listings, or anywhere else you want a "before" and "after" presentation. Your tv mods tend to be heavier for the 80-character line than the 64, and most often, the 64-character format will give you more pleasing results.

Double Stuffing

In a *double stuffed* display, we put down the *even* rows of character dots on one field and the *odd* rows of character dots on the second field. We do this by adding a few more words to the Scan program. No hardware changes are needed. Add-on changes for double stuffing are usually included in the interlace calculations made during the first blank line. This way, one program can serve for normal or double-stuffed Scans simply by changing a few words.

Fig. 2-11 shows an algorithm that gives us double stuffing. At the start of an *even* field, we initialize our character generator to start on the top blank row zero. We start scanning dots in the usual way, except that every time we go to a new row of dots, we *double* the amount usually added and *skip* one row. We move sequentially through lines 0,2,4, and 6. The entire field continues in the usual way, except for this skipping every second row of dots.

When we start the next *odd* field, we initialize our character generator to work on the first dot line or line one of our dots. We start scanning again, and again pick up every second row of dots. But this time, it is dot lines 1, 3, 5, and 7 that get put down.

Half of the character dots go down on the even field and half on the odd field. Characters are totally refreshed and appear whole 30 times a second.

If we only use interlace, we have been spending 18 lines to put

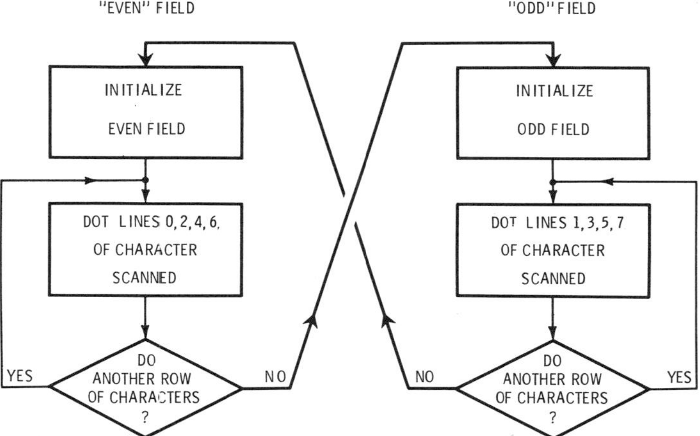

Fig. 2-11. Double-stuffing algorithm puts twice as many characters vertically on the screen.

down a row of characters, arranged as two fields of 9 lines each. Both fields were identical. Seven of these lines are for dots. One line is the top blank line. The final line is the blank line needed between characters to compute the next character address.

Now, if we use both interlace and double stuffing, we end up with only 10 lines per character, spending 5 per field. Four of these are dots, the fifth is the blank line between characters. So, double stuffing gives us eighteen tenths of the number of characters vertically. This can almost double the number of characters on the screen. Alternately, this can almost double the other-program throughput during transport operation.

If you have extra blanking lines available, these can be borrowed to actually double the number of character rows on the screen. Thus you can usually go from 16 × 32 to 32 × 32; from 16 × 40 to 32 × 40; from 16 × 64 to 32 × 64; and from 12 × 80 to 24 × 80 character displays. While 32 × 80 is possible, there is no throughput left for transparency and that is a large number of characters to view at once.

32 × 64 Interlaced Scan

A double-stuffed 32 × 64 Scan program is shown in Fig. 2-12. Except for the new double stuffing calculations made during the first blank Scan, everything else is much the same as our earlier Interlaced-Scan program. We can see our blank Scans in 17d8 through 17E1, and our character dot row sequencing in 1780 through 178d. But notice 178A, where we add *twice* as much to our character dot counter so that we skip a dot row each time. New rows of characters are picked up as before in 178F through 17A1.

Our first blank Scan also has some familiar features. We get an interlace word at 17A3 and use it to set or clear the carry bit, steering us to an even or odd field. On the even field, we put down a short number of blank Scans and an early vertical-sync pulse. On the odd field, one extra blank Scan is loaded into the X register, followed by a late vertical-sync pulse.

> *Your Turn:*
>
> Design a double-stuffed 32 × 32 Scan program running at normal horizontal frequency. Do not let the Scan program go past 17E6, the maximum allowable RAM location in the KIM-1 scratchpad.

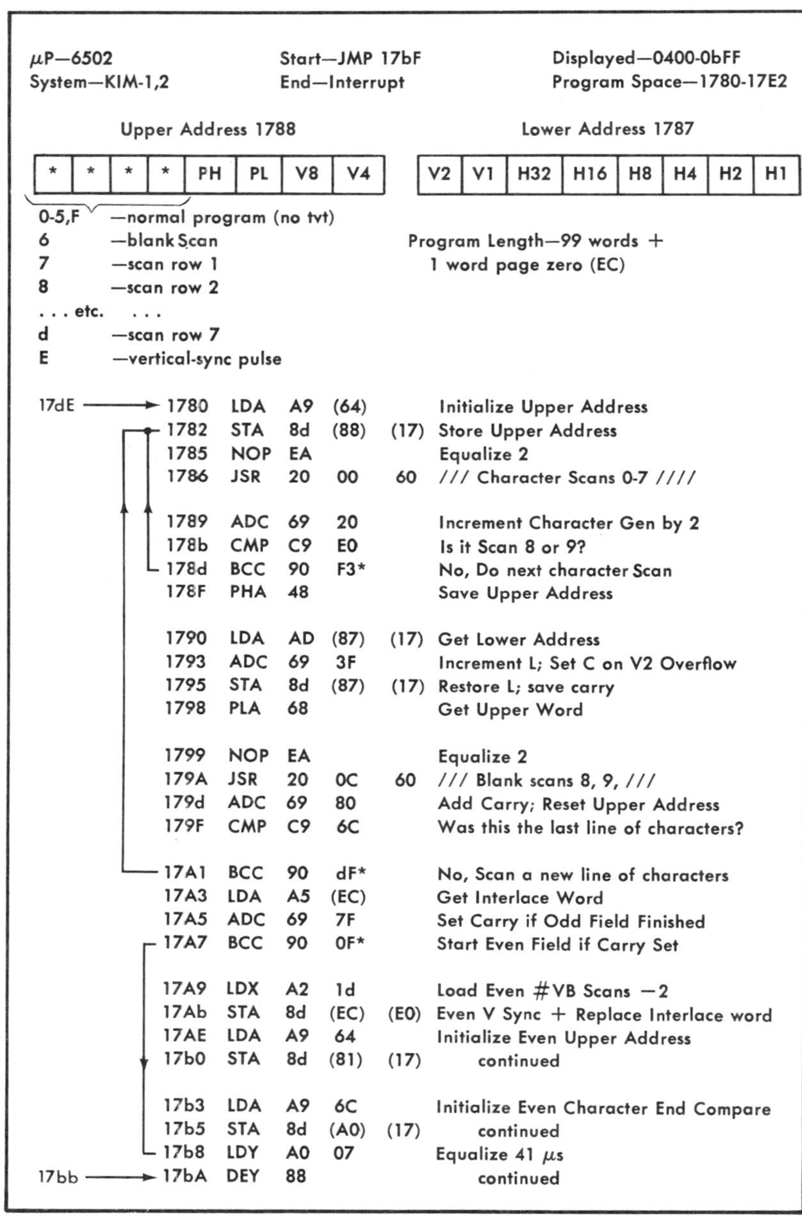

```
µP—6502                    Start—JMP 17bF          Displayed—0400-0bFF
System—KIM-1,2             End—Interrupt           Program Space—1780-17E2

          Upper Address 1788                           Lower Address 1787

| * | * | * | * | PH | PL | V8 | V4 |     | V2 | V1 | H32 | H16 | H8 | H4 | H2 | H1 |

0-5,F      —normal program (no tvt)
6          —blank Scan                   Program Length—99 words +
7          —scan row 1                     1 word page zero (EC)
8          —scan row 2
. . . etc.   . . .
d          —scan row 7
E          —vertical-sync pulse

17dE ———→ 1780  LDA  A9  (64)           Initialize Upper Address
          1782  STA  8d  (88)   (17)    Store Upper Address
          1785  NOP  EA                 Equalize 2
          1786  JSR  20   00     60     /// Character Scans 0-7 ////

          1789  ADC  69   20            Increment Character Gen by 2
          178b  CMP  C9   E0            Is it Scan 8 or 9?
          178d  BCC  90   F3*           No, Do next character Scan
          178F  PHA  48                 Save Upper Address

          1790  LDA  AD  (87)   (17)    Get Lower Address
          1793  ADC  69   3F            Increment L; Set C on V2 Overflow
          1795  STA  8d  (87)   (17)    Restore L; save carry
          1798  PLA  68                 Get Upper Word

          1799  NOP  EA                 Equalize 2
          179A  JSR  20   0C     60     /// Blank scans 8, 9, ///
          179d  ADC  69   80            Add Carry; Reset Upper Address
          179F  CMP  C9   6C            Was this the last line of characters?

          17A1  BCC  90   dF*           No, Scan a new line of characters
          17A3  LDA  A5  (EC)           Get Interlace Word
          17A5  ADC  69   7F            Set Carry if Odd Field Finished
          17A7  BCC  90   0F*           Start Even Field if Carry Set

          17A9  LDX  A2   1d            Load Even #VB Scans −2
          17Ab  STA  8d  (EC)   (E0)    Even V Sync + Replace Interlace word
          17AE  LDA  A9   64            Initialize Even Upper Address
          17b0  STA  8d  (81)   (17)        continued

          17b3  LDA  A9   6C            Initialize Even Character End Compare
          17b5  STA  8d  (A0)   (17)        continued
          17b8  LDY  A0   07            Equalize 41 µs
17bb ———→ 17bA  DEY  88                     continued
```

Fig. 2-12. Program for a 16- or 32-line,

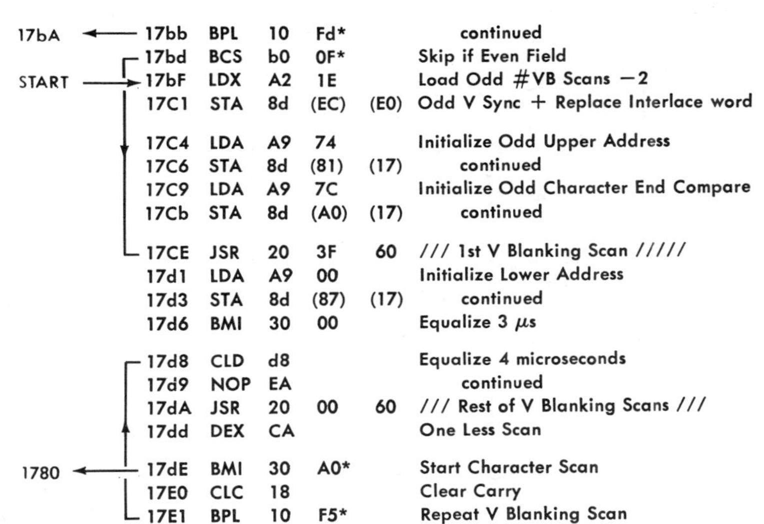

```
17bA  <---  17bb  BPL  10  Fd*         continued
          ┌ 17bd  BCS  b0  0F*         Skip if Even Field
START --->  17bF  LDX  A2  1E          Load Odd #VB Scans -2
            17C1  STA  8d  (EC)  (E0)  Odd V Sync + Replace Interlace word

            17C4  LDA  A9  74          Initialize Odd Upper Address
            17C6  STA  8d  (81)  (17)      continued
            17C9  LDA  A9  7C          Initialize Odd Character End Compare
            17Cb  STA  8d  (A0)  (17)      continued

          └ 17CE  JSR  20  3F    60    /// 1st V Blanking Scan /////
            17d1  LDA  A9  00          Initialize Lower Address
            17d3  STA  8d  (87)  (17)      continued
            17d6  BMI  30  00          Equalize 3 µs

          ┌ 17d8  CLD  d8              Equalize 4 microseconds
            17d9  NOP  EA                  continued
            17dA  JSR  20  00    60    /// Rest of V Blanking Scans ///
            17dd  DEX  CA              One Less Scan

1780  <---  17dE  BMI  30  A0*         Start Character Scan
            17E0  CLC  18              Clear Carry
          └ 17E1  BPL  10  F5*         Repeat V Blanking Scan
```

NOTES:

TVT 6 5/8 must be connected and both the Scan 658-KS64 and Decode 658-KD8 PROMS must be in circuit for program to run.

Both 17Ab and 17C1 require that page 00 be enabled when page E0 is addressed. This is done automatically in the KIM-1 decode circuitry.

Location 00EC on page zero is reserved as an interlace storage bit.

Step 1786 goes to where the upper address stored in 1788 and the lower address stored in 1787 tells it to. Values in these slots continuously change throughout the program.

Values in slots 1781 (Upper address start) and 17A0 (Character end compare) alternate with the field being scanned.

Horizontal Scan Frequency is 11.494 kHz; Vertical frequency 60.0222 Hz. 87 µs per line, 191.5 lines per field; 2 fields per frame, 383 lines total.

TVT 6 5/8 switch must be in the "64" position.

( ) Denotes an absolute address that is program location sensitive.

* Denotes a relative branch that is program length sensitive.

Continued on next page.

64-character-per-line, interlaced TVT 6 5/8 Raster Scan.

Program may be used for 16 × 64 large characters or 32 × 64 small characters by changing the following code:

Code	Function	16 × 64	32 × 64
178A	dot row spacing	10	20
17AA	even # VB Scans −2	2d	1d
17AF	even start address	64	64
17b4	even end compare	68	6C
17C0	odd # VB Scans −2	2E	1E
17C5	odd start address	64	74
17CA	odd end compare	68	7C

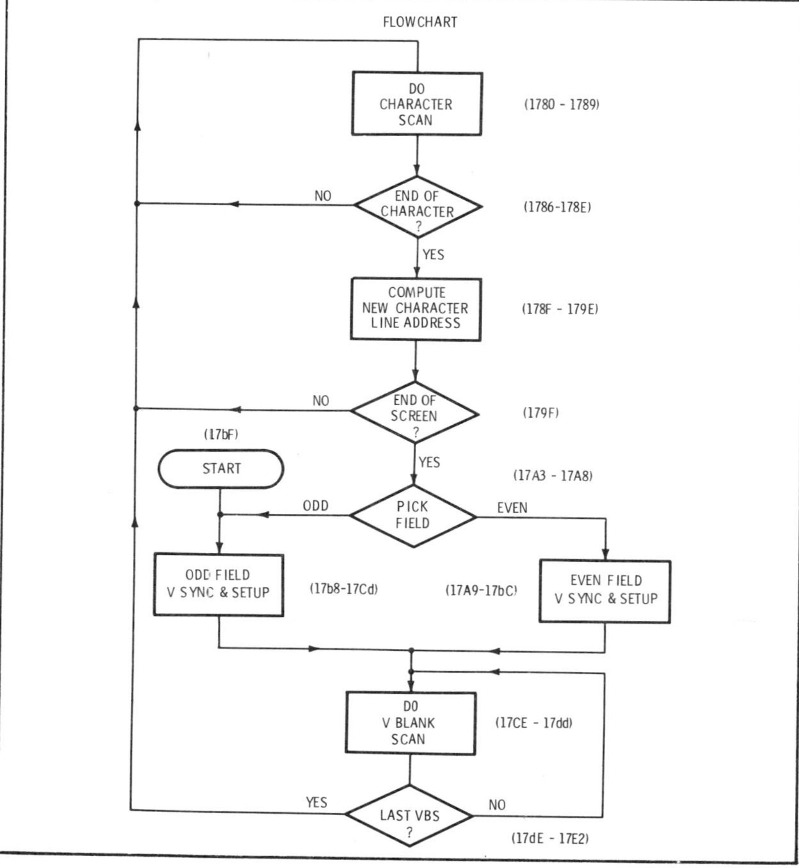

Fig. 2-12 *Continued.* Program for a 16- or 32-line, 64-character-per-line, interlaced TVT 6 5/8 Raster Scan.

The new things we need to pick up double stuffiing are also put in this first blank Scan line sequence. On the odd fields, we initialize to dot row one in 17C4-17C8. We also set up an end-of-screen odd compare in 17C9 through 17Cd. The end-of-screen condition differs for even and odd fields and must be separately set up if the same number of characters are going to be put down on both fields.

Similarly, we initialize to even dot row 0 in 17AE-17b2, and set up the end-of-screen even compare in 17b3-17b7.

The table in Fig. 2-12 also shows us how to change just six memory locations to use this program as a 16 × 64 or a 32 × 64 display. A hundred words are needed for this Scan program, 99 in the usual 1780 stash and one on page zero for interlace storage.

Memory Repacking

As Fig. 2-13 shows, our 32- and 64-character lines completely fill our display memory. The end of one line butts up against the start

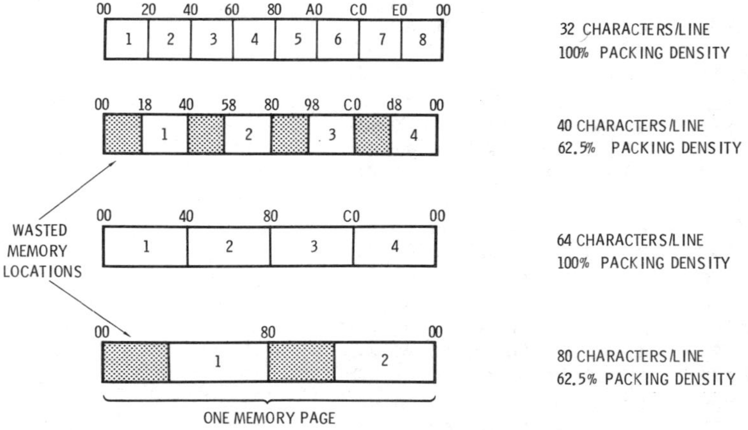

(A) Normal Scan program and microinstruction uses memory inefficiently during 40- or 80-character-per-line format.

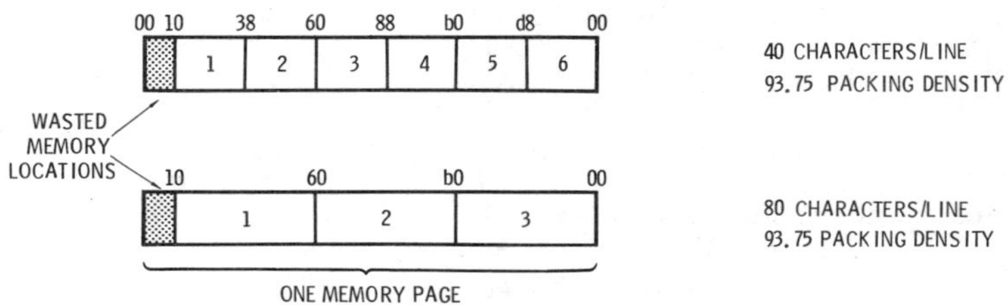

(B) Repacked Scan program and microinstruction greatly improves memory packing density.

Fig. 2-13. Improving memory packing density on 40- and 80-character lines.

of the next line. Since all display memory locations are used, we say we have a *memory packing efficiency* of 100%, the best we can do.

But, if we use the Scan programs we have so far on a 40- or 80-character line, it is a very different story. On a 40-character line, 24 out of every 64 words of display memory are wasted. On an 80-character line, 48 words out of every 128 are wasted. This is a packing density of only 62.5%.

Conceivably, we could use these wasted locations for other programs. But they are disjointed and short. Worse yet, they are dangerous, because a simple or poorly thought out Cursor-control program could override these locations and wipe them out, particularly on clear or scrolling. We could also simply ignore the

Chart 2-7. A 6502 Repacked Scan Microinstruction Coding for a Page of Six Scans of 40 Characters Each

XX00	A0	A0	A0	A0	A0	A0	A0	A0
XX08	A0	A0	A0	A0	A0	A0	A0	A0
XX10	A0	A0	A0	A0	A0	A0	A0	A0
XX18	A0	A0	A0	A0	A0	A0	A0	A0
XX20	A0	A0	A0	A0	A0	A0	A0	A0
XX28	A0	A0	A0	A0	A0	A0	A0	A0
XX30	A0	A0	A0	A0	A0	A0	**60**	**60**
XX38	A0	A0	A0	A0	A0	A0	A0	A0
XX40	A0	A0	A0	A0	A0	A0	A0	A0
XX48	A0	A0	A0	A0	A0	A0	A0	A0
XX50	A0	A0	A0	A0	A0	A0	A0	A0
XX58	A0	A0	A0	A0	A0	A0	**60**	**60**
XX60	A0	A0	A0	A0	A0	A0	A0	A0
XX68	A0	A0	A0	A0	A0	A0	A0	A0
XX70	A0	A0	A0	A0	A0	A0	A0	A0
XX78	A0	A0	A0	A0	A0	A0	A0	A0
XX80	A0	A0	A0	A0	A0	A0	**60**	**60**
XX88	A0	A0	A0	A0	A0	A0	A0	A0
XX90	A0	A0	A0	A0	A0	A0	A0	A0
XX98	A0	A0	A0	A0	A0	A0	A0	A0
XXA0	A0	A0	A0	A0	A0	A0	A0	A0
XXA8	A0	A0	A0	A0	A0	A0	**60**	**60**
XXb0	A0	A0	A0	A0	A0	A0	A0	A0
XXb8	A0	A0	A0	A0	A0	A0	A0	A0
XXC0	A0	A0	A0	A0	A0	A0	A0	A0
XXC8	A0	A0	A0	A0	A0	A0	A0	A0
XXd0	A0	A0	A0	A0	A0	A0	**60**	**60**
XXd8	A0	A0	A0	A0	A0	A0	A0	A0
XXE0	A0	A0	A0	A0	A0	A0	A0	A0
XXE8	A0	A0	A0	A0	A0	A0	A0	A0
XXF0	A0	A0	A0	A0	A0	A0	A0	A0
XXF8	A0	A0	A0	A0	A0	A0	**60**	**60**

Note:
"XX" is any high address that activates the Scan instruction decoder.

A0 — LDY
60 — RTS

locations. On a 24 × 80 display, well over a thousand locations would go unused.

One way to *repack* memory is shown in Fig. 2-13B. We put six lines of 40 characters or three lines of 80 characters per computer page of 256 locations. We make each page the same to keep the scanning and cursor activities reasonable and straightforward. We still waste 16 locations out of 256, but this gives us a memory packing of almost 94%. Even in the long 24 × 80 display, only 128 locations are wasted, a 10:1 improvement.

Memory repacking is not free. We have to change the Scan microinstruction coding, and no longer can use the PROM that is coded in Chart 2-4. The correct coding for six Scans of 40 characters per

Chart 2-8. A 6502 Repacked Scan Microinstruction Coding for a Page of Three Scans of 80 Characters Each

XX00	A0	A0	A0	A0	A0	A0	A0	A0
XX08	A0	A0	A0	A0	A0	A0	A0	A0
XX10	A0	A0	A0	A0	A0	A0	A0	A0
XX18	A0	A0	A0	A0	A0	A0	A0	A0
XX20	A0	A0	A0	A0	A0	A0	A0	A0
XX28	A0	A0	A0	A0	A0	A0	A0	A0
XX30	A0	A0	A0	A0	A0	A0	A0	A0
XX38	A0	A0	A0	A0	A0	A0	A0	A0
XX40	A0	A0	A0	A0	A0	A0	A0	A0
XX48	A0	A0	A0	A0	A0	A0	A0	A0
XX50	A0	A0	A0	A0	A0	A0	A0	A0
XX58	A0	A0	A0	A0	A0	A0	**60**	**60**
XX60	A0	A0	A0	A0	A0	A0	A0	A0
XX68	A0	A0	A0	A0	A0	A0	A0	A0
XX70	A0	A0	A0	A0	A0	A0	A0	A0
XX78	A0	A0	A0	A0	A0	A0	A0	A0
XX80	A0	A0	A0	A0	A0	A0	A0	A0
XX88	A0	A0	A0	A0	A0	A0	A0	A0
XX90	A0	A0	A0	A0	A0	A0	A0	A0
XX98	A0	A0	A0	A0	A0	A0	A0	A0
XXA0	A0	A0	A0	A0	A0	A0	A0	A0
XXA8	A0	A0	A0	A0	A0	A0	**60**	**60**
XXb0	A0	A0	A0	A0	A0	A0	A0	A0
XXb8	A0	A0	A0	A0	A0	A0	A0	A0
XXC0	A0	A0	A0	A0	A0	A0	A0	A0
XXC8	A0	A0	A0	A0	A0	A0	A0	A0
XXd0	A0	A0	A0	A0	A0	A0	A0	A0
XXd8	A0	A0	A0	A0	A0	A0	A0	A0
XXE0	A0	A0	A0	A0	A0	A0	A0	A0
XXE8	A0	A0	A0	A0	A0	A0	A0	A0
XXF0	A0	A0	A0	A0	A0	A0	A0	A0
XXF8	A0	A0	A0	A0	A0	A0	**60**	**60**

Note:
"XX" is any high address that activates the Scan instruction decoder.

A0 — LDY
60 — RTS

page appears in Chart 2-7, while the coding for three Scans of 80 characters per page is shown in Chart 2-8.

At first glance, it would look like we now need an eight input PROM for our Scan microinstruction generation. Once again, with a 6502 we can ignore the least significant address line A0 and do everything "by twos." This helps a little. Now, if you go through the logic you will find that we can use a simple AND of address lines A1, A2, and A3 to form a *precoded* input for our PROM. So, we are once again down to a five input 32 × 8 PROM.

The new gate seems to be needed for the 40-line Scans. But, on the 80-line Scans, if we are willing *not* to display characters 75 through 80 on each line, we can simply ignore A1 and A2 as well, routing A3 directly to the PROM. This leaves things as simple as they were before, except for the use of a different PROM and different socket address interconnections. When we do this, we retain the 80-line Teletype software compatibility, and also pick up a magic number that hits a stable hum bar with a shorter horizontal line and a stock crystal. So, this strange sounding compromise may turn out to be a useful simplification.

Repacking will also add complications to the Cursor-control program, particularly on the carriage return and backspace. Your Scan program also gets lengthened by seven words. If you decide you want the 40- or 80-character lines instead of the simpler 64- and 32-length binary counterparts, the price of repacking memory usually pays for itself, even with the complications.

The Scan program needs one seven-word addition for repacking. The addition is needed to bridge the wasted locations every time the page overflows.

Normally, on a 40-character line, we add 40_{10} to each starting location to get to the next starting location for a new Scan. Except, when we go from line 6 to line 7 (the first line on the next page), we have to add 40_{10} *plus* 16_{10} to get across the unused locations. Very fortunately, the carry bit sets every time we overflow the page, so we can use this as a flag to tell us to add an extra sixteen.

Our Scan program repacking correction goes like this:

* On a 40-character Scan line, add 40_{10} to get to the start of the next character line. If the page overflows, add 16_{10} more.
* On an 80-character Scan line, add 80_{10} to get to the start of the next character line. If the page overflows, add 16_{10} more.

24 × 80 Scan Program

Memory repacking, double stuffing, and interlace are combined in the 24 × 80 Scan program of Fig. 2-14. By now, your program areas of blank Scans (17db–17E2), active-character Scans (1780–

178C), next character row computation (178E–17A4), and first blank-line interlace and double-stuffing setup (17A6–17d9) should be obvious to you.

Our bridging, needed for the memory repacking, is done in 1794. Should there be no page overflow, the carry remains clear, and the program goes from 1794 to 17E4 to 1799 and takes 6 μs to do so. Should you have a page overflow, we know we have to add an extra 16_{10} to get to the next lower starting address, besides the usual change of upper address. So, if carry is set, we go from 1794 to the "add sixteen" of 1796 and the carry restoration of 1798, again taking 6 μs.

This program takes a special PROM coding 658-KS80 similar to Chart 2-8, and special connections to that PROM. As Fig. 2-14 shows, you have several ways you can use the Scan program.

If you are willing to display only the first 76 characters on each 80-character line, you end up with a near-stationary hum bar and no extra gating. If you want the full 80 characters, you add an extra AND gate. The full 80-character display has a rather fast hum bar of 5.5 seconds. You can stop this by speeding up your clock to 1.003 MHz, either by pulling the old crystal or changing to a new one.

Either setup works compatibly with 80 line existing tty software. Locations are changed as shown to get the right operation for either mode.

You can change back to a 12 × 80 display by making the six word changes as noted in the program.

> *Your Turn:*
>
> Design a 32 × 40 double stuffed, interlaced, and memory repacked TVT 6 5/8 Scan running at a normal horizontal frequency.

Note that custom Cursor programs will be needed for memory repacked Scans.

GRAPHICS SCAN PROGRAMS

Graphics displays are usually a lot simpler to design than alphanumeric ones. We do not have the hassles of a character generator and repeat trips for the character dot rows. We actually display

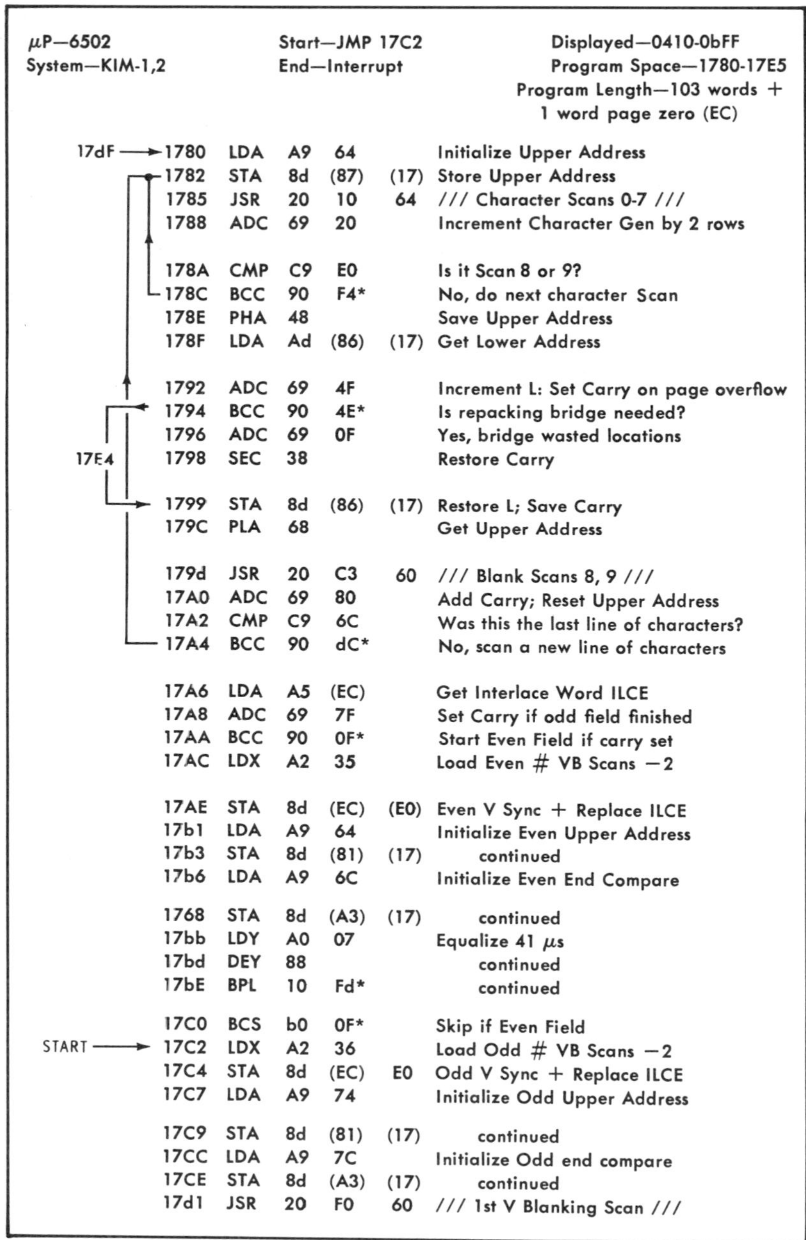

μP—6502
System—KIM-1,2

Start—JMP 17C2
End—Interrupt

Displayed—0410-0bFF
Program Space—1780-17E5
Program Length—103 words +
1 word page zero (EC)

```
17dF →  1780  LDA  A9  64          Initialize Upper Address
        1782  STA  8d  (87)  (17)  Store Upper Address
        1785  JSR  20  10    64    /// Character Scans 0-7 ///
        1788  ADC  69  20          Increment Character Gen by 2 rows

        178A  CMP  C9  E0          Is it Scan 8 or 9?
        178C  BCC  90  F4*         No, do next character Scan
        178E  PHA  48              Save Upper Address
        178F  LDA  Ad  (86)  (17)  Get Lower Address

        1792  ADC  69  4F          Increment L: Set Carry on page overflow
        1794  BCC  90  4E*         Is repacking bridge needed?
        1796  ADC  69  0F          Yes, bridge wasted locations
17E4    1798  SEC  38              Restore Carry

        1799  STA  8d  (86)  (17)  Restore L; Save Carry
        179C  PLA  68              Get Upper Address

        179d  JSR  20  C3    60    /// Blank Scans 8, 9 ///
        17A0  ADC  69  80          Add Carry; Reset Upper Address
        17A2  CMP  C9  6C          Was this the last line of characters?
        17A4  BCC  90  dC*         No, scan a new line of characters

        17A6  LDA  A5  (EC)        Get Interlace Word ILCE
        17A8  ADC  69  7F          Set Carry if odd field finished
        17AA  BCC  90  0F*         Start Even Field if carry set
        17AC  LDX  A2  35          Load Even # VB Scans −2

        17AE  STA  8d  (EC)  (E0)  Even V Sync + Replace ILCE
        17b1  LDA  A9  64          Initialize Even Upper Address
        17b3  STA  8d  (81)  (17)      continued
        17b6  LDA  A9  6C          Initialize Even End Compare

        1768  STA  8d  (A3)  (17)      continued
        17bb  LDY  A0  07          Equalize 41 μs
        17bd  DEY  88                  continued
        17bE  BPL  10  Fd*             continued

        17C0  BCS  b0  0F*         Skip if Even Field
START → 17C2  LDX  A2  36          Load Odd # VB Scans −2
        17C4  STA  8d  (EC)  E0    Odd V Sync + Replace ILCE
        17C7  LDA  A9  74          Initialize Odd Upper Address

        17C9  STA  8d  (81)  (17)      continued
        17CC  LDA  A9  7C          Initialize Odd end compare
        17CE  STA  8d  (A3)  (17)      continued
        17d1  JSR  20  F0    60    /// 1st V Blanking Scan ///
```

Fig. 2-14. Program for a 12- or 24-line, 80-character-per-line,

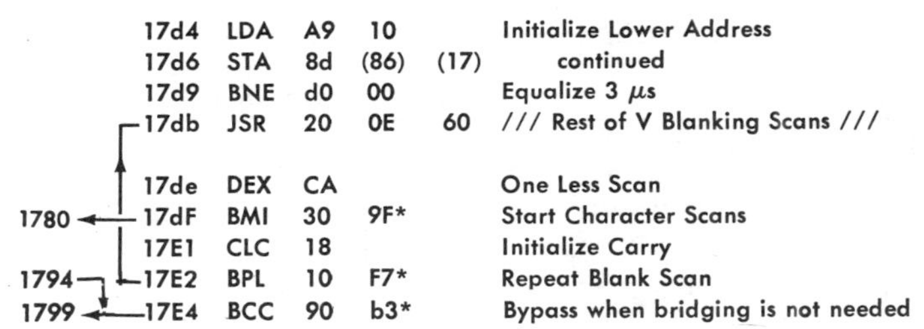

```
         17d4  LDA  A9  10          Initialize Lower Address
         17d6  STA  8d  (86)  (17)       continued
         17d9  BNE  d0  00          Equalize 3 µs
       ┌-17db  JSR  20  0E    60    /// Rest of V Blanking Scans ///
       |
       | 17de  DEX  CA              One Less Scan
1780 <-+-17dF  BMI  30  9F*         Start Character Scans
       | 17E1  CLC  18              Initialize Carry
1794-┐ └-17E2  BPL  10  F7*         Repeat Blank Scan
1799 <-----17E4  BCC  90  b3*       Bypass when bridging is not needed
```

NOTES:

TVT 6 5/8 must be connected and both the Scan 658-KS80 and Decode 658-KD8 PROMS must be in circuit for program to run.

Both 17AE and 17C4 require that page 00 be enabled when page E0 is addressed. This is done automatically in the KIM-1 decode circuitry.

Location 00EC on page zero is reserved as an interlace storage bit.

Step 1785 goes to where the upper address stored in 1787 and the lower address stored in 1786 tells it to. Values in these slots continuously change throughout the program.

Values in slots 1781 (Upper Address start) and 17A3 (Character end compare) alternate with the field being scanned.

TVT 6 5/8 switch must be in the "64" position.

( ) Denotes an absolute address that is program location sensitive.

* Denotes a relative branch that is program length sensitive.

One of the two following operation modes should be picked:

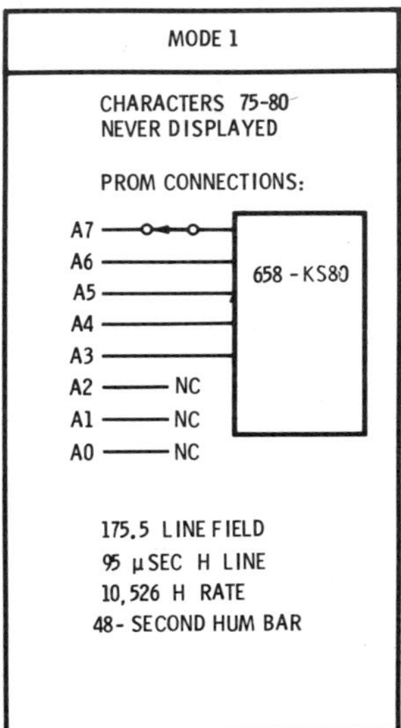

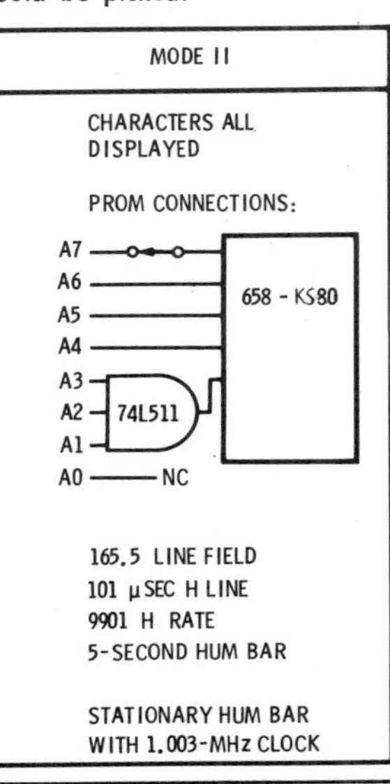

Continued on next page.

interlaced, double-stuffed, memory repacked TVT 6 5/8 Raster Scan.

Code should be changed as follows:

Location	Function	12 × 80 MODE I	12 × 80 MODE II	24 × 80 MODE I	24 × 80 MODE II
1789	dot spacing	10	10	20	20
17Ad	even VB scans −2	41	C7	35	26
17b7	even end compare	68	68	6C	6C
17C3	odd VB scans −2	42	C8	36	27
17C8	odd start address	64	64	74	74
17Cd	odd end compare	68	68	7C	7C

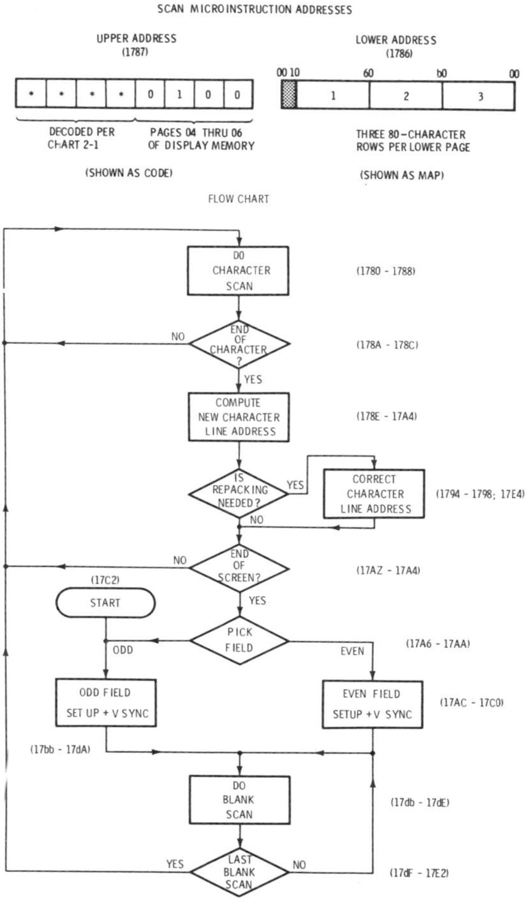

SCAN MICROINSTRUCTION ADDRESSES

UPPER ADDRESS (1787)

*	*	*	*	0	1	0	0

DECODED PER CHART 2-1 — PAGES 04 THRU 06 OF DISPLAY MEMORY

(SHOWN AS CODE)

LOWER ADDRESS (1786)

00 10 — 60 — b0 — 00

	1	2	3

THREE 80-CHARACTER ROWS PER LOWER PAGE

(SHOWN AS MAP)

FLOW CHART

DO CHARACTER SCAN (1780 - 1788)
END OF CHARACTER ? (178A - 178C) — NO / YES
COMPUTE NEW CHARACTER LINE ADDRESS (178E - 17A4)
IS REPACKING NEEDED? — YES / NO
CORRECT CHARACTER LINE ADDRESS (1794 - 1798; 17E4)
END OF SCREEN? (17AZ - 17A4) — NO / YES
(17C2) START
PICK FIELD (17A6 - 17AA) — ODD / EVEN
ODD FIELD SET UP + V SYNC (17bb - 17dA)
EVEN FIELD SETUP +V SYNC (17AC - 17C0)
DO BLANK SCAN (17db - 17dE)
LAST BLANK SCAN (17dF - 17E2) — YES / NO

Fig. 2-14 *Continued.* Program for a 12- or 24-line, 80-character-per-line, interlaced, double-stuffed, memory repacked TVT 6 5/8 Raster Scan.

the code stored in memory rather than converting it to something else. All the graphics displays we will be showing you run at a normal horizontal rate. Cursors, double stuffing, and memory repacking are no longer needed. We can still use the same Scan (658-KS64) and Decode (658-KD8) PROMS we used for most of the alphanumeric Scans as well. A plug-in module on our TVT 6⅝ converts it for graphics-output modes.

One thing our graphics displays will need, though, is plenty of available RAM for your display memory. The 512 locations on pages 02 and 03 of a bare bones KIM is only enough for a 64 × 64 black and white or a 64 × 48 color display. This is big enough to be interesting and a good way to learn graphics. It may also be handy for simple games and color art displays. But, for many applications, we will want more memory and lots of it.

The minimum workable graphics size is somewhere around 128 × 128 elements, which needs 2K of display memory. You can do a lot more with a high resolution 256 × 256 display, but this takes a full 8K of memory provided with the usual upstream tap. Super displays up to 400 × 512 or so are possible, but you will have to be a real graphics freak to provide the 25K or so of RAM you will need; rapid changes of this much information will also be rather tricky to accomplish.

Two medium resolution graphics formats that will use the same Scan program are shown in Fig. 2-15. We call the word stored in display memory and its presentation on the display a *chunk*. For our 128 × 128 format, we use a "four over four" chunk that puts down four dots or undots on one Scan and then another four directly below on the next Scan line. The four-dots-per-microsecond rate gives us very modest bandwidth needs (about half of what we needed for alphanumerics). We also have the option of double-height elements stored in only a single memory location. This is especially handy for a moving ball or puck in a game display as only a single calculation and storage is needed.

The three-over-three 128 × 96 color format gives us about the same resolution. The video (luminance) bandwidth is now even lower since we only put down three dots or undots per microsecond. Only six bits per word are used for dots. The two remaining display memory bits are used for one-of-four color information. The reduced rate is picked up by changing a *width* control on the TVT 6⅝. The *entire* chunk lights to *one* selected color, but the individual *bits* have the option of being lit or black. This nicely resolves the dilemma of the color (chrominance) bandwidth of a tv set being *much* lower than the video (luminance) bandwidth. This way, we get a sharp display with still a reasonable number of color changes per horizontal line.

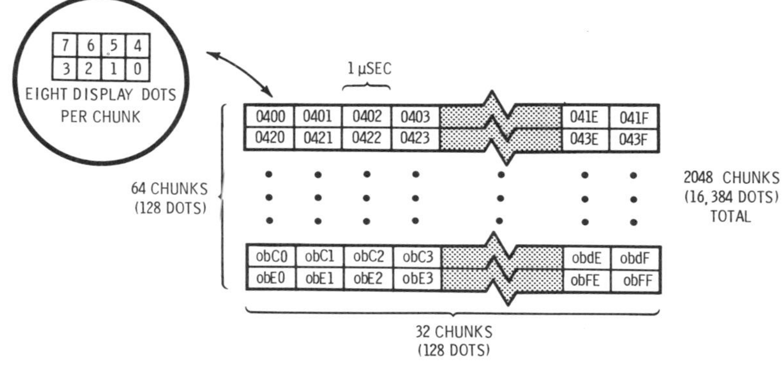

(A) "Four over four" 128 × 128 black and white.

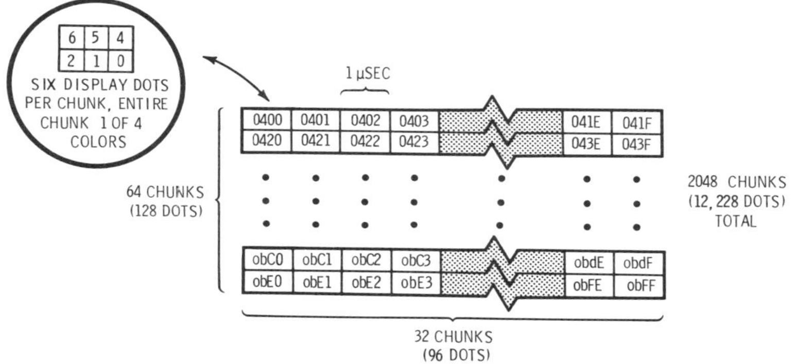

(B) "Three over three" 128 × 96 color. Each chunk may be one of four colors.

Fig. 2-15. Medium resolution graphics formats.

128 × 128 Format

The Scan program for either the 128 × 128 or 128 × 96 color format is shown in Fig. 2-16. Our magic numbers use a standard horizontal frequency and interlace, and are the same as we used in the utility 16 × 32 alphanumeric Scan of Fig. 2-10. In fact, if you want to, you can use a variation of double stuffing in which you put the graphics down on one field and the alphanumerics (scores, annotation, time, etc. . . .) on a second field, simply by going to a custom module on the TVT 6⅝.

Everything about the first blank line and interlace setup, along with the remaining blank Scans, remains as before. Our live Scans, of course, are substantially different. We call a pass that is putting down the upper chunk row of dots an "A" Scan, and the pass that is working on the lower chunk row of dots a "B" Scan. We set up a correct starting address. Then we do an A Scan. Then we change to a B Scan. After a B Scan, we change to a new initial chunk address and on to the next A Scan, repeating the process.

There is not quite enough time available between one B Scan and the next A Scan to do everything we would like to, so we use pipelining in which we borrow some of the extra time available in going from an A Scan to a B Scan to help out. When we go from A to B, we tell the TVT 6⅝ and its graphics module "C" to switch to its B output side. We also make a test for the end of the display screen, getting this detail out of the critical B to A timing loop.

We also calculate the *next* upper A address as pipelining to save us time. But we do not restore this calculation; we save it in the accumulator till the B Scan is done. It is there, ready and waiting, the instant the B to A Scan loop calculations need it.

The *same* JSR instruction is used to do either an A or a B Scan. This saves us from having to compute and store two separate sets of absolute addresses. The carry bit is used as a flag to tell us whether we are doing an A Scan or a B Scan. The carry is set during an A Scan and is cleared during a B Scan.

The TVT 6⅝ is hardware programmed by module "C" to alternately be able to pick up four bit A and B Scans. For 128 × 128 black and white use, the width control is set to *four* dots per microsecond; for 128 × 96 color use, you set it to *three* dots per microsecond. The format of the data stored in the display memory is also changed to pick up the color information.

> *Your Turn:*
>
> Design a TVT 6 5/8 64 × 64 black and white and a 64 × 48 color Scan program using pages 02 and 03 of a KIM as a display memory. Change only the Scan program and make no adjustments to do this.

256 × 256 Format

The 256 × 256 high-resolution format of Fig. 2-17 puts down eight dots per microsecond, all in sequence on a single horizontal line. A total of 32 chunks are used per line, giving us 256 dots horizontally. A new set of chunks is needed for each line.

This program needs an 8K memory located at 0400 through 05FF, with a continuous upstream tap. You can do this with a KIM-3 or another 8K memory. You can also easily rewrite the program to use less memory, but ending with fewer lines. For instance, a 128 × 256 format can be done with 4K of memory.

There is a sneaky and sticky detail involved in this 256 × 256 format. Your memory address space and decode space overlap. *During the live portions of the Scan, you have to be able to call both the proper memory locations* AND *call for a live Scan.* Fortunately, your 658-KD8 instruction decoder is redundantly decoded during a high-resolution mode, with codes 1000, 1001, 1100 and 1101 all calling a live Scan. Note that code 1100 simultaneously calls memory page 4000 (as far as the upstream tap) and that code 1101 simultaneously calls page 5000. If you move your memory or shorten it, be sure you are still able to call a live graphics Scan for all needed memory addresses. This overlap usually happens only when you have *more* than 4K of display memory in use.

You will find the 256 × 256 Scan program in Fig. 2-18. Since this program is relatively short, we have thrown in an optional

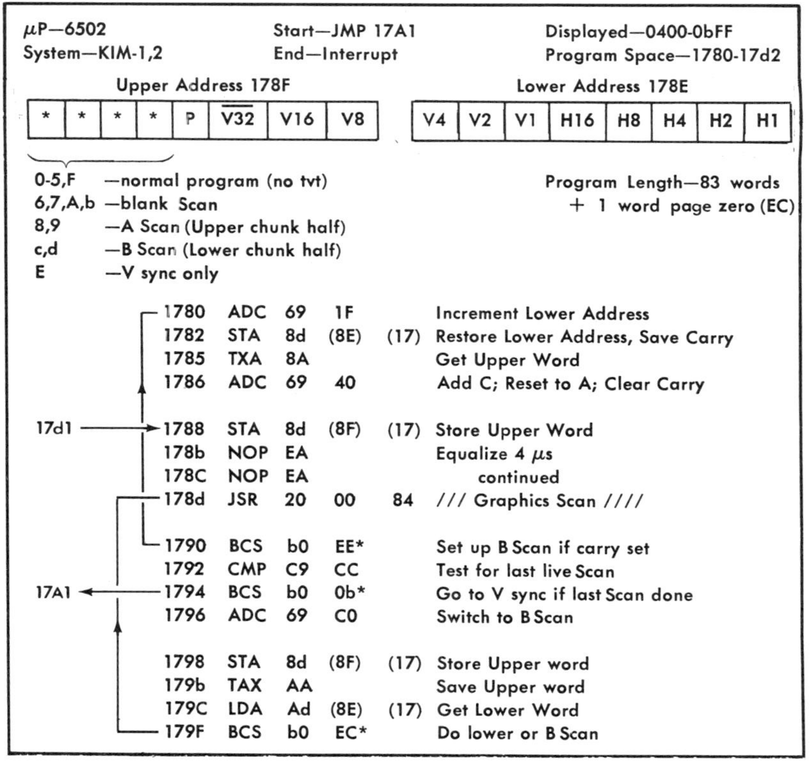

μP—6502 | Start—JMP 17A1 | Displayed—0400-0bFF
System—KIM-1,2 | End—Interrupt | Program Space—1780-17d2

Upper Address 178F: | * | * | * | * | P | $\overline{V32}$ | V16 | V8 |

Lower Address 178E: | V4 | V2 | V1 | H16 | H8 | H4 | H2 | H1 |

0-5,F —normal program (no tvt)
6,7,A,b —blank Scan
8,9 —A Scan (Upper chunk half)
c,d —B Scan (Lower chunk half)
E —V sync only

Program Length—83 words + 1 word page zero (EC)

```
        1780  ADC  69  1F          Increment Lower Address
        1782  STA  8d  (8E)  (17)  Restore Lower Address, Save Carry
        1785  TXA  8A              Get Upper Word
        1786  ADC  69  40          Add C; Reset to A; Clear Carry

17d1 -> 1788  STA  8d  (8F)  (17)  Store Upper Word
        178b  NOP  EA              Equalize 4 μs
        178C  NOP  EA                   continued
        178d  JSR  20  00    84    /// Graphics Scan ////

        1790  BCS  b0  EE*         Set up B Scan if carry set
        1792  CMP  C9  CC          Test for last live Scan
17A1 <- 1794  BCS  b0  0b*         Go to V sync if last Scan done
        1796  ADC  69  C0          Switch to B Scan

        1798  STA  8d  (8F)  (17)  Store Upper word
        179b  TAX  AA              Save Upper word
        179C  LDA  Ad  (8E)  (17)  Get Lower Word
        179F  BCS  b0  EC*         Do lower or B Scan
```

Fig. 2-16. A 128 × 127 interlaced graphics Scan program for

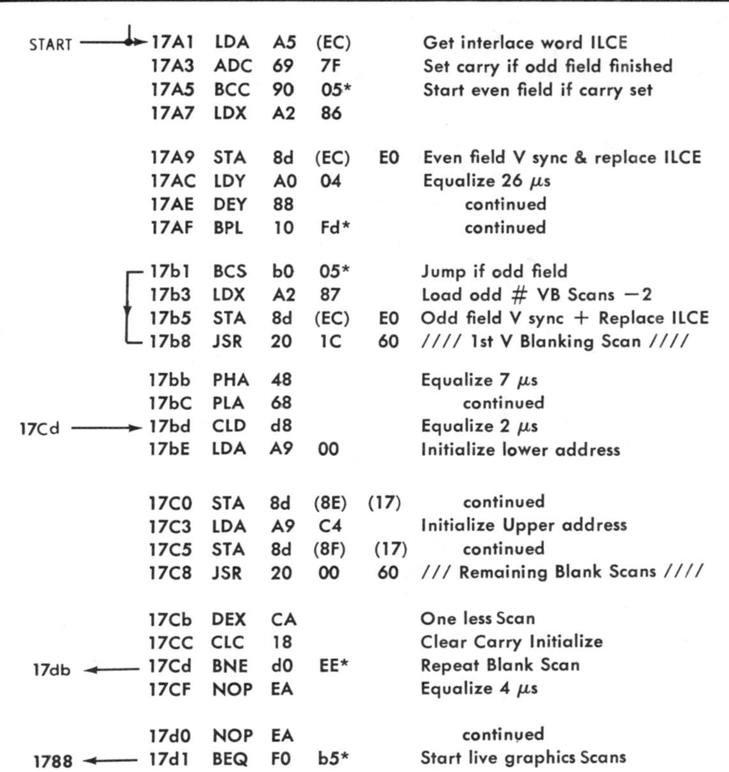

```
START ──┬─► 17A1  LDA  A5  (EC)        Get interlace word ILCE
            17A3  ADC  69   7F         Set carry if odd field finished
            17A5  BCC  90   05*        Start even field if carry set
            17A7  LDX  A2   86

            17A9  STA  8d  (EC)   E0   Even field V sync & replace ILCE
            17AC  LDY  A0   04         Equalize 26 µs
            17AE  DEY  88                   continued
            17AF  BPL  10   Fd*             continued

         ┌─ 17b1  BCS  b0   05*        Jump if odd field
         │  17b3  LDX  A2   87         Load odd # VB Scans -2
         ▼  17b5  STA  8d  (EC)   E0   Odd field V sync + Replace ILCE
         └─ 17b8  JSR  20   1C    60   //// 1st V Blanking Scan ////

            17bb  PHA  48              Equalize 7 µs
            17bC  PLA  68                   continued
17Cd ────►  17bd  CLD  d8              Equalize 2 µs
            17bE  LDA  A9   00         Initialize lower address

            17C0  STA  8d  (8E)  (17)       continued
            17C3  LDA  A9   C4         Initialize Upper address
            17C5  STA  8d  (8F)  (17)       continued
            17C8  JSR  20   00    60   /// Remaining Blank Scans ////

            17Cb  DEX  CA              One less Scan
            17CC  CLC  18              Clear Carry Initialize
17db  ◄──── 17Cd  BNE  d0   EE*        Repeat Blank Scan
            17CF  NOP  EA              Equalize 4 µs

            17d0  NOP  EA                   continued
1788  ◄──── 17d1  BEQ  F0   b5*        Start live graphics Scans
```

NOTES:

TVT 6 5/8 must be connected and both the Scan PROM 658-KS64 and the Decode PROM 658-KD8 must be in the circuit for the program to run.

Both 17A7 and 17b5 require that page 00 be enabled when page C0 is addressed. This is done automatically in the KIM-1 decode circuitry.

Location 00EC on page zero is reserved as an interlace storage bit.

Step 178d goes to where the upper address stored in 178F and the lower address stored in 178E tells it to. These values continuously change throughout the program.

An upper or "A" graphics scan is done with the carry *set* during step 178d; a lower or "B" graphics scan is done with the carry *cleared* during 178d.

Program Horizontal frequency is 15,873.015 kHz; vertical is 60.0114 Hz. 88.5-second hum bar; 63 µs per line, 264.5 lines per field. 2 fields per frame; 529 lines total.

TVT 6 5/8 width control must be set to deliver 4 dots per microsecond for B/W use and 3 dots per microsecond for color use. Switches should be set to "32"; "off"; "slow"; "+". Use module "C."

( ) Denotes an absolute location that is program location sensitive.

* Denotes a relative branch that is program length sensitive.

Continued on next page.

"four over four" black and white or "three over three" color TVT-6 5/8.

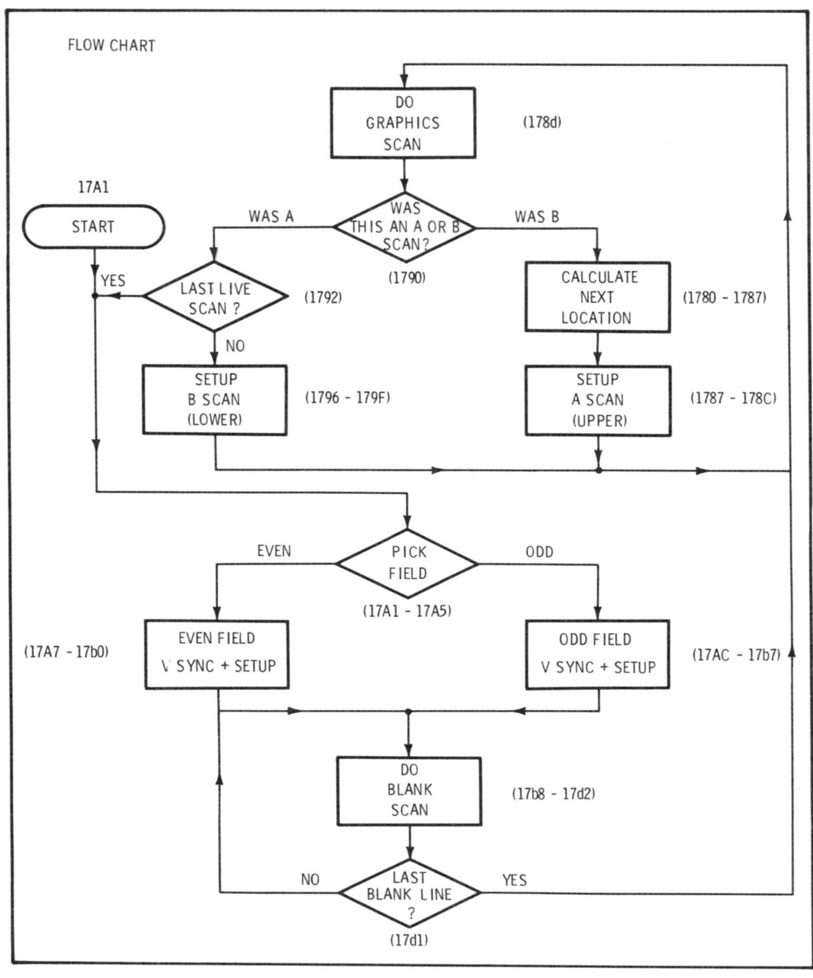

Fig. 2-16 *Continued.* A 128 × 128 interlaced graphics Scan program for "four over four" black and white or "three over three" color TVT-6 5/8.

software-controlled vertical position. You might find this useful for centering if you chose a shorter version (fewer lines; less memory) of this high-resolution display. It also has some animation possibilities.

The time to compute a new row address after a live Scan is once again critical. This time, there is no place to pipeline anything from. But, we can get out of this bind by noting that we never have to change the upper address by more than one count at a time.

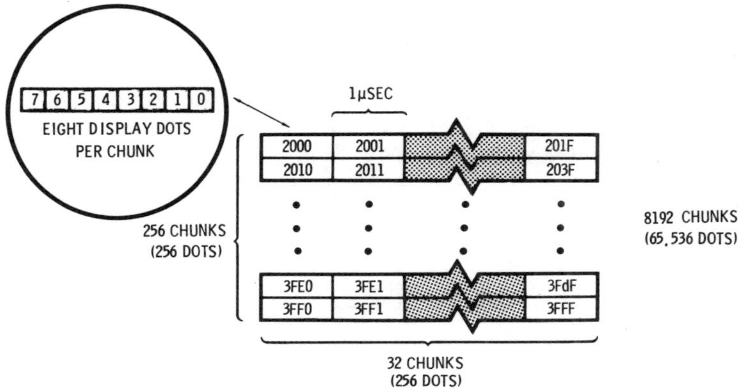

Fig. 2-17. High-resolution 256 × 256 graphics format.

This is unlike all the earlier Scan programs where we used the upper address also to pick a row of dots or do an A/B chunk select for us. We can now leave the upper address where it is normally stashed in the JSR instruction and use the powerful INC (increment memory) command. This lets us keep the *lower* memory address in the accumulator for immediate use, restoring it immediately before each live Scan.

After each live Scan, we increment the lower address. If no carry is produced, we go on to another live Scan, wheel spinning enough to make up the needed time. If a carry is produced, we test for end of screen, then increment the upper address in place, and go on to another live Scan.

> *Your Turn:*
>
> * Show how this program can be used as a 64 × 256 display using RAM starting at 0400. Demonstrate the use of software position and animation.
> * Design a 256 × 256 graphics Scan that uses double stuffing to put down half the dots on one field and half on the second. This will maximize the available blank Scan time which, in turn, can be used to improve transparency and increase throughput.

But, how on earth can we tell the end of the screen if we cannot test the upper address? A different approach is clearly needed. Before we get into the live Scans, but after the blank Scans are finished, we load the X register with a number equal to *one eighth* of the desired number of live Scans. Every eight live Scans, a carry is produced to signal a change of upper address, since there are eight 32-chunk lines per 256 word page. We decrement X every eight live Scans, and when X goes negative, we have reached the end of the live Scan.

Our software-position control throws in some extra blank Scans after the live ones and before the vertical-sync pulse. For vertical

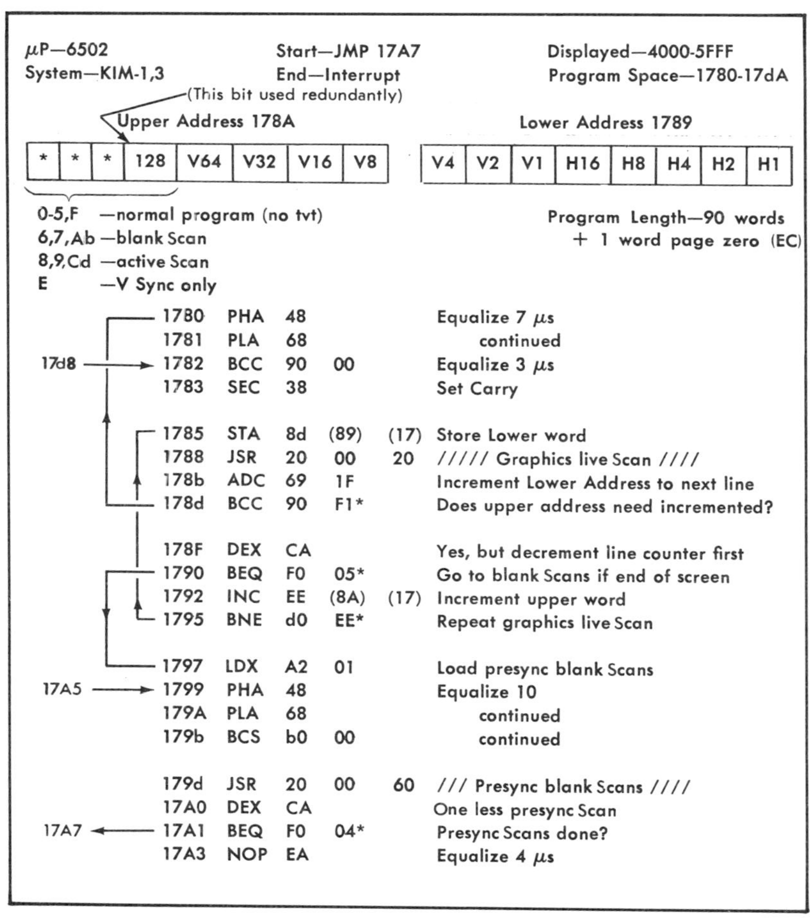

```
μP—6502                 Start—JMP 17A7          Displayed—4000-5FFF
System—KIM-1,3          End—Interrupt           Program Space—1780-17dA
              (This bit used redundantly)
      Upper Address 178A                          Lower Address 1789
| * | * | * | 128 | V64 | V32 | V16 | V8 |   | V4 | V2 | V1 | H16 | H8 | H4 | H2 | H1 |

0-5,F  —normal program (no tvt)                 Program Length—90 words
6,7,Ab —blank Scan                                + 1 word page zero (EC)
8,9,Cd —active Scan
E      —V Sync only

        1780  PHA  48                 Equalize 7 μs
        1781  PLA  68                      continued
17d8 →  1782  BCC  90  00             Equalize 3 μs
        1783  SEC  38                 Set Carry

        1785  STA  8d  (89)  (17)     Store Lower word
        1788  JSR  20  00    20       ///// Graphics live Scan ////
        178b  ADC  69  1F             Increment Lower Address to next line
        178d  BCC  90  F1*            Does upper address need incremented?

        178F  DEX  CA                 Yes, but decrement line counter first
        1790  BEQ  F0  05*            Go to blank Scans if end of screen
        1792  INC  EE  (8A)  (17)     Increment upper word
        1795  BNE  d0  EE*            Repeat graphics live Scan

        1797  LDX  A2  01             Load presync blank Scans
17A5 →  1799  PHA  48                 Equalize 10
        179A  PLA  68                      continued
        179b  BCS  b0  00                  continued

        179d  JSR  20  00    60       /// Presync blank Scans ////
        17A0  DEX  CA                 One less presync Scan
17A7 ←  17A1  BEQ  F0  04*            Presync Scans done?
        17A3  NOP  EA                 Equalize 4 μs
```

Fig. 2-18. A 256 × 256 interlaced graphics

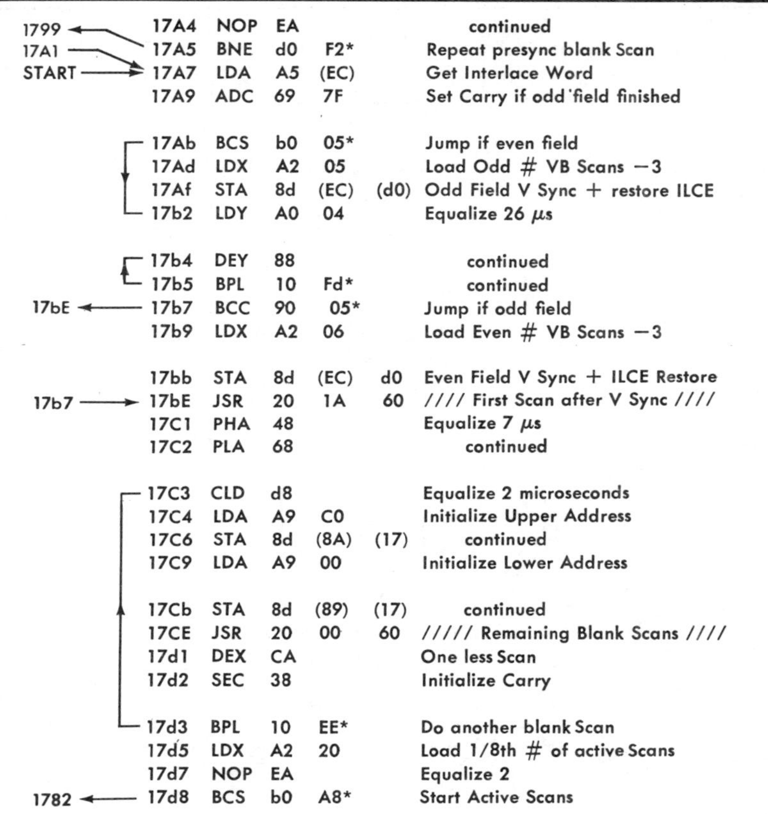

```
1799 ←┐      17A4  NOP  EA                  continued
17A1 ─┼──→   17A5  BNE  d0   F2*          Repeat presync blank Scan
START ───→   17A7  LDA  A5   (EC)         Get Interlace Word
             17A9  ADC  69   7F           Set Carry if odd field finished

         ┌── 17Ab  BCS  b0   05*          Jump if even field
         │   17Ad  LDX  A2   05           Load Odd # VB Scans −3
         ↓   17Af  STA  8d   (EC)  (d0)   Odd Field V Sync + restore ILCE
         └── 17b2  LDY  A0   04           Equalize 26 μs

         ┌── 17b4  DEY  88                  continued
         └── 17b5  BPL  10   Fd*            continued
17bE ←────── 17b7  BCC  90   05*          Jump if odd field
             17b9  LDX  A2   06           Load Even # VB Scans −3

             17bb  STA  8d   (EC)  d0     Even Field V Sync + ILCE Restore
17b7 ──────→ 17bE  JSR  20   1A    60     //// First Scan after V Sync ////
             17C1  PHA  48                Equalize 7 μs
             17C2  PLA  68                  continued

         ┌── 17C3  CLD  d8                Equalize 2 microseconds
         │   17C4  LDA  A9   C0           Initialize Upper Address
         │   17C6  STA  8d   (8A)  (17)     continued
         │   17C9  LDA  A9   00           Initialize Lower Address
         │
         ↑   17Cb  STA  8d   (89)  (17)     continued
         │   17CE  JSR  20   00    60     ///// Remaining Blank Scans ////
         │   17d1  DEX  CA                One less Scan
         │   17d2  SEC  38                Initialize Carry
         │
         └── 17d3  BPL  10   EE*          Do another blank Scan
             17d5  LDX  A2   20           Load 1/8th # of active Scans
             17d7  NOP  EA                Equalize 2
1782 ←────── 17d8  BCS  b0   A8*          Start Active Scans
```

NOTES:

TVT 6 5/8 must be connected and both the Scan PROM 658-KS64 and the Decode PROM 658-KD8 must be in the circuit for the program to run.

Both 17AF and 17bb require that page 00 be enabled when page d0 is addressed. This is done automatically in the KIM-1 decode circuitry.

Location 00EC on page zero is reserved as an interlace storage bit.

Step 1788 goes to where the upper address stored in 178A and the lower address stored in 178E tells it to. These values continuously change throughout the program.

The V Sync pulse can be delayed under software control by adding to 1798 the same number of scan lines that is removed from 17b1 and 17bA.

TVT 6 5/8 width control must be set to deliver 8 dots per microsecond. Set switches to "32"; "off"; "fast"; "+." Use graphics module "B."

Program horizontal frequency is 15,873.015 Hz; vertical 60.0114 Hz. 88.5-second hum bar. 63 μs per line, 264.5 lines per field 2 fields per frame, 529 lines total.

( ) denotes an absolute location that is program location sensitive.

* denotes a relative branch that is program length sensitive.

Continued on next page.

Scan program for TVT 6 5/8.

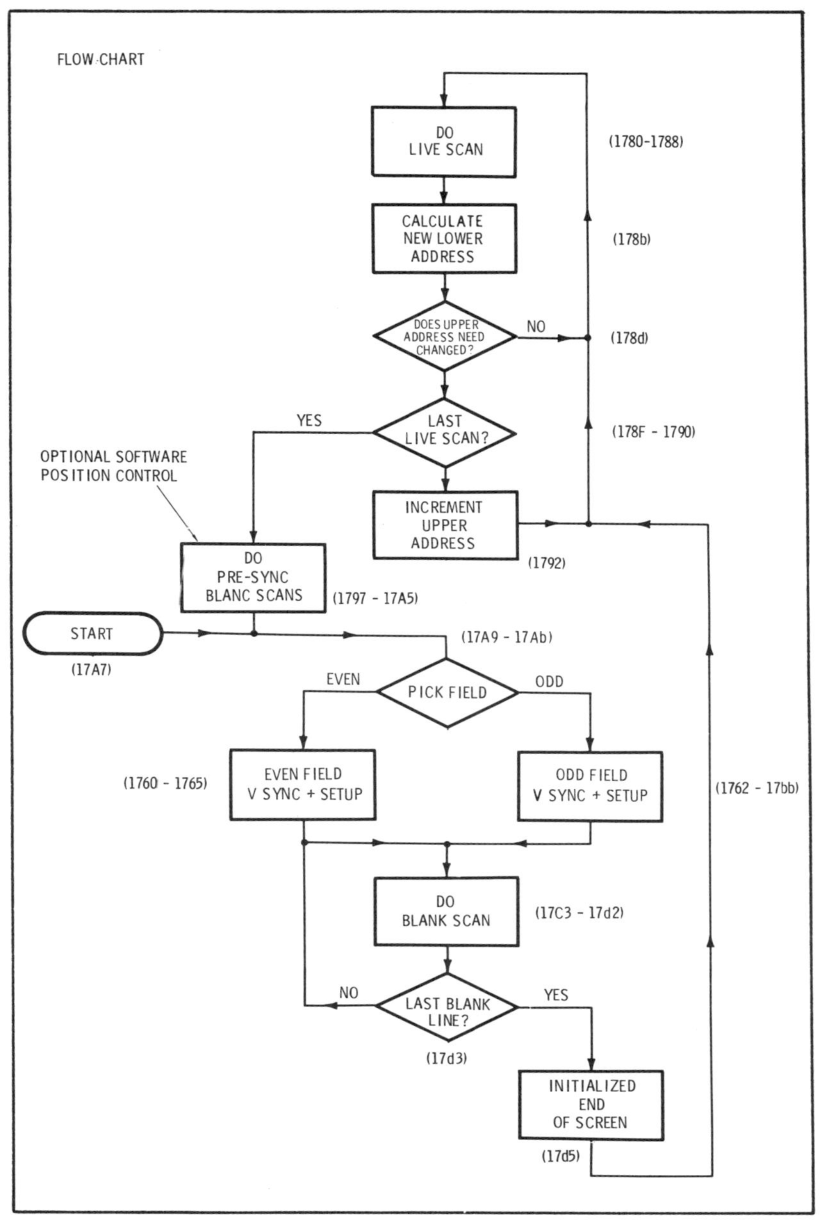

Fig. 2-18 *Continued.* A 256 × 256 interlaced graphics Scan program for TVT 6 5/8.

motion on shorter displays, you remove counts from the usual even (17b1) and odd (17bA) blank Scan loadings and add these counts to the new presync blank Scan (1798). Since 17b1 and 17bA are used on alternate fields, and 1798 is used on all fields, you move the same number of lines *per field*. Thus, to move the screen up by four lines, remove four from both 17b1 and 17bA, and add four to 1798.

This software position control is also one key to a "gentle" or crawling Cursor scrolling on an alphanumeric display. How would you do this?

CURSOR SOFTWARE

Your *Cursor software* decides when and how characters are to be put on or taken off the screen. Cursor software also gives you the fancy editing motions needed to move around the screen without making changes, to erase portions of the screen, to scroll up, and so on. Cursor software is often a different program than your Scan Program. The Scan Program causes characters already stored in memory to appear on the screen; the Cursor software puts the characters into memory as needed.

Our cheap video displays give us access to a very powerful software-controlled Cursor system. This lets us get anything onto or off of the display memory at any time for any reason at zero hardware cost and extreme flexibility. This is far more powerful and more versatile than traditional terminals with fixed-hardware Cursors, particularly when you want to get one or two values back off the screen or display a real time clock.

Since your display memory is in every way ordinary compared to any other RAM in your computer, any old software you want can work as a Cursor. You can even build a cursor with Extended BASIC or some other higher-level language if you have the *Peek* and *Poke* ability to change machine locations.

Cursor Guidelines

Since your Cursor is ordinary software, there are various ways to do the job. Anything that works can be used. Your obvious goals should be to get by with a reasonably short program and to limit the total time needed for any action to times that are short enough that we do not get into transparency problems.

Here are some hints and guidelines that will help you simplify your Cursor designs:

1. **Always test for a valid Cursor location.**
   If the memory locations that hold your "next character" loca-

tion ever get *off* the display memory pages, you are in deep trouble. Your next character entry will plow up some other program rather than get entered. Always test for a valid location first. If you are in the display memory space, go ahead with your entry. If you are out of range, home the Cursor immediately!

2. **Erase, change, then replace the Cursor.**
   The lower seven bits of a display memory word are usually used to store an ASCII character. The eighth most-significant bit is used as a Cursor. If this most-significant bit is a one, the Cursor is optionally displayed. If it is a zero, it is not. Rather than try to figure out what happens to your Cursor for each and every possible screen motion, always erase the old Cursor first. Then make any changes you want. Then find out where the new Cursor belongs. Finally, restore the Cursor at the new location.

3. **Use Subroutines.**
   If several Cursor motions need the same operation, combine these in subroutine code. Three useful subroutines are Enter Character and Increment; Enter Spaces; and Home Cursor.
   Enter Character and Increment is obviously used to enter characters and move on to the next location. It is also used to enter spaces during a screen erase, scrolling, or an erase to end of paragraph. By jumping into the middle of this subroutine, you can increment only. This is useful during Cursor right commands and carriage return. A carriage return can be done by moving to the extreme right-hand character of the old line and then incrementing one to get to the start of the next line.
   Enter Spaces is useful for clearing, erasing to end of line, erasing to end of screen, and to erase the bottom line after scrolling. It may be used to call a nested Enter and Increment subroutine.
   Home Cursor is used by itself to move the Cursor to the upper left. It is also used at the start and finish of an Erase Screen command. You also need it if you are in a wraparound mode when the screen overflows, and it is used to get an out-of-range Cursor back onto the screen.
   One time you do NOT want to use a subroutine is if time gets out of hand for long, repetitive programs. A transparent scrolling Cursor is one design where nested subroutines should be avoided.

4. **Use memory remapping from scrolling.**
A scrolling display moves up one from the bottom each time a bottom line is completed. In cheap video systems, you can do a powerful scrolling by reading a memory location and then storing it on the next line up, repeating the process for the entire screen.

Fig. 2-19 shows a simplified flowchart for a typical Cursor. We can enter our Scan program by way of an interrupt, any time a key is pressed. We then test for a valid Cursor location. If we are somewhere legal on the screen, we erase the old Cursor. We then decode the keypressed entry. If it is a character, we go ahead and enter it. If it is a machine command, we decode this command to see if it applies to us. We then carry out any valid command. Typical machine commands include *Clear* (CAN), *Carriage Return* (CR), *Backspace* (BS), and so on.

After the character is entered or removed or after your machine instruction is carried out, we find the new Cursor location and write the Cursor back into it. You then return from the interrupt and resume scanning.

We also have the option of including the Cursor in the main Scan program. This eliminates any need for interruptions. If carefully

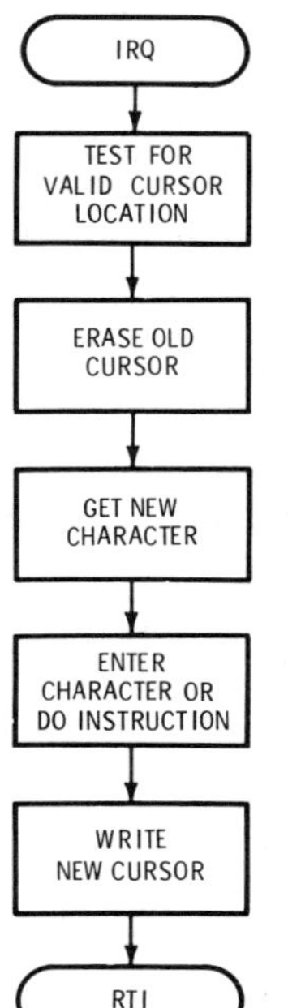

Fig. 2-19. Simplified flowchart of a typical Cursor control program.

designed, this also gives you complete transparency. You can also do things like scan a keyboard at the same time and eliminate the need for a hardware encoder. We call this an *Integrated* Scan program. Integrated programs often take more code, are harder to write, and harder to change. But they are probably what you will eventually want to get.

For now, we will stick with the interrupt-driven Cursor. You can pick up the fancier versions once you have your basics up and properly working. Details on this will appear in the last chapter.

A Full-Performance Scrolling Cursor

Fig. 2-20 gives a 6502 coded program for a full-performance scrolling Cursor. It is useful for 16 × 32, 16 × 64, and 32 × 64 alphanumeric display formats. It gives you a choice of scrolling or wraparound Cursor by changing a single software word. You can similarly protect or not protect the screen as well as display or not display your Cursor.

As Fig. 2-20 shows, you enter your ASCII character on the parallel A inputs on your KIM. An interrupt driven from the keypressed output causes character entry or Cursor motions. This IRQ signal should be a negative-going pulse that lasts 10 μs. The Cursor program is located on KIM page 01 below the stack.

In operation, any key pressed causes an interrupt which stops the scanning and jumps us to location 0100. The Cursor is tested to make sure it is on a legal display memory page location, and then the old Cursor is erased. Refer to the flowchart in Fig. 2-20 for actual locations of all these operations. If the Cursor location is legal, a new character is picked up from the A parallel interface. If it is a character, it is directly entered. If it is a control command, it is decoded. If it is a valid command, that command is acted on. If not, the command gets entered as a screen character.

After the command or character is completed, the Cursor is restored to its new locations and the interrupt is halted with a RTI command that jumps us back to the main Scan program.

Here is how the individual commands work:

* *Enter a Character*—Character is stored in a memory location using Cursor values in 00Ed (low) and 00EE (high). Cursor values are then incremented, starting with the lower page (always) and the upper page (if needed). On screen overflow, program jumps to a home Cursor command for wraparound, or to a scrolling sequence.
* *Home Cursor*—Subroutine is used to load upper and lower page values in locations 00Ed and 00EE.
* *Clear Screen*—Cursor is sent home with subroutine. An ASCII

space (20) is loaded in the accumulator and stored sequentially in all locations using the enter spaces subroutine which calls a nested enter and increment subroutine. Entry continues till screen is filled. Cursor is then sent home to complete clearing.

* *Carriage Return*—Cursor location is moved to extreme right of old line, using ORA 1F for a 32-character line and ORA 3F for a 64-character line. Cursor location is then incremented by jumping into middle of enter-and-increment subroutine. This moves you to the start of the next line. If the Cursor overflows display memory, program jumps to scrolling or wraparound as selected.
* *Cursor Up*—One line of characters is subtracted from old Cursor location. If the Cursor location goes off the screen by underflowing, the Cursor is sent home with a subroutine.
* *Cursor Down*—One line of characters is added to the old Cursor location. If the Cursor location goes off the screen by overflowing, the program jumps to a selected wraparound or scroll sequence.
* *Cursor Right*—Increment portion of enter and increment subroutine is used. If Cursor overflows display memory, wraparound or scrolling sequence is picked up.
* *Cursor Left*—Cursor is decremented. If page underflows, upper Cursor page is decremented. If screen underflows, Cursor is sent home with subroutine.
* *Erase to End of Screen*—Present Cursor location is saved on stack. Screen is erased from present location to end. Present Cursor location is retrieved from stack and reused.
* *Wraparound*—If wraparound is selected, any overflow of memory homes Cursor.
* *Scrolling*—A page overflow that results from a character entry or a Cursor motion activates the scrolling sequence. Scrolling is NOT permitted on clear screen or erase to end of screen to prevent a permanent loop. When scrolling is called for and allowed, an indirect address is used to get a character and move it up one line, storing the character 32 or 64 slots earlier in memory. When scrolling is complete, the old top line is gone, and everything else has moved up one line. The bottom and next to bottom lines are identical. The bottom line is next erased by doing an Erase to End of Screen, starting with the first character on the bottom line. The Cursor is then returned to the first character on the bottom line.

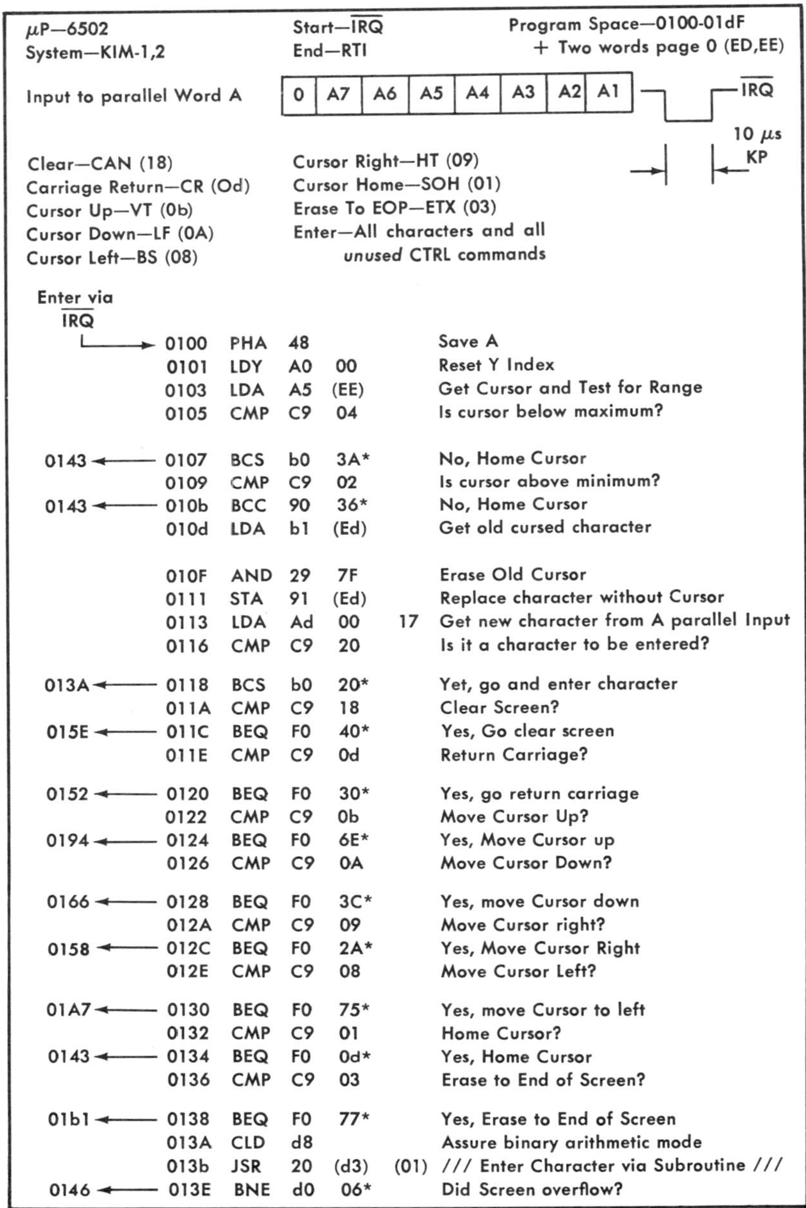

```
μP—6502                        Start—IRQ             Program Space—0100-01dF
System—KIM-1,2                 End—RTI                 + Two words page 0 (ED,EE)

Input to parallel Word A   | 0 | A7 | A6 | A5 | A4 | A3 | A2 | A1 |  IRQ (10 μs KP)

Clear—CAN (18)                 Cursor Right—HT (09)
Carriage Return—CR (Od)        Cursor Home—SOH (01)
Cursor Up—VT (Ob)              Erase To EOP—ETX (03)
Cursor Down—LF (0A)            Enter—All characters and all
Cursor Left—BS (08)                  unused CTRL commands

 Enter via
  IRQ
   └──────→ 0100  PHA  48                   Save A
            0101  LDY  A0  00               Reset Y Index
            0103  LDA  A5  (EE)             Get Cursor and Test for Range
            0105  CMP  C9  04               Is cursor below maximum?

 0143 ←──── 0107  BCS  b0  3A*              No, Home Cursor
            0109  CMP  C9  02               Is cursor above minimum?
 0143 ←──── 010b  BCC  90  36*              No, Home Cursor
            010d  LDA  b1  (Ed)             Get old cursed character

            010F  AND  29  7F               Erase Old Cursor
            0111  STA  91  (Ed)             Replace character without Cursor
            0113  LDA  Ad  00   17          Get new character from A parallel Input
            0116  CMP  C9  20               Is it a character to be entered?

 013A ←──── 0118  BCS  b0  20*              Yet, go and enter character
            011A  CMP  C9  18               Clear Screen?
 015E ←──── 011C  BEQ  F0  40*              Yes, Go clear screen
            011E  CMP  C9  0d               Return Carriage?

 0152 ←──── 0120  BEQ  F0  30*              Yes, go return carriage
            0122  CMP  C9  0b               Move Cursor Up?
 0194 ←──── 0124  BEQ  F0  6E*              Yes, Move Cursor up
            0126  CMP  C9  0A               Move Cursor Down?

 0166 ←──── 0128  BEQ  F0  3C*              Yes, move Cursor down
            012A  CMP  C9  09               Move Cursor right?
 0158 ←──── 012C  BEQ  F0  2A*              Yes, Move Cursor Right
            012E  CMP  C9  08               Move Cursor Left?

 01A7 ←──── 0130  BEQ  F0  75*              Yes, move Cursor to left
            0132  CMP  C9  01               Home Cursor?
 0143 ←──── 0134  BEQ  F0  0d*              Yes, Home Cursor
            0136  CMP  C9  03               Erase to End of Screen?

 01b1 ←──── 0138  BEQ  F0  77*              Yes, Erase to End of Screen
            013A  CLD  d8                   Assure binary arithmetic mode
            013b  JSR  20  (d3)  (01)       /// Enter Character via Subroutine ///
 0146 ←──── 013E  BNE  d0  06*              Did Screen overflow?
```

Fig. 2-20. Full-performance scrolling Cursor for TVT 6 5/8 KIM

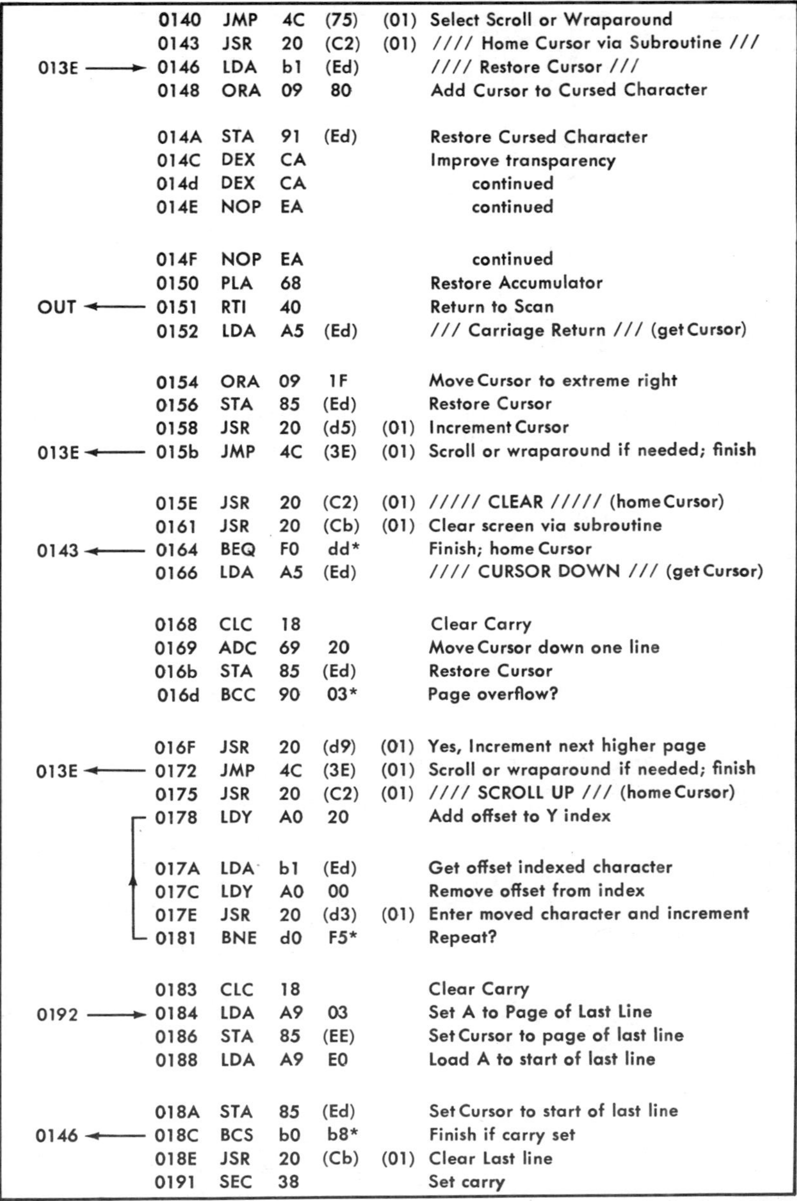

	Address	Instr.	Op	Operand		Comment
	0140	JMP	4C	(75)	(01)	Select Scroll or Wraparound
	0143	JSR	20	(C2)	(01)	//// Home Cursor via Subroutine ///
013E →	0146	LDA	b1	(Ed)		//// Restore Cursor ///
	0148	ORA	09	80		Add Cursor to Cursed Character
	014A	STA	91	(Ed)		Restore Cursed Character
	014C	DEX	CA			Improve transparency
	014d	DEX	CA			continued
	014E	NOP	EA			continued
	014F	NOP	EA			continued
	0150	PLA	68			Restore Accumulator
OUT ←	0151	RTI	40			Return to Scan
	0152	LDA	A5	(Ed)		/// Carriage Return /// (get Cursor)
	0154	ORA	09	1F		Move Cursor to extreme right
	0156	STA	85	(Ed)		Restore Cursor
	0158	JSR	20	(d5)	(01)	Increment Cursor
013E ←	015b	JMP	4C	(3E)	(01)	Scroll or wraparound if needed; finish
	015E	JSR	20	(C2)	(01)	///// CLEAR ///// (home Cursor)
	0161	JSR	20	(Cb)	(01)	Clear screen via subroutine
0143 ←	0164	BEQ	F0	dd*		Finish; home Cursor
	0166	LDA	A5	(Ed)		//// CURSOR DOWN /// (get Cursor)
	0168	CLC	18			Clear Carry
	0169	ADC	69	20		Move Cursor down one line
	016b	STA	85	(Ed)		Restore Cursor
	016d	BCC	90	03*		Page overflow?
	016F	JSR	20	(d9)	(01)	Yes, Increment next higher page
013E ←	0172	JMP	4C	(3E)	(01)	Scroll or wraparound if needed; finish
	0175	JSR	20	(C2)	(01)	//// SCROLL UP /// (home Cursor)
┌	0178	LDY	A0	20		Add offset to Y index
│	017A	LDA	b1	(Ed)		Get offset indexed character
↑	017C	LDY	A0	00		Remove offset from index
│	017E	JSR	20	(d3)	(01)	Enter moved character and increment
└	0181	BNE	d0	F5*		Repeat?
	0183	CLC	18			Clear Carry
0192 →	0184	LDA	A9	03		Set A to Page of Last Line
	0186	STA	85	(EE)		Set Cursor to page of last line
	0188	LDA	A9	E0		Load A to start of last line
	018A	STA	85	(Ed)		Set Cursor to start of last line
0146 ←	018C	BCS	b0	b8*		Finish if carry set
	018E	JSR	20	(Cb)	(01)	Clear Last line
	0191	SEC	38			Set carry

Continued on next page.

based 16 × 32, 16 × 64, and 32 × 64 alphanumeric displays.

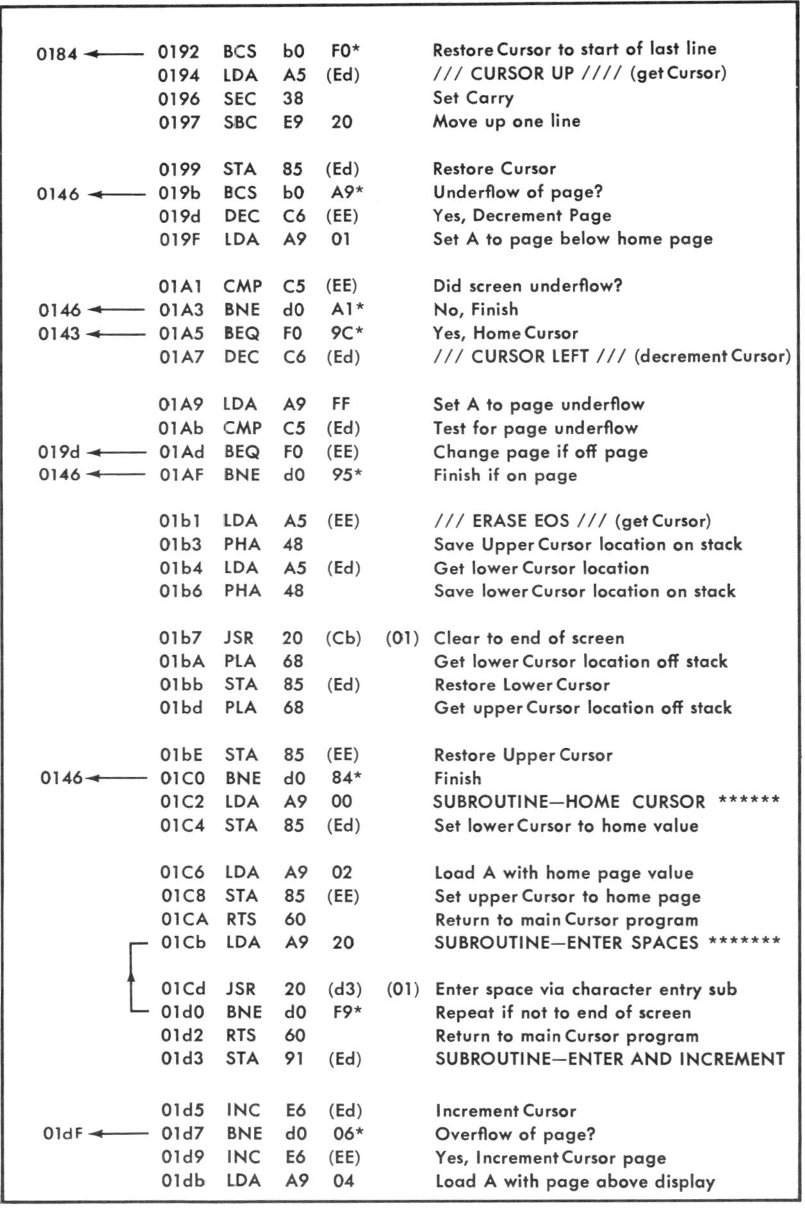

```
0184 <------ 0192  BCS  b0  F0*        Restore Cursor to start of last line
             0194  LDA  A5  (Ed)       /// CURSOR UP //// (get Cursor)
             0196  SEC  38             Set Carry
             0197  SBC  E9  20         Move up one line

             0199  STA  85  (Ed)       Restore Cursor
0146 <------ 019b  BCS  b0  A9*        Underflow of page?
             019d  DEC  C6  (EE)       Yes, Decrement Page
             019F  LDA  A9  01         Set A to page below home page

             01A1  CMP  C5  (EE)       Did screen underflow?
0146 <------ 01A3  BNE  d0  A1*        No, Finish
0143 <------ 01A5  BEQ  F0  9C*        Yes, Home Cursor
             01A7  DEC  C6  (Ed)       /// CURSOR LEFT /// (decrement Cursor)

             01A9  LDA  A9  FF         Set A to page underflow
             01Ab  CMP  C5  (Ed)       Test for page underflow
019d <------ 01Ad  BEQ  F0  (EE)       Change page if off page
0146 <------ 01AF  BNE  d0  95*        Finish if on page

             01b1  LDA  A5  (EE)       /// ERASE EOS /// (get Cursor)
             01b3  PHA  48             Save Upper Cursor location on stack
             01b4  LDA  A5  (Ed)       Get lower Cursor location
             01b6  PHA  48             Save lower Cursor location on stack

             01b7  JSR  20  (Cb) (01)  Clear to end of screen
             01bA  PLA  68             Get lower Cursor location off stack
             01bb  STA  85  (Ed)       Restore Lower Cursor
             01bd  PLA  68             Get upper Cursor location off stack

             01bE  STA  85  (EE)       Restore Upper Cursor
0146 <------ 01C0  BNE  d0  84*        Finish
             01C2  LDA  A9  00         SUBROUTINE—HOME CURSOR ******
             01C4  STA  85  (Ed)       Set lower Cursor to home value

             01C6  LDA  A9  02         Load A with home page value
             01C8  STA  85  (EE)       Set upper Cursor to home page
             01CA  RTS  60             Return to main Cursor program
          +- 01Cb  LDA  A9  20         SUBROUTINE—ENTER SPACES *******
          ^
          |  01Cd  JSR  20  (d3) (01)  Enter space via character entry sub
          +- 01d0  BNE  d0  F9*        Repeat if not to end of screen
             01d2  RTS  60             Return to main Cursor program
             01d3  STA  91  (Ed)       SUBROUTINE—ENTER AND INCREMENT

             01d5  INC  E6  (Ed)       Increment Cursor
01dF <------ 01d7  BNE  d0  06*        Overflow of page?
             01d9  INC  E6  (EE)       Yes, Increment Cursor page
             01db  LDA  A9  04         Load A with page above display
```

Fig. 2-20 *Continued.* Full-performance scrolling Cursor for TVT 6 5/8 KIM

```
             01dd  CMP  C5  (EE)        Test for Overflow
01d7 ——————► 01dF  RTS  60              Return to main Cursor program
```

NOTES:

For auto-scrolling, use 0141 75. For wraparound use 0141 43. To protect page, load 00F3 04. To enable entry, use 00F3 00. To display Cursor, load 0149 80. For no display use 0149 00.

IRQ vector must be stored in 17FE 00 and 17FF 01.

Cursor address is stored at 00Ed low and 00EE high.

Total available stack length is 32 words. Approximately 16 are used by operating system, Cursor, and Scan program. Stack must be initialized to 01FF as is done in KIM operating system. For 30 more stack locations, relocate subroutines starting at 01C2 elsewhere. For total stack availability, relocate entire program elsewhere.

* Denotes a relative branch that is program length sensitive.

( ) Denotes an absolute address that is program location sensitive.

To match this program to your Scan program, change the following slots:

Location	Function	16 × 32 0200-03FF	16 × 32 0400-05FF	16 × 64 0400-07FF	32 × 64 0400-0bFF
0106	Cursor max + 1	04	06	08	0C
010A	Cursor minimum	02	04	04	04
0155	CR line length	1F	1F	3F	3F
016A	LF line length	20	20	40	40
0179	Scroll Offset	20	20	40	40
0185	Scroll last page	03	05	07	0A
0189	Scroll last line	E0	E0	C0	C0
0198	VT line length	20	20	40	40
01A0	Underflow page	01	03	03	03
01C7	Home page	02	04	04	04
01dC	Overflow page	04	06	08	0C

Continued on next page.

based 16 × 32, 16 × 64, and 32 × 64 alphanumeric displays.

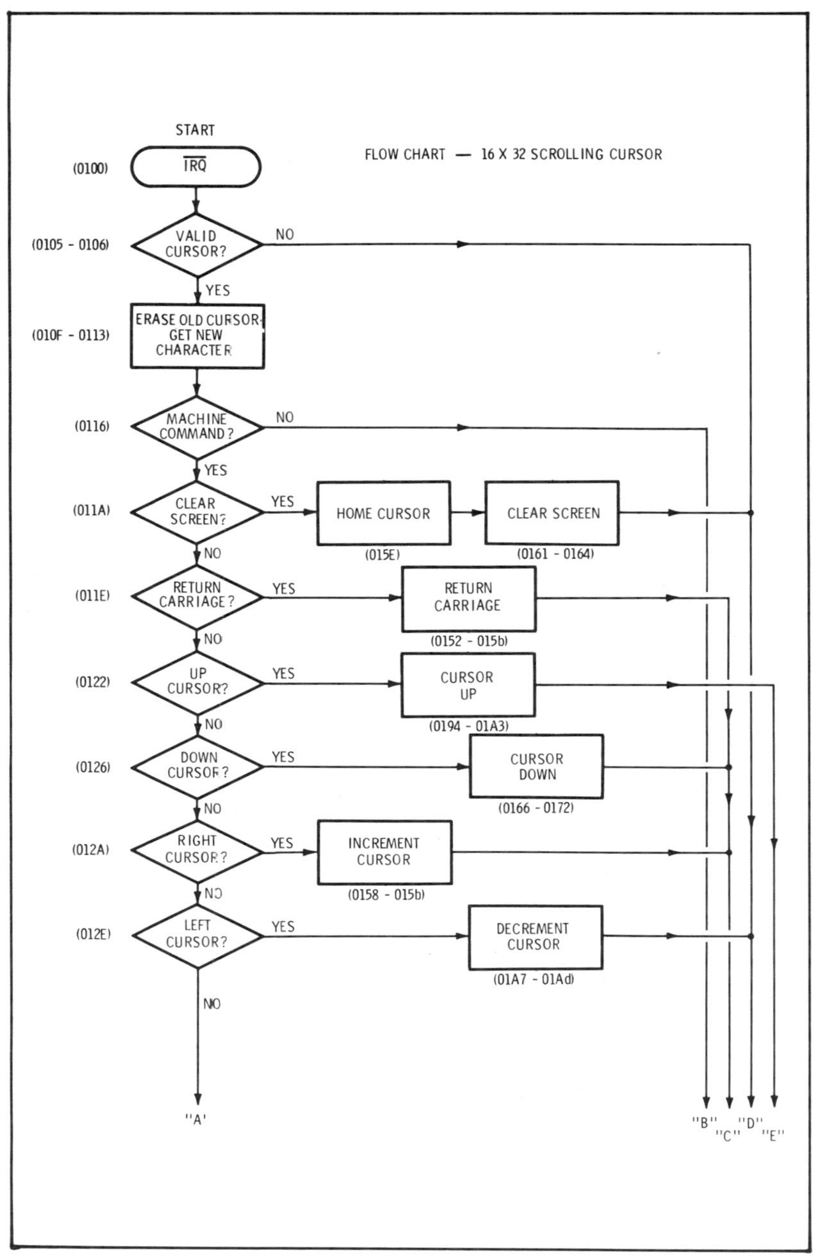

Fig. 2-20 *Continued.* Full-performance scrolling Cursor for TVT 6 5/8 KIM

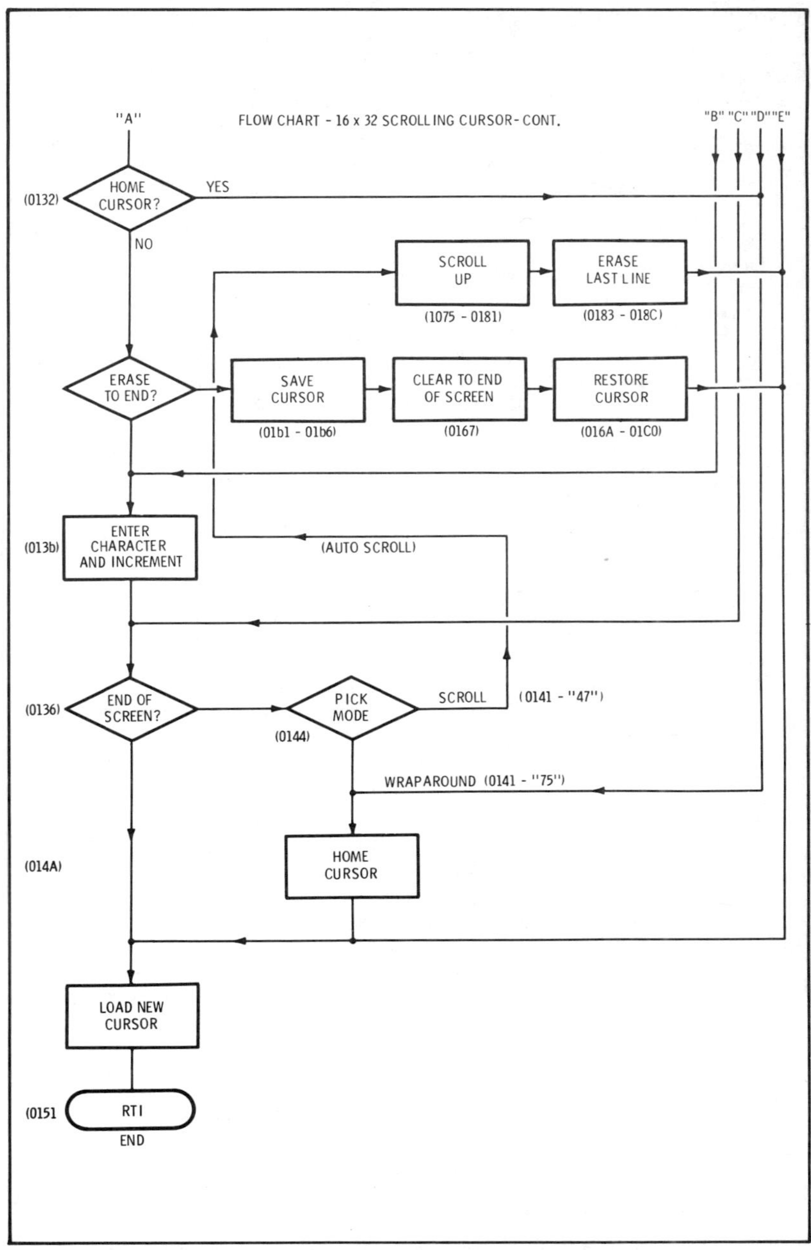

based 16 × 32, 16 × 64, and 32 × 64 alphanumeric displays.

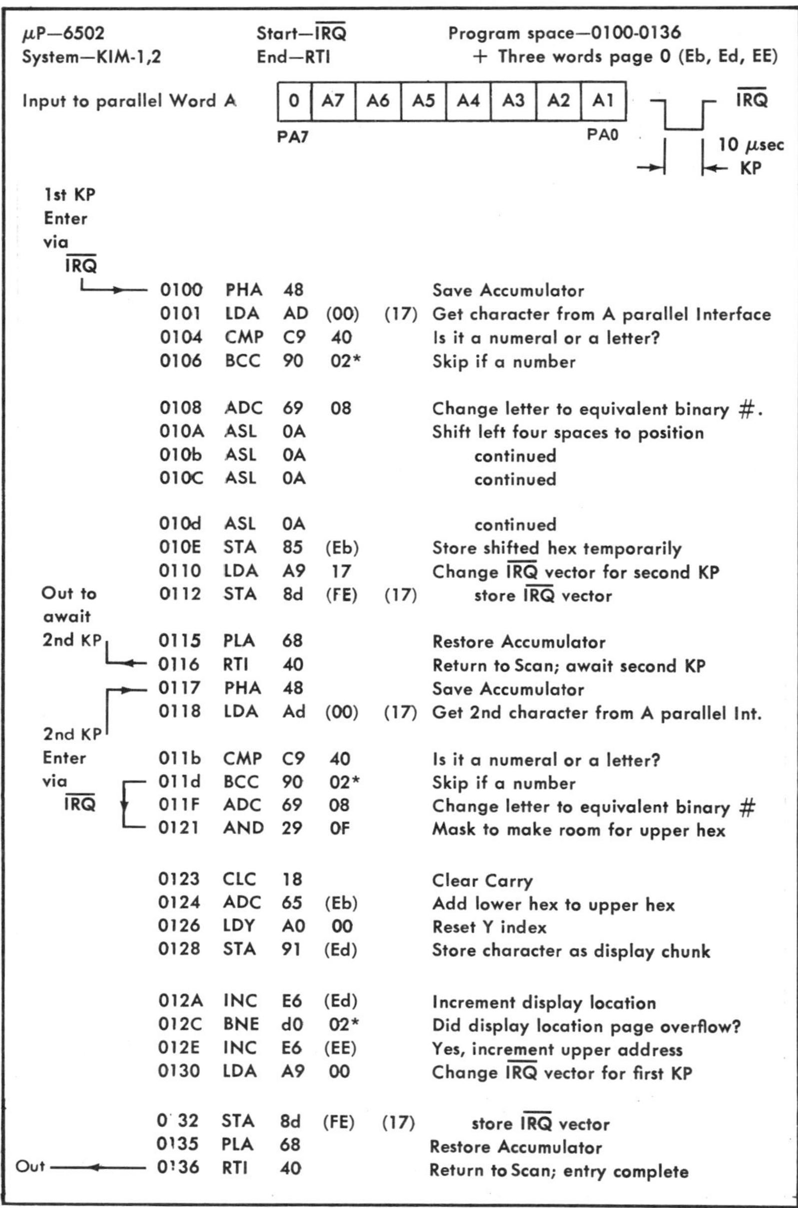

μP—6502 Start—$\overline{IRQ}$ Program space—0100-0136
System—KIM-1,2 End—RTI + Three words page 0 (Eb, Ed, EE)

Input to parallel Word A

0	A7	A6	A5	A4	A3	A2	A1

PA7 ... PA0

$\overline{IRQ}$ — 10 μsec — KP

```
1st KP
Enter
via
IRQ  --> 0100  PHA  48              Save Accumulator
         0101  LDA  AD  (00)  (17)  Get character from A parallel Interface
         0104  CMP  C9  40          Is it a numeral or a letter?
         0106  BCC  90  02*         Skip if a number

         0108  ADC  69  08          Change letter to equivalent binary #.
         010A  ASL  0A              Shift left four spaces to position
         010b  ASL  0A                   continued
         010C  ASL  0A                   continued

         010d  ASL  0A                   continued
         010E  STA  85  (Eb)        Store shifted hex temporarily
         0110  LDA  A9  17          Change IRQ vector for second KP
Out to   0112  STA  8d  (FE)  (17)       store IRQ vector
await
2nd KP   0115  PLA  68              Restore Accumulator
     <-- 0116  RTI  40              Return to Scan; await second KP
     --> 0117  PHA  48              Save Accumulator
         0118  LDA  Ad  (00)  (17)  Get 2nd character from A parallel Int.
2nd KP
Enter    011b  CMP  C9  40          Is it a numeral or a letter?
via      011d  BCC  90  02*         Skip if a number
IRQ      011F  ADC  69  08          Change letter to equivalent binary #
         0121  AND  29  0F          Mask to make room for upper hex

         0123  CLC  18              Clear Carry
         0124  ADC  65  (Eb)        Add lower hex to upper hex
         0126  LDY  A0  00          Reset Y index
         0128  STA  91  (Ed)        Store character as display chunk

         012A  INC  E6  (Ed)        Increment display location
         012C  BNE  d0  02*         Did display location page overflow?
         012E  INC  E6  (EE)        Yes, increment upper address
         0130  LDA  A9  00          Change IRQ vector for first KP

         0132  STA  8d  (FE)  (17)       store IRQ vector
         0135  PLA  68              Restore Accumulator
Out <--- 0136  RTI  40              Return to Scan; entry complete
```

Fig. 2-21. Simple graphics

Several program words have to be changed to customize your Cursor for the location and the size of the display memory as shown. Other words are changed to select scrolling or wraparound; visible or invisible Cursor; and protected or usable screen.

> *Your Turn:*
>
> Show the modifications needed to let this Cursor program run with a 40- and 80-character repacked memory Scan.

Our particular cursor example is a medium complexity one taking 200 odd words of code. To do all this with hardware would be a real mess, not to say anything about flexibility. You can greatly simplify this Cursor for simple character entry, or you can go the other way and add lots of extra functions for super fancy editing. Typical things you might like to add include erase to end of line, insert and delete words, lines, or characters, ring bells near line end, interchange lines, and so on.

A GRAPHICS LOADER

A *graphics loader* is the equivalent of an alphanumeric Cursor program. It lets you build up and modify a graphics display a chunk at a time, actually viewing the final result as chunks are put down. A rather primitive graphics loader is shown in Fig. 2-21.

To operate the loader, you put the starting address of what you want to modify on your display in 00Ed and 00EE. Every time you

Starting display location is placed in 00Ed (low) and 00EE (high). Typing a pair of hex characters enters the characters as a graphics chunk, then goes on to the next chunk location.

NOTES:

$\overline{\text{IRQ}}$ vector must be initialized as 17FE 00 and 17FF 01.

Starting display address must be set as 00Ed (low) and 00EE (high).

Loader must be stopped before leaving display memory space.

Characters must be entered as pairs. Characters other than 0-9 and A through F will be erroneously entered.

* Denotes a relative branch that is program length sensitive.

( ) Denotes an absolute address that is program location sensitive.

loader for TVT 6 5/8.

type a pair of hex characters, that chunk gets entered and the display changes as needed.

The program works by getting a character, converting it to hexadecimal, and shifting it left four spaces. This character is temporarily saved. A new character is gotten and hex converted. It is then masked to make room for the old shifted character. The old and the new character are added together into a composite 8-bit data chunk. The chunk is then entered in the desired location and the starting address is incremented one location.

The $\overline{\text{IRQ}}$ entry location is changed every time, so that the first KP gives us the rightmost hex character and the second the leftmost one and the actual screen update. Since this is a very simple program, you always have to load your starting address before you start, and always have to stop before you run out of display-memory space.

Your Turn:

Add the following bells and whistles to your graphics loader: Off display protection; home to starting address; four way Cursor motion; a visible Cursor; ability to complement cursed code; and a bell to indicate two-character chunk completion.

One thing you might like to look into is storing your graphics symbols as a *subroutine file of subelements.* In other words, you stash a basic set of symbols somewhere and then call them from your "library" as needed for display. This gives you tremendous software simplification since you can now call an entire symbol, such as a chess piece, and load it into the display memory with a single software word. Loading the screen and display design becomes much less of a hassle. Now, instead of having to individually load as many as 64,000 bits of screen information, you simply call larger blocks of ready-to-go elements as needed and let the computer do the work.

TRANSPARENCY

The Scan programs we have looked at so far make continuous 100% use of the microcomputer during a display. The Cursor-control software interrupts the Scan anytime a change is needed. The amount of interruption varies, so this results in a brief to long dropout of the Scan operation. You will see this on a screen as a flash, a blank, or tearing of the display. Usually you will alternate your compute and display modes.

For many simple uses, this brief tearing or dropout is acceptable. For others it is not. There are several ways to make our display totally *transparent,* so that time is left to do things like simultaneously run a BASIC program or complicated game calculations. One obvious but complicated way to make a Cursor program transparent is to *integrate* it into the Scan program so that Cursor motions are carried out during the vertical blanking time without interruption of the Scan timing.

We will be looking at alternate ways of picking up partial to full transparency in Chapter 5.

VOLATILITY—RAM versus ROM

Almost all the programs shown to you in this chapter use RAM memory. The nice thing about RAM is that it is uncommitted and undedicated. This makes things flexible and easy to change. The bad thing about RAM is that we have to reload all the programs every time the power goes off. Programs stored in RAM can also be wiped out if they or another program goes berserk and decides to plow up memory locations.

There is no problem in putting the Cursor software into ROM or PROM once you have decided exactly what you want your cursor to do and have in fact debugged it. This will restrict you to fixed formats of operation, but often this is exactly what you want for final use applications.

Note that even with a ROM cursor, a few RAM locations will be needed in the stack and for the cursor location.

Putting your Scan programs in ROM or PROM is a bit stickier. Some PROMs slow down the microprocessor cycle time and could introduce timing and magic number problems. But the crucial hangup is that all our Scan programs rely on a jump to subroutine at a 16-bit–wide *absolute calculated address.* At least for the 6502, the two slots following the JSR command *MUST* be RAM. There usually is not time enough to jump down to page zero or some similar stunt each time we want a new Scan. Our back is usually to the wall with Scan loop timing, as you should be aware by now.

How do we get out of this bind? Is there any way to put our Scan programs permanently in ROM or PROM?

The simplest way is to notice that the Scan programs are usually only a hundred words or less long. So, you *simply move the whole program from ROM to RAM anytime you need it.* A simple "move the next hundred words to 1780" loader that goes before the actual Scan program in ROM or PROM does the job for us.

How often you reload the RAM depends on your system. This can be done once on system reset. Just have the NMI vector go to the Scan PROM first, and then to the usual operating system reset. Or, you can do a load by calling a starting address any time you need one. You could even automatically reload every vertical blanking time, but this probably is too much. Another obvious possibility is to store your Scan program on a floppy disc or other file and transfer it to RAM as you need and use it.

Yet another route is to use brute force coding that calls, rather than calculates, JSR addresses. This will take many more words of coding but it can still fit in a reasonably priced PROM.

CHAPTER 3

Hardware Design

Our most obvious cheap video hardware concern is the interface card that goes between the microcomputer and the tv set. Important parts of a typical interface card include the *instruction decoder;* the *Scan microprogram PROM; a character generator* (for alphanumerics) or a *data formatter* (for graphics); *high-frequency timing; output circuitry;* and *sync positioning* circuits.

Two other important hardware problem areas are the interface to the television set itself, and the modification and interconnections you need between the microcomputer and the interface card. In this chapter, we will look at these hardware concepts in more detail. Once we have this background, we can go on to the complete system construction details of the TVT 6⅝ in Chapter 4.

INTERFACE CARD HARDWARE DESIGN

Our interface card has to hold most of the dedicated circuitry needed between a microprocessor and a tv set. You will find a block diagram of a typical card shown in Fig. 3-1. Depending on its design details and plug-in modules, you can use this type of card with graphics, alphanumerics, or a combination of the two.

The *instruction decoder* is the central controller of a cheap video display. It is usually a small bipolar PROM. When activated by the Scan program, the instruction decoder decides when a Scan of video is needed and what video is going to be produced. Control signals are delivered to the rest of the interface circuitry by the instruction decoder. These signals include sync pulses and disabling signals that go back to make certain nothing else tries to use the microcomputer at the same instant the tvt needs it.

The *Scan microprogram* generator is a second PROM that outputs a Scan microinstruction to the microprocessor. This PROM is activated by the instruction decoder every time a Scan of video is wanted.

The *data-to-video converter* is usually a dot-matrix character generator integrated circuit for alphanumeric use and is usually a shift register or a shift register and data selector combination for graphics use. This converter block converts code stored in the display memory of the computer and received by way of the new upstream tap into serial video that you can display. The instruction decoder controls the data-to-video converter by telling it which row of dots to output on a character or which part of a word to output for a graphics format. By making this circuit on a plug-in module, the same interface card may be used for alphanumerics or graphics.

High-frequency timing controls when the serial video dots are to be output and at what rate. This block can be a hex inverter gated oscillator driven from the main clock in the microcomputer. A *Cursor* circuit is often used in alphanumeric tvt's. The Cursor introduces the "winking" underline or box that shows us the next character location. The Cursor circuit usually is made up of a low-frequency oscillator and some gating.

The *sync and position* block takes horizontal- and vertical-timing signals from the instruction decoder. It then delays these timing signals as needed for positioning. After this, it goes on to shape these sync commands into the proper time widths for tv use.

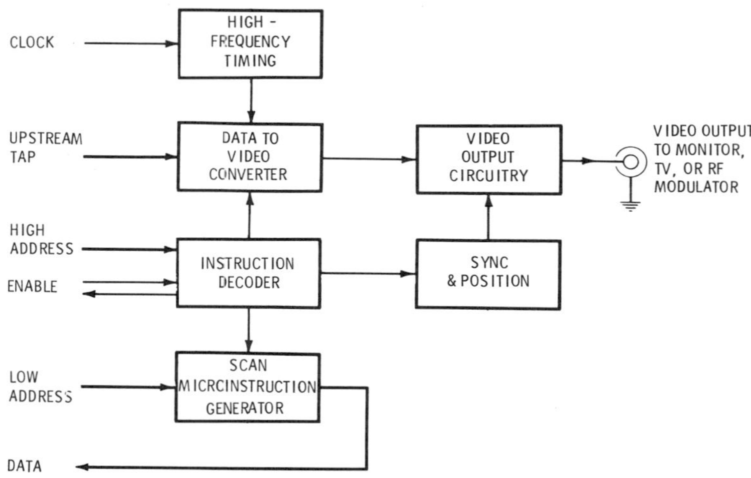

Fig. 3-1. Block diagram of a typical interface card.

Our *video-output circuitry* combines video and sync and then provides a composite output suitable for monitor, rf modulator, or direct video interface. One important part of the output circuitry is the *bandwidth enhancer.* This simple compensation circuit is usually included to predistort the output video in anticipation of how the tv set will try to mess it up. The result is denser and sharper characters for a given tv bandwidth.

Bandwidth enhancement is one of the keys to displaying long character lines on an ordinary tv set.

Let's take a closer look at these interface hardware blocks and see just what is involved in their design and use.

Instruction Decoder

Our instruction decoder PROM is the control center for tvt use of a microprocessor. The important things the instruction decoder has to do are summarized in Fig. 3-2. The instruction decoder has

The

INSTRUCTION DECODER

must:

* ACTIVATE THE SCAN MICROPROGRAM WHEN A SCAN IS NEEDED.
* DISABLE EVERYTHING ELSE TRYING TO USE THE COMPUTER CPU WHEN A SCAN IS NEEDED.
* SELECT THE RIGHT GRAPHICS FORMAT OR ALPHANUMERIC DOT ROW.
* OUTPUT SYNC PULSES AS NEEDED.
* OTHERWISE NOT INTERFERE WITH NORMAL COMPUTER OPERATION.

Fig. 3-2. Instruction Decoder PROM is key controlling block of the interface hardware.

to tell the microprocessor when to generate a Scan of characters. It has to pick the right part of whatever it is you are going to display. And, it has to firmly take over command of the microcomputer when the tvt is in use. When *not* in use, the instruction decoder has to make the interface hardware appear invisible to normal computer operation.

A 256-bit bipolar PROM of 32 words of 8 bits each is a good choice as an instruction decoder. This is the smallest PROM you can buy, costing under two dollars. Important advantages of using a PROM for the instruction decoder are the flexibility of assigning what each address does, the ease of making changes, and the single IC simplicity of board layout.

Fig. 3-3 shows us one good way to use a 32 × 8 PROM as an instruction decoder. We input high order address lines A15, A14, A13, and A12.

There are eight output leads available. One of these is used for a *decode enable* that takes over command from the normal address decoding of the computer. On a KIM, this is line K0 and is low for normal computer use and high for tvt use. A second output is a chip-select command which goes low when we want to activate the display memory as far as the upstream tap. A third output drives our Scan microprogram generator, going low to produce a Scan microinstruction. Two sync outputs are needed, one horizontal and one vertical. Often the *decode enable* output can double as a horizontal-sync output, saving us a pin.

The remaining four output lines can be used to format the output data. In alphanumerics, these can be the three or four "what line is it?" row commands that go to the character generator. For graphics, we can use the same pins as a blanking output and an upper/lower output.

Our 32 × 8 PROM has a fifth input. We can pick just what we are going to do with it. In Fig. 3-3, an external AND gate was used

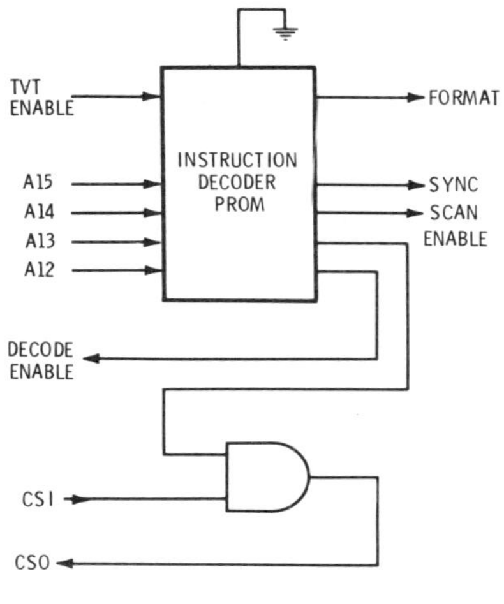

Fig. 3-3. Instruction Decoder PROM using external gate for display memory chip select.

to combine the normal computer chip select with the tvt chip select to provide a composite CSO that activates the display memory as needed. This external gate is physically an AND gate and is shown with its usual positive logic symbol but, in reality, it is used as an "either input low gives a low output," or as its DeMorgan equivalent *negative logic* OR gate.

We can call our fifth PROM input a *tvt enable,* and activate this input from some external logic. This lets you use the higher order memory slots for other things besides tvt use (see Fig. 2-2). A low tvt enable lets the tvt work; when the enable is high, the tvt remains inactive and the computer is free to do whatever else it wants to do with its high address lines. For all-the-time tvt use, you can simply ground this input.

Note that we have to keep our instruction decoder outputs active at all times to prevent messing up the decode-enable commands. This usually means that the usual enable input of the PROM must stay grounded at all times. Thus, we must switch our PROM outputs from an "active" to a "passive" state as far as tvt operation is concerned, but we must never actually float the tristate outputs.

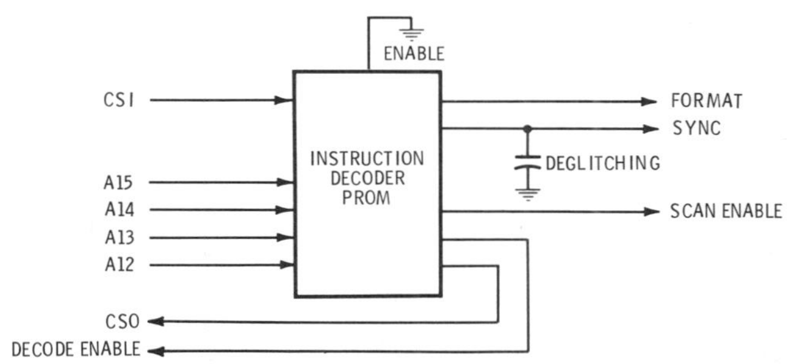

Fig. 3-4. Instruction Decoder PROM with internal gating for display memory chip select.

We also have the option of using our fifth PROM address input as a chip-select input from the computer. This internalizes the AND gate used for the chip selects. A diagram of this is shown in Fig. 3-4. We did this in the older TVT-6L as part of the mania for doing an entire video display in only six integrated circuits. There are two penalties to pay when you use internal-display memory CS selection. One is that your outputs glitch, which means you have to filter the sync outputs crudely. The second is that you cannot use many of the higher address locations for anything except tvt use. The TVT 6⅝ offers a choice of external or internal CS gating.

Fig. 3-5 shows the truth table for an instruction decoder having an internal-chip select. This is the PROM to be used on the TVT 6⅝.

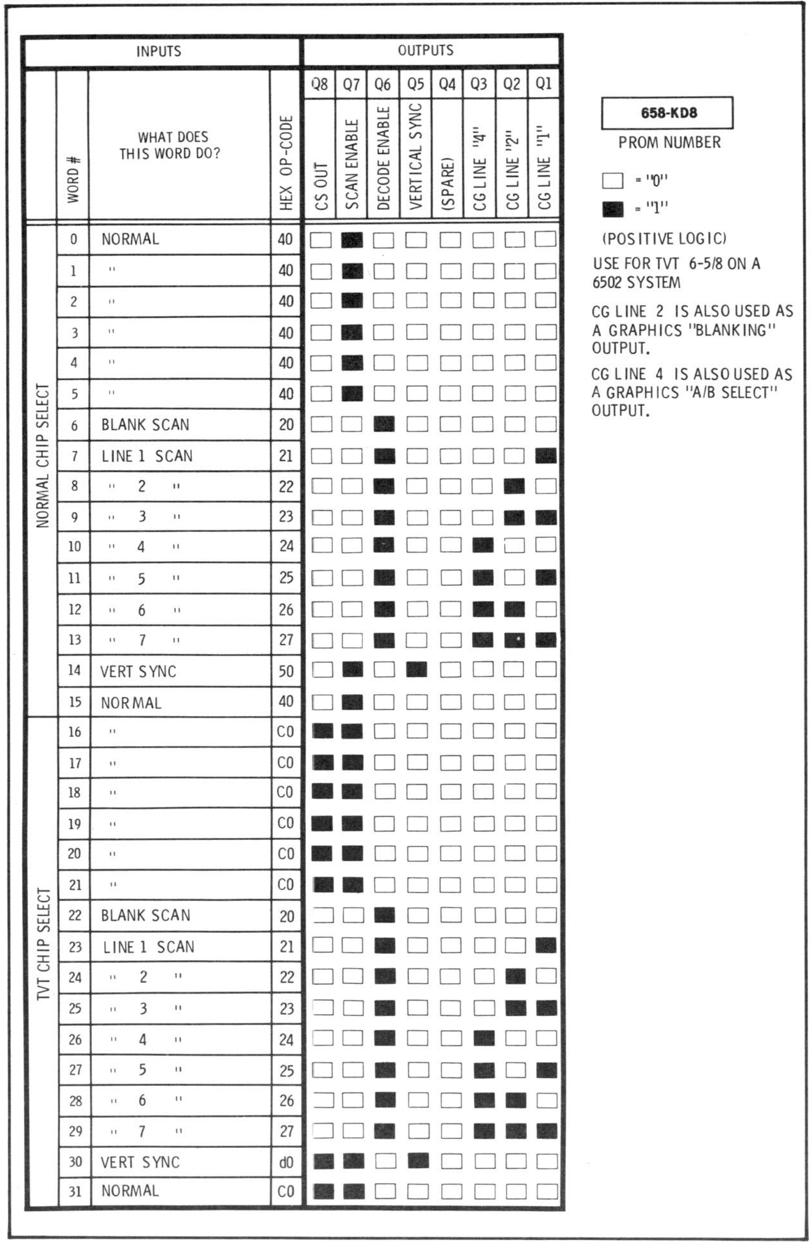

INPUTS				OUTPUTS							
	WORD #	WHAT DOES THIS WORD DO?	HEX OP-CODE	Q8 CS OUT	Q7 SCAN ENABLE	Q6 DECODE ENABLE	Q5 VERTICAL SYNC	Q4 (SPARE)	Q3 CG LINE "4"	Q2 CG LINE "2"	Q1 CG LINE "1"
NORMAL CHIP SELECT	0	NORMAL	40	□	■	□	□	□	□	□	□
	1	"	40	□	■	□	□	□	□	□	□
	2	"	40	□	■	□	□	□	□	□	□
	3	"	40	□	■	□	□	□	□	□	□
	4	"	40	□	■	□	□	□	□	□	□
	5	"	40	□	■	□	□	□	□	□	□
	6	BLANK SCAN	20	□	□	■	□	□	□	□	□
	7	LINE 1 SCAN	21	□	□	■	□	□	□	□	■
	8	" 2 "	22	□	□	■	□	□	□	■	□
	9	" 3 "	23	□	□	■	□	□	□	■	■
	10	" 4 "	24	□	□	■	□	□	■	□	□
	11	" 5 "	25	□	□	■	□	□	■	□	■
	12	" 6 "	26	□	□	■	□	□	■	■	□
	13	" 7 "	27	□	□	■	□	□	■	■	■
	14	VERT SYNC	50	□	■	□	■	□	□	□	□
	15	NORMAL	40	□	■	□	□	□	□	□	□
TVT CHIP SELECT	16	"	C0	■	■	□	□	□	□	□	□
	17	"	C0	■	■	□	□	□	□	□	□
	18	"	C0	■	■	□	□	□	□	□	□
	19	"	C0	■	■	□	□	□	□	□	□
	20	"	C0	■	■	□	□	□	□	□	□
	21	"	C0	■	■	□	□	□	□	□	□
	22	BLANK SCAN	20	□	□	■	□	□	□	□	□
	23	LINE 1 SCAN	21	□	□	■	□	□	□	□	■
	24	" 2 "	22	□	□	■	□	□	□	■	□
	25	" 3 "	23	□	□	■	□	□	□	■	■
	26	" 4 "	24	□	□	■	□	□	■	□	□
	27	" 5 "	25	□	□	■	□	□	■	□	■
	28	" 6 "	26	□	□	■	□	□	■	■	□
	29	" 7 "	27	□	□	■	□	□	■	■	■
	30	VERT SYNC	d0	■	■	□	■	□	□	□	□
	31	NORMAL	C0	■	■	□	□	□	□	□	□

658-KD8

PROM NUMBER

□ = "0"

■ = "1"

(POSITIVE LOGIC)

USE FOR TVT 6-5/8 ON A 6502 SYSTEM

CG LINE 2 IS ALSO USED AS A GRAPHICS "BLANKING" OUTPUT.

CG LINE 4 IS ALSO USED AS A GRAPHICS "A/B SELECT" OUTPUT.

Fig. 3-5. Truth table for 6502 decode PROM (used on KIM 1,2).

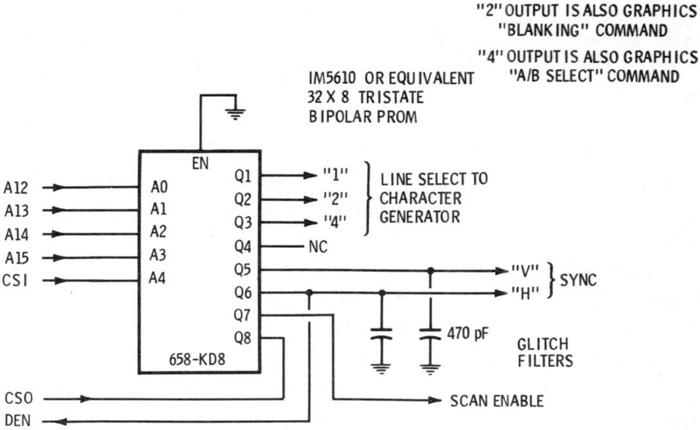

Fig. 3-6. Connections for decode PROM 658-KD8.

Locations 0-15 are selected if the decoder is to pass through an existing low CSI. Locations 16-31 are selected if the tvt is only to provide its own CSO when needed to the display memory. The only output difference you will see between these two halves of the truth table is the CSO output itself.

The remaining inputs are driven from A12 through A15 and select normal computer operation, a blank Scan, a vertical-sync pulse, or Scan of lines one through seven. Outputs include the character generator line commands (which double as graphics commands), the vertical-sync output, the Scan enable for the microprogram generator, the decode enable for the computer, and the chip-select output for the display memory. Typical connections are shown in Fig. 3-6.

Your Turn:

Show a truth table for a similar decode PROM whose fifth input is a tvt enable line. Show how external logic can switch between tvt operation and other use of high order address slots.

Scan Microprogram Generator

The Scan microprogram generator is a second PROM used as part of our interface hardware. Its purpose is to force a Scan microinstruction onto the microprocessor. The microprocessor, in turn, gives us a sequential one-character-per-microsecond code output that lasts for as many characters or chunks as you want in a horizontal line. Fig. 3-7 sums up what our Scan microprogram generator has to do.

To produce a Scan, our Scan software program from Chapter 2 calls a subroutine at an address that activates the instruction decoder. The instruction decoder then activates the Scan microprogram generator, which produces the microcode needed for a sequential Scan. As we saw in Chapter 2, the 6502 coding can be a sequence of LDY commands, followed by a RTS.

When a Scan is wanted, the instruction decoder provides a ground on its Scan Enable output line. This ground is used to activate the tristate PROM that generates our Scan microinstruction.

Once it is activated, this PROM take over control of the computer data bus. When not activated, the tristate outputs float and remain transparent to the data bus. This lets your computer behave normally during nonscan times. When you are scanning, it is very important that anything else that might want to use the data bus is disabled—this is what the DEN output on the instruction decoder is for. This output disables everything except the Scan microprogram PROM when a scan is needed. The DEN output goes low for normal computer use and high for Scan microinstruction times.

Typical coding for a Scan microprogram PROM is shown in Fig. 3-8. Our code consists of 31 LDY commands followed by a

The

SCAN MICROPROGRAM GENERATOR

must:

* GENERATE THE RIGHT CODING TO SEQUENTIALLY SCAN A ROW OF VIDEO.

* OPTIONALLY PROVIDE FOR ALPHANUMERIC MEMORY REPACKING.

* BE TRANSPARENT DURING OTHER COMPUTER USES.

Fig. 3-7. The Scan microprogram PROM generates the long miscroinstruction needed to sequentially output a row of characters or graphics dots.

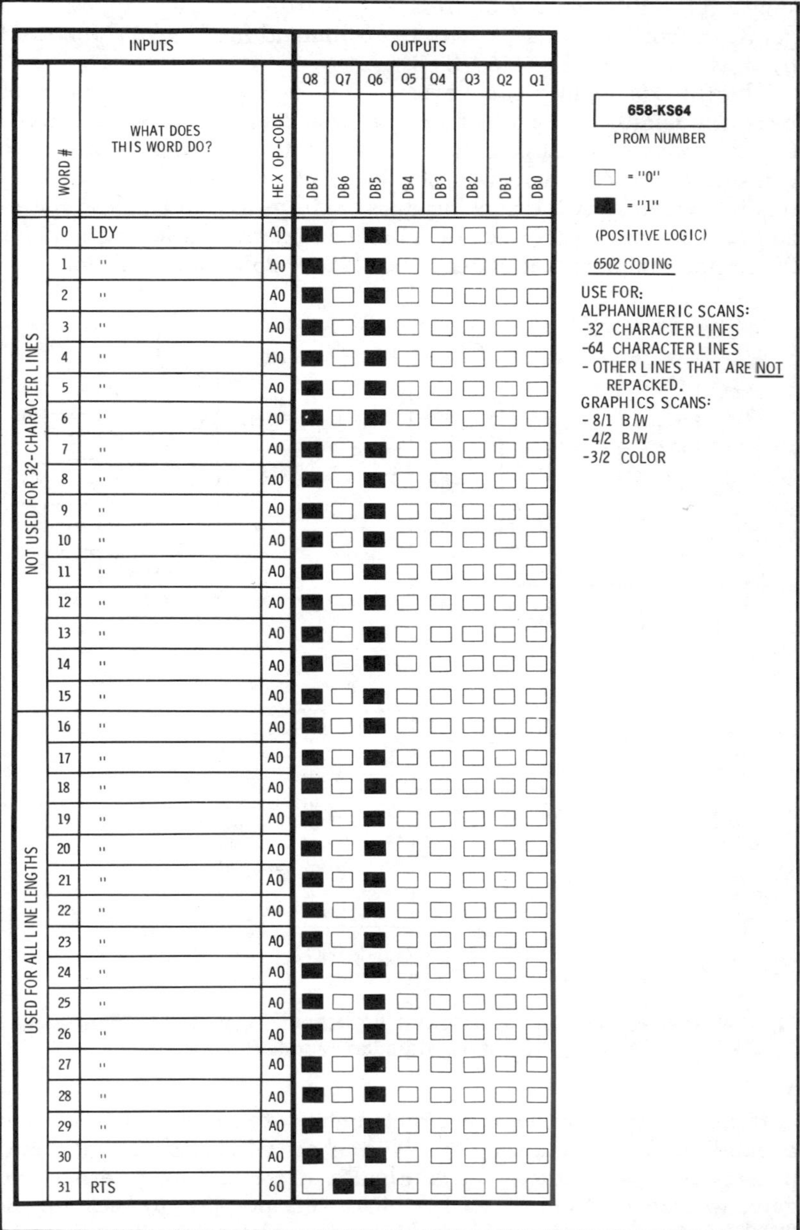

	INPUTS			OUTPUTS							
	WORD #	WHAT DOES THIS WORD DO?	HEX OP-CODE	Q8 DB7	Q7 DB6	Q6 DB5	Q5 DB4	Q4 DB3	Q3 DB2	Q2 DB1	Q1 DB0
NOT USED FOR 32-CHARACTER LINES	0	LDY	A0	■	□	■	□	□	□	□	□
	1	"	A0	■	□	■	□	□	□	□	□
	2	"	A0	■	□	■	□	□	□	□	□
	3	"	A0	■	□	■	□	□	□	□	□
	4	"	A0	■	□	■	□	□	□	□	□
	5	"	A0	■	□	■	□	□	□	□	□
	6	"	A0	■	□	■	□	□	□	□	□
	7	"	A0	■	□	■	□	□	□	□	□
	8	"	A0	■	□	■	□	□	□	□	□
	9	"	A0	■	□	■	□	□	□	□	□
	10	"	A0	■	□	■	□	□	□	□	□
	11	"	A0	■	□	■	□	□	□	□	□
	12	"	A0	■	□	■	□	□	□	□	□
	13	"	A0	■	□	■	□	□	□	□	□
	14	"	A0	■	□	■	□	□	□	□	□
	15	"	A0	■	□	■	□	□	□	□	□
USED FOR ALL LINE LENGTHS	16	"	A0	■	□	■	□	□	□	□	□
	17	"	A0	■	□	■	□	□	□	□	□
	18	"	A0	■	□	■	□	□	□	□	□
	19	"	A0	■	□	■	□	□	□	□	□
	20	"	A0	■	□	■	□	□	□	□	□
	21	"	A0	■	□	■	□	□	□	□	□
	22	"	A0	■	□	■	□	□	□	□	□
	23	"	A0	■	□	■	□	□	□	□	□
	24	"	A0	■	□	■	□	□	□	□	□
	25	"	A0	■	□	■	□	□	□	□	□
	26	"	A0	■	□	■	□	□	□	□	□
	27	"	A0	■	□	■	□	□	□	□	□
	28	"	A0	■	□	■	□	□	□	□	□
	29	"	A0	■	□	■	□	□	□	□	□
	30	"	A0	■	□	■	□	□	□	□	□
	31	RTS	60	□	■	■	□	□	□	□	□

658-KS64
PROM NUMBER

□ = "0"
■ = "1"
(POSITIVE LOGIC)

6502 CODING

USE FOR:
ALPHANUMERIC SCANS:
-32 CHARACTER LINES
-64 CHARACTER LINES
- OTHER LINES THAT ARE NOT REPACKED.
GRAPHICS SCANS:
- 8/1 B/W
- 4/2 B/W
- 3/2 COLOR

Fig. 3-8. Truth table for Scan PROM 658-KS64.

single RTS. By ignoring address A0, we double this capability to get 62 μs worth of "Load Y with the command for Load Y," followed by 2 μs worth of advancing RTS.

This PROM coding can be used anywhere you want a Scan of most any length, so long as memory repacking is not needed. Some typical connections appear in Fig. 3-9. With input A4 positive, we can scan 32 or less characters per line. Any *even* number of characters is possible, but the packing density drops as you use less chara-acters. This PROM is used for 32 alphanumeric characters, and for 32 graphics chunks that result in 96, 128, or 256 horizontal dots.

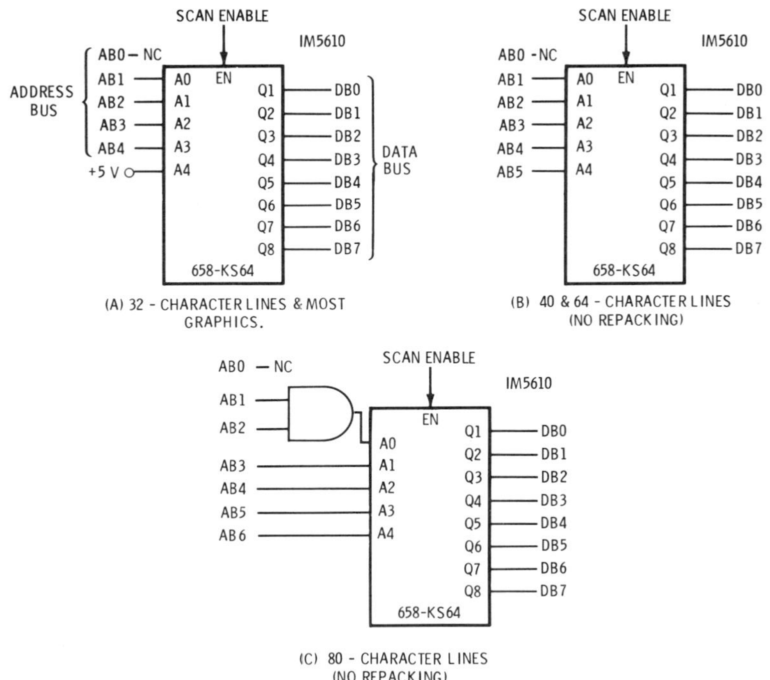

Fig. 3-9. Connections for Scan PROM 658-KS64 SCAN enable input comes from the instruction decoder.

If all five inputs are used, we pick up a 34- to 64-character-per-line capability. This includes densely packed 64-character lines and nonrepacked 40-character lines. Finally, if we add an external AND gate, we can go from 68 to 128 characters per line to pick up an 80-character, nonrepacked capability. Line lengths with this gate must be some multiple of *four*.

> *Your Turn:*
>
> Show the PROM connections and memory map for densely packed lines of 8 and 16 characters.

Note that this PROM *must* have tristate outputs, since it is absolutely essential to float the outputs going to the data bus during non-tvt times. Note further, that your coding will change with any change in the microprocessor family.

Somewhat fancier and more specialized PROM coding is needed if we are going to densely repack 40- or 80-character lines, following the guidelines of the last chapter. Fig. 3-10 shows the 6502 coding for a 40-character Scan, while Fig. 3-11 shows the coding for an 80-character Scan. Both PROMs provide for repacking so that each page of 256 words has three 80-character lines or six 40-character lines.

Connections for either repacked PROM are shown in Fig. 3-12. An external three-input AND gate is normally used that lets us get the needed 128 equivalent words out of a 32-word PROM.

> *Your Turn:*
>
> Show how three switches or jumpers may be added to Fig. 3-12 to allow the same interface circuit board to work with any of the three Scan truth tables shown.

Be sure to notice the difference in how the enable input is treated between the *Decode* PROM and the Scan PROM. In the instruction decoder, the outputs must always be active, so we permanently enable this PROM. In the Scan microprogram PROM, we have to be able to tristate float the outputs for all non-tvt times, and we drive the chip enable of the PROM from an instruction-decoder output, going low only when a Scan is wanted. The instruction-decoder PROM could be tristate, open collector, or even permanently internally enabled, but the Scan microprogram PROM *must* be tristate.

The instruction decoder and the Scan microprogram PROMs, and possibly an AND gate or two, are usually all we need to get a

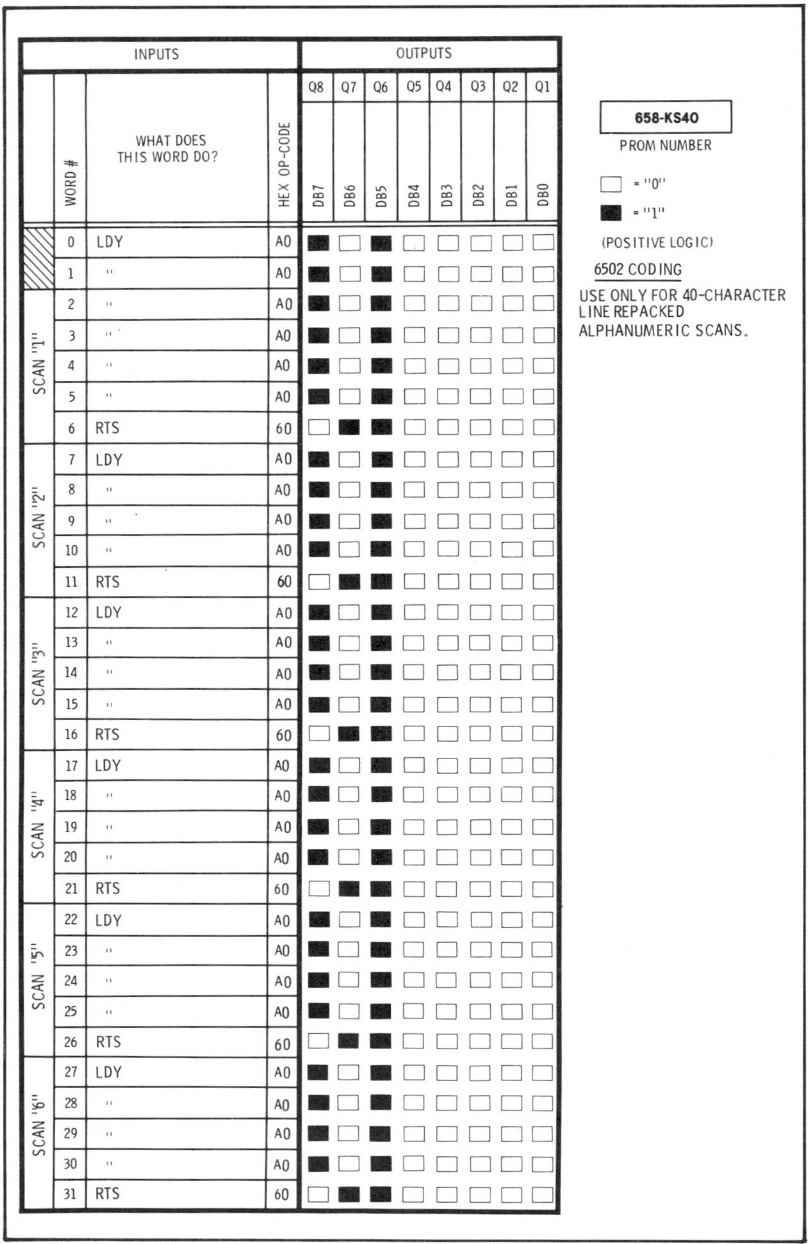

		INPUTS		OUTPUTS							
				Q8	Q7	Q6	Q5	Q4	Q3	Q2	Q1
	WORD #	WHAT DOES THIS WORD DO?	HEX OP-CODE	DB7	DB6	DB5	DB4	DB3	DB2	DB1	DB0
	0	LDY	A0	■	□	■	□	□	□	□	□
	1	"	A0	■	□	■	□	□	□	□	□
SCAN "1"	2	"	A0	■	□	■	□	□	□	□	□
SCAN "1"	3	"	A0	■	□	■	□	□	□	□	□
SCAN "1"	4	"	A0	■	□	■	□	□	□	□	□
SCAN "1"	5	"	A0	■	□	■	□	□	□	□	□
SCAN "1"	6	RTS	60	□	■	■	□	□	□	□	□
SCAN "2"	7	LDY	A0	■	□	■	□	□	□	□	□
SCAN "2"	8	"	A0	■	□	■	□	□	□	□	□
SCAN "2"	9	"	A0	■	□	■	□	□	□	□	□
SCAN "2"	10	"	A0	■	□	■	□	□	□	□	□
SCAN "2"	11	RTS	60	□	■	■	□	□	□	□	□
SCAN "3"	12	LDY	A0	■	□	■	□	□	□	□	□
SCAN "3"	13	"	A0	■	□	■	□	□	□	□	□
SCAN "3"	14	"	A0	■	□	■	□	□	□	□	□
SCAN "3"	15	"	A0	■	□	■	□	□	□	□	□
SCAN "3"	16	RTS	60	□	■	■	□	□	□	□	□
SCAN "4"	17	LDY	A0	■	□	■	□	□	□	□	□
SCAN "4"	18	"	A0	■	□	■	□	□	□	□	□
SCAN "4"	19	"	A0	■	□	■	□	□	□	□	□
SCAN "4"	20	"	A0	■	□	■	□	□	□	□	□
SCAN "4"	21	RTS	60	□	■	■	□	□	□	□	□
SCAN "5"	22	LDY	A0	■	□	■	□	□	□	□	□
SCAN "5"	23	"	A0	■	□	■	□	□	□	□	□
SCAN "5"	24	"	A0	■	□	■	□	□	□	□	□
SCAN "5"	25	"	A0	■	□	■	□	□	□	□	□
SCAN "5"	26	RTS	60	□	■	■	□	□	□	□	□
SCAN "6"	27	LDY	A0	■	□	■	□	□	□	□	□
SCAN "6"	28	"	A0	■	□	■	□	□	□	□	□
SCAN "6"	29	"	A0	■	□	■	□	□	□	□	□
SCAN "6"	30	"	A0	■	□	■	□	□	□	□	□
SCAN "6"	31	RTS	60	□	■	■	□	□	□	□	□

658-KS40

PROM NUMBER

□ = "0"

■ = "1"

(POSITIVE LOGIC)

6502 CODING

USE ONLY FOR 40-CHARACTER LINE REPACKED ALPHANUMERIC SCANS.

Fig. 3-10. Truth table for Scan PROM 658-KS40.

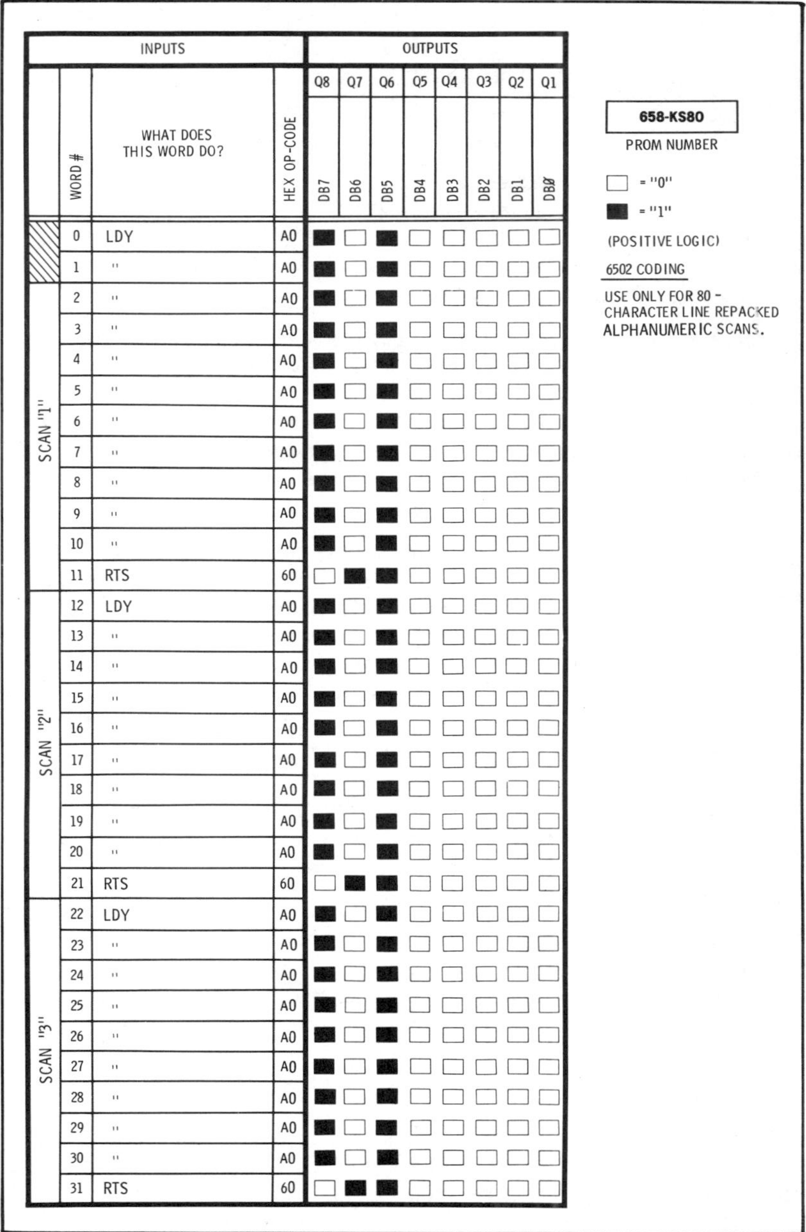

INPUTS				OUTPUTS							
	WORD #	WHAT DOES THIS WORD DO?	HEX OP-CODE	Q8 DB7	Q7 DB6	Q6 DB5	Q5 DB4	Q4 DB3	Q3 DB2	Q2 DB1	Q1 DBØ
	0	LDY	A0	■	□	■	□	□	□	□	□
	1	"	A0	■	□	■	□	□	□	□	□
SCAN "1"	2	"	A0	■	□	■	□	□	□	□	□
	3	"	A0	■	□	■	□	□	□	□	□
	4	"	A0	■	□	■	□	□	□	□	□
	5	"	A0	■	□	■	□	□	□	□	□
	6	"	A0	■	□	■	□	□	□	□	□
	7	"	A0	■	□	■	□	□	□	□	□
	8	"	A0	■	□	■	□	□	□	□	□
	9	"	A0	■	□	■	□	□	□	□	□
	10	"	A0	■	□	■	□	□	□	□	□
	11	RTS	60	□	■	■	□	□	□	□	□
SCAN "2"	12	LDY	A0	■	□	■	□	□	□	□	□
	13	"	A0	■	□	■	□	□	□	□	□
	14	"	A0	■	□	■	□	□	□	□	□
	15	"	A0	■	□	■	□	□	□	□	□
	16	"	A0	■	□	■	□	□	□	□	□
	17	"	A0	■	□	■	□	□	□	□	□
	18	"	A0	■	□	■	□	□	□	□	□
	19	"	A0	■	□	■	□	□	□	□	□
	20	"	A0	■	□	■	□	□	□	□	□
	21	RTS	60	□	■	■	□	□	□	□	□
SCAN "3"	22	LDY	A0	■	□	■	□	□	□	□	□
	23	"	A0	■	□	■	□	□	□	□	□
	24	"	A0	■	□	■	□	□	□	□	□
	25	"	A0	■	□	■	□	□	□	□	□
	26	"	A0	■	□	■	□	□	□	□	□
	27	"	A0	■	□	■	□	□	□	□	□
	28	"	A0	■	□	■	□	□	□	□	□
	29	"	A0	■	□	■	□	□	□	□	□
	30	"	A0	■	□	■	□	□	□	□	□
	31	RTS	60	□	■	■	□	□	□	□	□

658-KS80
PROM NUMBER

□ = "0"
■ = "1"
(POSITIVE LOGIC)

6502 CODING

USE ONLY FOR 80 - CHARACTER LINE REPACKED ALPHANUMERIC SCANS.

Fig. 3-11. Truth table for Scan PROM 658-KS80.

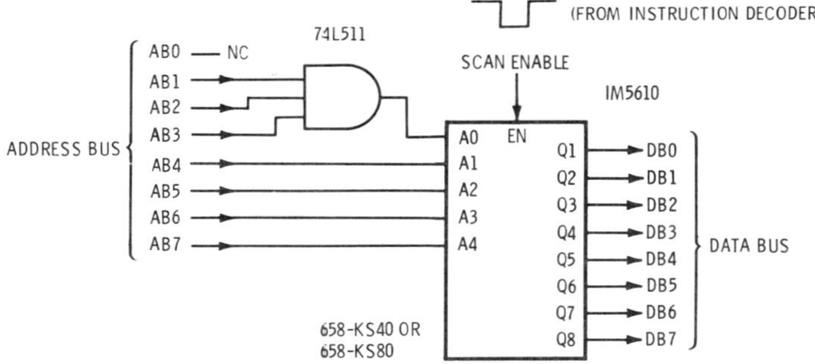

Fig. 3-12. Connections for 658-KS40 and 658-KS80 Scan PROMs that give densely repacked 40- or 80-character lines.

microprocessor outputting character or chunk words in a sequence and a form that eventually will give us good video. *The only signals fed back from the interface hardware to the microcomputer originate in these two PROMs.* These signals are:

DEN —The *Decode Enable* that goes high whenever a Scan is to be produced, and stops anything else from grabbing the data bus during Scan times.

CSO —The *Chip-Select Output* that enables the display memory, either when the computer wants it for normal use, or when the tvt wants to get characters out the upstream tap.

DB0-DB7—The *Data Bus* outputs from the Scan microprogram generator that are active whenever a Scan is wanted, but tristate floated otherwise.

The important thing to note is that *these two PROMs plus any supporting gating always should be designed, tested, and debugged first in any microprocessor-based cheap video display system.* If the PROMs cannot make the computer behave the way you want it to, nothing else you add in the way of interface hardware is going to work either.

Data-to-Video Conversion

The next most important block in our interface hardware is the data-to-video converter. This block gets us from code sent out the upstream tap to serial raw video.

Graphics data-to-video conversion is usually simpler than alphanumeric conversion. For graphics use, we can sometimes get by with nothing but a shift register that converts the parallel chunk code into serial video. To this we might add blanking or an electronic selector to rearrange the chunk as needed for other formats. This selector can be a 4pdt switch that picks the upper or lower part of a chunk on a given Scan.

For alphanumeric tvt's, there is no "one-on-one" relationship between the ASCII and Cursor stored code in the display memory and the dots on the screen. Somehow, we have to irrationally "fluff up" our 6-, 7-, or 8-bit code into a 35-dot serial video code. Since the character dots do not have any logical relationship to the ASCII code, any bits-and-pieces logic scheme is bound to be a complex disaster.

Instead, we go to the code conversion capabilities of a read only memory or ROM. You can use your own PROM for this, but code converting read only memories called *dot matrix character* generators are easy to get, usually cheaper, and often a better choice. Details on these character generators appear in the *TV Typewriter Cookbook* (SAMS 21313). Character generators can offer a choice of upper case or combined upper and lower case. They will either do the entire conversion to serial video by themselves, or else they will have multiple outputs that have to go to an external video-shift register for final conversion.

For tvt use, your character generator must be of the *row scan* type. There is another type called a *column Scan* character generator, but this is only good for strip printers, advertising signs, and similar uses where the serial or parallel output runs up and down rather than back and forth.

An alphanumeric data-to-video converter using a 2513 character generator is shown in Fig. 3-13. The character generator accepts ASCII words from the upstream tap on the display memory. These ASCII words change once each microsecond for each new character to be output. The 2513 also accepts three "what line is it" commands from the instruction decoder. In exchange for these inputs, five dots are output at once, corresponding to one row on a 5 × 7 dot matrix character. An eight input, one output shift register then converts these dots, along with spacing undots from grounded inputs, into raw serial output video. The input ASCII character coding repeats itself at least seven times to generate the entire seven dot rows involved in a row of characters. Our shift register is driven by a high-frequency timing circuit that outputs a narrow Load pulse once each microsecond, along with a Clock output that runs continuously at the desired dot rate.

An optional Cursor is shown in the lower right of Fig. 3-13. The 4585 is a 3-Hz oscillator that sets up the Cursor winking rate. If ASCII input bit No. 8 is high, the CUR input will go high and a white line is output on leads Q1 through Q5. The right diode causes

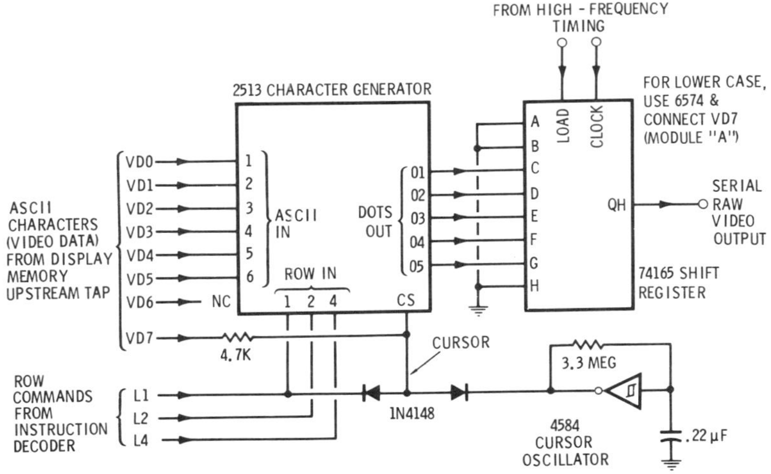

Fig. 3-13. Alphanumeric data-to-video converter using 2513 character generator.

this line to blink off and on, while the left diode allows winking Cursors only during valid character times.

Since lower case is not available on a 2513, ASCII bit No. 7 remains unused. Note that if you want to display lower-case characters as upper case, you must add a simple external gate, for the lower six bits of a lower case "u" are the same as a "5," and not a capital "U," and some conversion is needed. (See Chapter 4.)

The 2513 is cheap and easy to get. The newer, single supply +5-V versions by *General Instruments* and others are far easier to use than the old +5-V, ground −5-V, −12-V versions. This is particularly important since the rest of the interface hardware all can run on a +5-volt supply. Lower case versions of the 2513 are also available. You can use a pair of 2513s, one upper, one lower, for full alphabet capability.

> *Your Turn:*
>
> Show how switching may be added to Fig. 3-13 to give you manual control of Cursor visibility.

An alphanumeric data-to-video converter using the Motorola 6674 character generator is used as the module "A" plug-in for the TVT

6⅝. This circuit gives you both upper and lower case. Input VD6 (Fig. 3-13) is used to pick up the new characters.

Your serial video output is called *raw video* because it contains only character dots when and where needed and blank logic zeros everywhere else. To get from here to something a tv set, monitor, or rf modulator can handle, we have to add the sync pulses and predistort the raw video for improved clarity. We call everything compensated and combined in our *composite video*.

Fig. 3-14 shows us our first graphics interface. This is used as module "B" in the TVT 6⅝ whenever eight dots per chunk in a

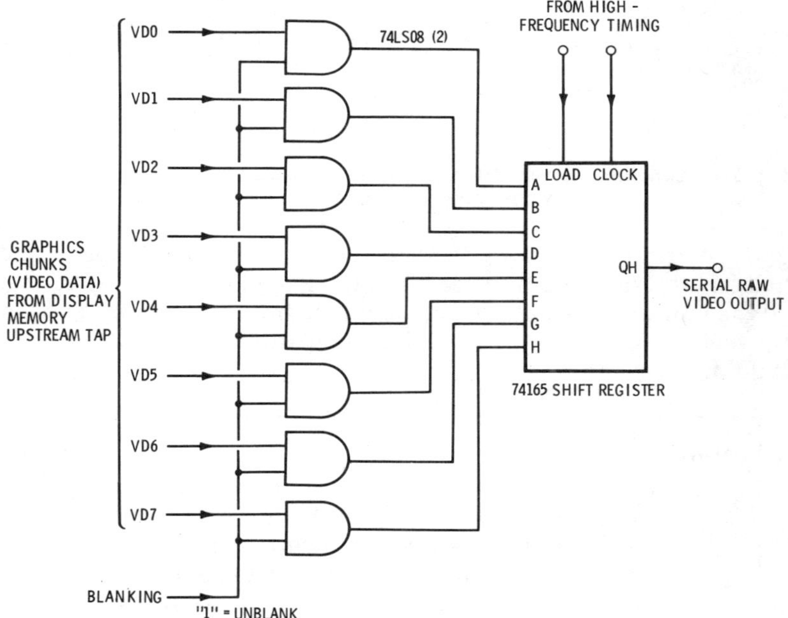

Fig. 3-14. Graphics data-to-video converter to display eight horizontal dots per chunk.

row are needed. Input video data chunks from the display memory are routed to the eight inputs of a shift register by way of a blanking gate. High-frequency timing applies just the right Load and Clock commands to output continuous dots during graphics display times. Timing is adjusted for minimum over- or underlap between sequential chunks.

Fig. 3-15 shows us a graphics interface used for three or four dots per chunk output. This is plug-in module "C" on the TVT 6⅝ upper- and lower-chunk halves alternate for sequential lines or line

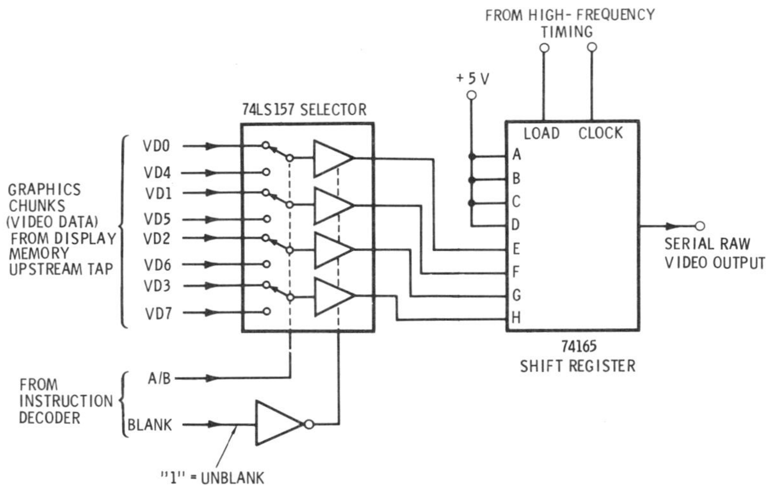

Fig. 3-15. Graphics data-to-video converter to display three or four horizontal dots per chunk on alternate line pairs.

pairs. A data selector is added to the inputs to pick upper-chunk halves, lower-chunk halves, or blanking. Blanking is done by forcing all the inputs of the shift register low. The inverter gives us a system convention of low = blanked for compatibility with the decode PROM.

> *Your Turn:*
>
> Show how modular plug-ins can be used to let one interface hardware card serve for upper- or upper- and lower-case alphanumerics, 1 × 8, 2 × 4, 2 × 3 graphics, and combined alphanumerics and graphics.

Color can be added to the circuit in Fig. 3-15 with an external color modulator. The color format can be three dots on top of three dots, with the remaining two-chunk bits letting us call any of four colors plus black.

High-Frequency Timing

It is up to the high-frequency timing to give the Load and Clock signals needed for serial output of video from our data-to-video converter. Traditionally, these circuits use crystal oscillators and counter-dividers for this job. All we really need in a cheap video system is to borrow the existing microprocessor clock and add a simple gated oscillator using a hex inverter to get our Load and Clock waveforms.

Fig. 3-16 tells what our high-frequency timing has to do, while Fig. 3-17 shows a circuit that works with any of the three data-to-video converters we have already looked at. The waveforms involved are shown in Fig. 3-18.

The

HIGH-FREQUENCY TIMING

must:

* DELIVER A "LOAD" PULSE TO THE VIDEO SHIFT REGISTER.
* TIME THE "LOAD" PULSE TO ARRIVE ONLY WHEN DATA IS VALID.
* DELIVER "CLOCK" PULSES TO SET THE VIDEO DOT RATE.
* LOCK "LOAD" AND "CLOCK" PULSES TOGETHER TO PREVENT JITTER.

Fig. 3-16. High-frequency timing traditionally has used crystals and divider chains, but a hex inverter gated oscillator is often all that is needed.

The Load output of the timing circuit has to transfer parallel dots into the video shift register. **This Load pulse must be carefully timed to arrive only when data is ready and settled from earlier portions of the data-to-video converter.** Often you will have two choices of input clock available; if one phase does not do it, the other one probably will. Usually, it is best to arrange the load command so that it always arrives 1 μs after the addresses change. This gives you a nearly maximum processing time and minimizes any settling or bad data problems. Note that the Cursor and blanking of individual characters should be introduced *before* this 1-μs delay takes place; otherwise, the Cursor and blanking will be skewed by one or more characters.

The Load command must be normally high and go briefly low when driving a 74165 shift register. The load command also should be as narrow as possible. This is particularly important in graphics modes where too long a load pulse or a misplaced one can cause dot underlap or overlap.

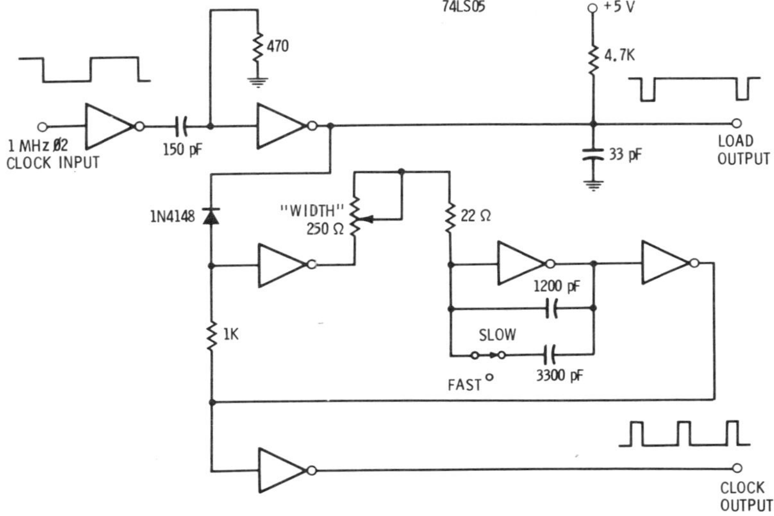

Fig. 3-17. High-frequency timing is derived from 1.0-MHz computer clock with gated oscillator.

Your Clock line decides how fast the dots are going to come out as serial video. The WIDTH control and the FAST-SLOW switch set the clock rate. Slow is used for the 4/2 and 3/2 graphics modes, while Fast is used for the 8/1 graphics and both alphanumeric modes. The WIDTH control is adjusted for proper spacing and a stable display in alphanumeric modes, while it is set for the right number of dots and proper dot matching (no overlap or underlap) in graphic modes.

Clock and Load must be locked together to prevent the dot locations from jittering or otherwise smearing. It is also especially important to make sure the Load command does not distort the clock graphics displays; otherwise clockings end up wider or narrower with respect to each other.

In Fig. 3-17 the first inverter acts as a buffer to make us independent of system clock rise and fall times. The second inverter is a

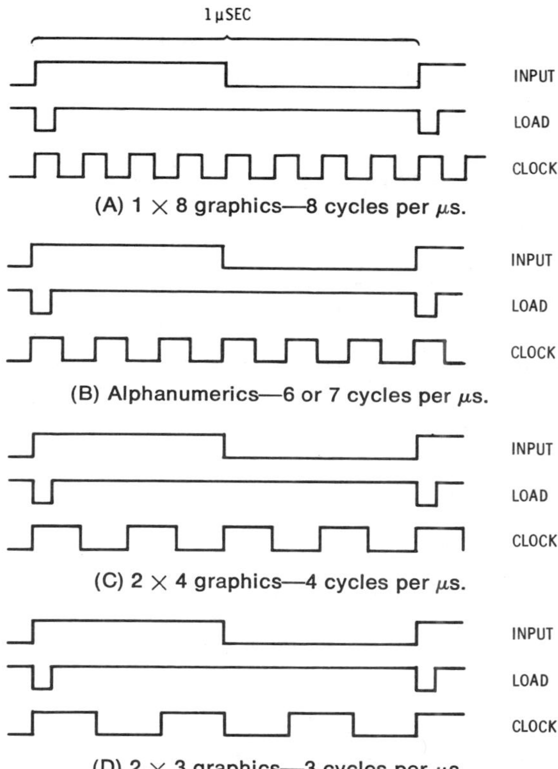

Fig. 3-18. High-frequency timing is adjusted to suit operating mode. These are typical waveforms.

half monostable device whose output briefly drops to ground for 30 nanoseconds on the falling edge of the clock input. The three inverters in the center are a gated ring oscillator. The frequency of this oscillator is coarsely set with the extra capacitor that is switched

> *Your Turn:*
>
> Show a way of raising and lowering the microprocessor clock frequency to allow locking of the video display vertical rate to the power line. This will give you a stationary hum bar.

in by the "FAST-SLOW" switch, and finely adjusted with the WIDTH control. The diode gates the oscillator and locks it to the Load command. A final buffer and inverter is used to square up the clock line. The RC network on the Load output is a glitch filter used for added stability.

As a rough rule of thumb, the output-video frequency will be around one half of the dot rate set by the high-frequency timing clock. Thus, eight dots per microsecond gives around 4-MHz bandwidth, while three dots per microsecond needs only a 1.5-MHz bandwidth. A black and white tv set has a 4-MHz bandwidth, extendable somewhat by defeating the sound trap. The video bandwidth of a color set is limited to a 3-MHz bandwidth. As you can see, the output frequencies associated with your cheap video displays are compatible with most tv sets. This is a dramatic improvement over the much higher video bandwidths often demanded by traditional video terminal systems.

Sync and Position

When we run a properly debugged Scan program our instruction decoder will give us signals at the needed vertical (V SYNC) and horizontal (DEN) rates. We can then selectively delay these signals to gain control over position. This is then followed by pulse shaping to get the proper widths of the sync signals for tv use. Since the tv set locks itself to the sync pulses, backing up or moving these pulses forward has the effect of moving the entire display. Horizontal-delay changes cause back and forth position changes in the display. Vertical-sync changes control up and down positioning.

A typical circuit is shown in Fig. 3-19. Once again, it is six inverters to the rescue. Only, this time two of the inverters have to have open collectors and very low output impedances and are TTL, while four of them need extremely high input impedances and a snap action, so they are CMOS Schmitt inverters.

Our V-sync pulse starts out as a 1-μs positive pulse that is glitch filtered to get rid of anything that crops up during the PROM settling times. The 7405 discharges the 4700-pF capacitor completely once each $\frac{1}{60}$ of a second. This capacitor is recharged by a rate you set with the V POS control. When the recharging reaches one half the supply voltage, the Schmitt snaps on, and our second-stage output becomes a square wave delayed by the amount set on the position pot. Because of the extreme differences in charge to discharge times of the capacitor doing the positioning, the TTL/CMOS combination is called for. The delayed output is shaped into a positive going 200-μs pulse by the final Schmitt and RC network. The output resistor aids in interfacing the TTL stage that follows in the video-output circuitry.

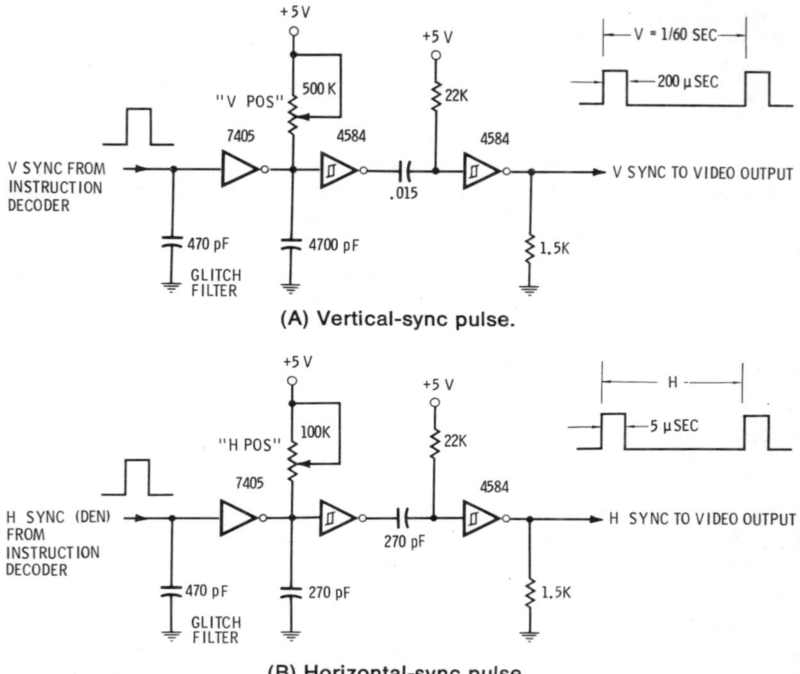

(A) Vertical-sync pulse.

(B) Horizontal-sync pulse.

Fig. 3-19. Sync and position circuitry.

The horizontal circuit is similar, with only the timing details changing. The DEN output of the instruction decoder can often be used instead of needing a special H SYNC line. Delay of a portion of the horizontal line is done with the first variable RC network, while the second RC combination gives us a 5-μs sync pulse once every horizontal line.

This particular sync and position circuit needs continuous arrival of H and V signals from the instruction decoder. This continuous need limits the transparency and throughput of the computer on other programs that are also active while the tvt is displaying.

Fig. 3-20 shows a different way to get horizontal-sync pulses. This *counter method* can free the computer for other uses during vertical-retrace times. This in turn can greatly increase the transparency and throughput. We will be looking at this in more detail in Chapter 5.

What we do is use a divide-by-H counter. H is set to the number of microseconds per horizontal line. Every overflow, an H sync pulse is delivered, regardless of what the computer happens to be up to. This counter is synchronized to the Scan program by resetting

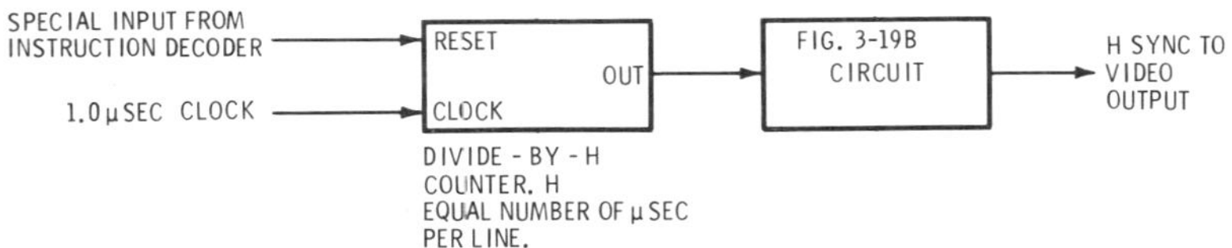

Fig. 3-20. Modified horizontal sync and position circuits give high transparency and throughput. (See Chapter 7.)

it with the instruction decoder. The synchronization and reset can take place on every active line, once during vertical retrace, or even only once during power up. Horizontal sync is maintained through vertical-retrace, even if the computer is busy working on something else.

Bandwidth Compensation and Video Output

We now have three signals available—raw video, vertical sync, and horizontal sync. We somehow have to combine these and pick up some line drive capability if we are going to interface a tv set, monitor, or rf modulator. This final interface is done with the video-output circuitry.

Our raw video first goes to a *bandwidth compensator*. This super important circuit tries to anticipate how the tv set is going to degrade the response and then predistorts the video in the opposite direction beforehand. Bandwidth compensation is done by making the dots longer than the undots. One way is to OR the raw video with a delayed replica of itself. A simpler but very sneaky way is shown in Fig. 3-21. An open-collector TTL inverter has a much lower output low ON impedance than its output high OFF impedance. If we add capacitance from this output to ground, the capacitor will discharge fast but its charge rate will be much slower and set by the value of the pull up resistor, which in this case is a CLARITY pot. Since this is an inverter, a white dot is *low* and a black undot is *high* at the capacitor. It takes longer to get out of the low state, so our dots automatically get lengthened.

How much lengthening is set by the CLARITY pot. This pot is adjusted for the densest, clearest characters on the final tv screen. The optimum setting is often the one that just barely closes the inside of an "M" or a "W" on the display. The use of this bandwidth compensator, taken together with our 1-μs constant character or chunk time are the two keys to display of quality characters or graphics on a tv set with unmodified video bandwidth.

Three more open-collector inverters are used for video combination. At the VIDEO output, sync pulses are nearly at ground, while black is at +0.5 volt, and white is near +2 volts. The ratios of these

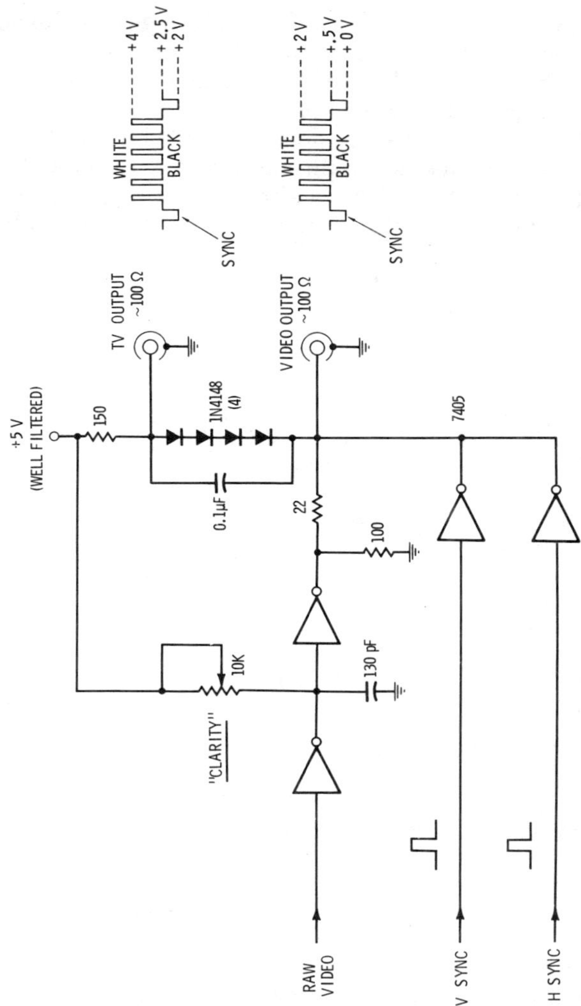

Fig. 3-21. Bandwidth compensator and video output circuit. "Video" output is for monitors and rf modulators, "TV" output is pretranslated for minimum set modification.

three values are set by the three resistors. This output is pretty much a standard form for video monitors, rf modulators, and tv sets that have been completely preconverted internally for direct-video monitor use.

But, we have also provided a new "tv" output. This tv output has the same waveform, but it is translated up so that white is at +4 volts and sync at +3 volts. The +4-volt white level is the normal bias level at the video detector of most solid-state tv sets. You can often use this tv output to go directly into the first video stage of many tv sets, without needing anything else in the way of translation or bias circuits. We will look at more details on this later in the chapter.

Some monitors have separate VIDEO and SYNC inputs. These are called *split sync systems,* and an alternate dual output circuit shown in Fig. 3-22 may be used if split sync is needed or wanted.

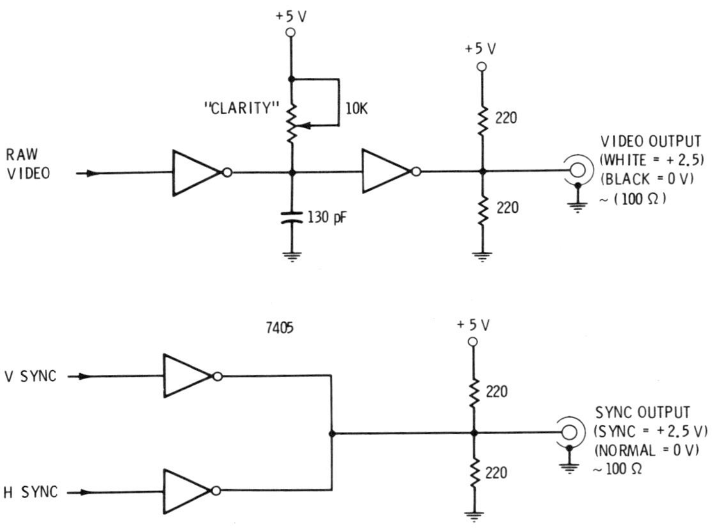

Fig. 3-22. Video-output circuit for monitors with separate sync input.

COMPUTER INTERFACE

You will find that there are about 32 connections you will have to make between your microcomputer and the interface hardware card. A lot of these connections are ready-to-go on existing bus lines and expansion connectors, but a few are not, and you will have to dig into the works to get at them. Most of these connections are "add on" connections, but the one involving the display memory chip enable is usually a "cut" that involves a change in the circuitry of your computer. If your interface card is to be removable, some sort of changeover switch might also be needed for non-tvt operation times.

It is far easier to add a microprocessor-based cheap video display to a new system design than it is to retrofit to an existing system.

Also, since most of our examples use the 6502 microprocessor, you will find computer interconnections easiest with 6502-based systems. Because of their similarities, 6800 series microcomputers will be only slightly more difficult to interface. The 8080 interface is somewhat more tricky and will take some creative work on your part.

As you go further afield from these "mainstream" microcomputer families, your interface and tvt operation will get harder and harder.

It is best to intimately associate the interface circuitry with the display memory. Preferably, both should be the same pc board, or at least a permanently connected pair of boards. There are two reasons for this. The first is that almost all of the "oddball" connections we need to get the tvt to work come from or go to the display memory upstream tap and chip enable. These are not available on bus lines, and even if you have an extra nine or ten pins as spares on your system bus, there are certainly better things to be doing with them than using them for the upstream tap. The second good reason to have the interface hardware and the display memory close together is that your upstream tap is often the bare output of an MOS memory chip. Any capacitive loading, particularly from an expansion cable, is almost certain to slow the memory down enough so that it will be erratic or even quit entirely. *Do not use extension cables on MOS upstream taps!*

In the case of a KIM, to display all or parts of pages 01 through 03, you can add a connector to the top of the main computer board that accepts the interface hardware card. On the TVT 6⅝, a 36-pin, single readout, 0.156-in (3.96-mm) connector can be used. To display part or all of pages 04 through 0F, a similar connector can be added to your KIM-2 4K add-on memory, or its equivalent.

Larger computer systems than the KIM-1 are usually bus oriented. Typical examples are the Heath H-8 system using the *Benton Harbor* 50-pin bus, and the MITS and IMSAI systems that use the *S-100* bus. For these bus-oriented systems, it's best to design a single card that contains *both* the display memory and the interface hardware. Another possibility is to add spacers to an existing 4K or 8K memory card and permanently attach the interface hardware so that they both plug into the bus through a single connector. Two slots may be needed.

As Chart 3-1 shows, we can logically group our interface connections. These groupings include the supply pins, the data bus, the address lines, the system clock, the upstream tap, the display memory chip enable lines, and the system decode enable. Let's take a general look at just what is involved with each group of interconnections; then we will find out how to interface the KIM-1 and KIM-2 to the TVT 6⅝ detailed in the following chapter.

Chart 3-1. Interconnections Needed Between Your Microcomputer and TVT Interface Hardware

Power Supply	Gives +5 volts and ground for tvt power. *Goes from μP to tvt.*
Address Bus	Runs tvt instruction and Scan PROMs. *Goes from μP to tvt.*
Data Bus	Receives Scan Microprogram from Scan PROM. *Goes from tvt to μP.*
Clock	Drives High Frequency Timing. *Goes from μP to tvt.*
Upstream Tap	Delivers characters or chunks to the data-to-video converter. *Goes from μP to tvt.*
Decode Enable	Disables other computer use during tvt Scan times. *Goes from tvt to μP.*
Chip Select	Enables Display memory either for normal or tvt operation. *CSI goes from μP to tvt; CSO goes from tvt to μP.*

Supply Pins

The supply lines are an obvious place to start. We often power our interface hardware from an existing +5-volt supply on the computer or display memory card. Approximately 250 milliamperes is usually needed. Reasonably heavy connections should be used for both the +5-volt and ground leads.

Your +5-volt line *must* be well regulated and well filtered. A local regulator and some extra bypassing is usually a good idea. Supply line noise can cause plenty of trouble. If noise gets into the position circuits, you get slanted or broken characters. If noise gets into the video output, you get variable character brightness. If noise gets into the high-frequency timing, fuzzy or sugar-coated characters can result. Since these circuits are essentially analog, the supply filtering requirements are more stringent than would usually be the case.

Address Lines

Around half the address lines of the computer may be needed. In the TVT 6⅝ we use A1 through A5 and A12 through A15, and optionally use A6 and A7.

Each address line drives the input of a bipolar PROM. This is less than one LS TTL load, so extra buffering just for the tvt interface often is not needed.

But, if you are tapping a display memory card or something else that has its own address drivers, it pays to use the buffered side rather than adding extra load on the microcomputer itself. Address lines are usually easy to get to and often have available pins on the system bus or expansion connector.

Some bus systems use complements of the address lines, expecting you to use inverting bus drivers on everything that plugs onto the bus. If this occurs, you can add your own drivers, borrow existing ones, or else redefine the truth tables on your PROMs to work with complementary code.

If you are retrofiting an existing microcomputer or memory card, use a wiring pencil for your interconnections. This is far and away the neatest, simplest, and fastest way to make needed add-on connections. You can use wiring-pencil connections for everything *except* the supply lead and ground.

Data Bus

Data-bus connections are as easy to do as the address-line connections. You can pick these off of your expansion connectors or system bus. The interface hardware drives your address bus from the tristate Scan microprogram PROM during Scan times, but floats its bus access otherwise. A typical PROM can drive eight regular TTL loads. Everything *else* hung on the data bus must be less than this, or you will need more buffering.

Clock

A 1-MHz clock is needed. If this is also your microprocessor system clock frequency, you are usually home free. The clock must have the capability to drive one LS TTL gate in the high-frequency timing.

It is extremely important to pick the right clock phase or delay to make sure that the video-shift register gets loaded during data-valid times. One timing scheme that usually works is to load your video shift register 1 μs after you change the addresses to your data-to-video converter.

If you do not have a megahertz floating around your system, you can usually get one by dividing down your system clock with a flip-flop or two. An inverter can give you the opposite clock phase, or a delay of one half a microsecond. Remember that this frequency must be exactly known and stable, since it defines the critical vertical-sync rate.

Upstream Tap

So far, all of our interconnections have been obvious and easy to do. The rest of them, however, have to go to special places in your microcomputer that are not normally brought out to system bus lines or expansion connectors.

Your new *upstream tap* (Fig. 1-8) consists of eight wires that come directly from the output of your display memory. A noninverting driver of some kind *must* be present between your memory output and the true data bus. This driver is present on the KIM-1 and on practically all plug-in static-memory cards.

If your microcomputer display-memory RAM outputs go directly to the data bus, you will have to add a noninverting buffer between that memory and the true data bus. Fig. 3-23 shows the typical con-

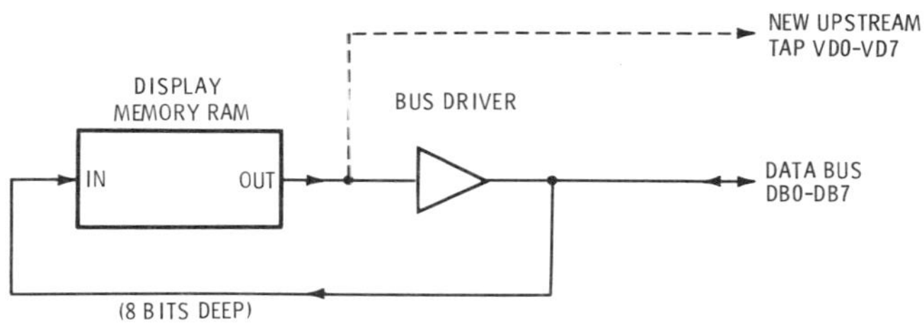

(A) Using existing bus drivers.

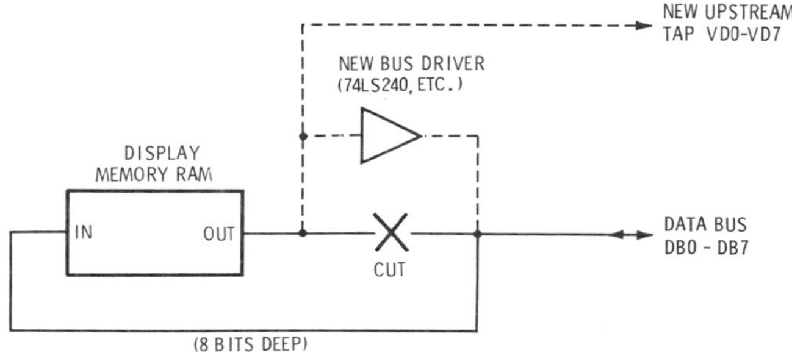

(B) Adding your own bus driver.

Fig. 3-23. Adding the upstream tap.

nections for your upstream tap using either an existing or a new bus driver. *The bus driver gets activated only when the computer wants to read the display memory. During Scan times, the display is* activated only as far as the upstream tap, letting the Scan microprogram PROM have control of the data bus.

> *Your Turn:*
>
> Show how to provide an external driver to a display memory RAM having common input/output pins.

The loading on your upstream tap varies with the application, but, at worst, it is about one LS TTL load per line. For graphics uses, we usually go directly to the LS inputs on a register, selector, or blanking driver. On alphanumerics, the botton six or seven lines go to the MOS inputs of a character generator, while the eighth line will source or sink one half a milliampere as part of the Cursor circuit.

Display Memory Chip Selects

During normal computer operation, your display memory must be enabled when it is wanted for a read or a write. During computer read times, *both* the memory and the output bus driver are activated. During tvt Scan times, the memory is activated *only as far as the upstream tap.* During Scan times, the Scan microprogram generator has control of the data bus.

So we have to break the existing memory chip-select connection and add a way to enable *only the memory* during Scan times, as well as retaining the normal chip selection needed for ordinary computer use.

Most memory chip selects or enables are active low. Thus, you want a negative logic OR circuit that gives a low output for either input low. This turns out to be the DeMorgan equivalent of a plain old positive logic AND gate. You can use a 74LS08 or its internal PROM equivalent.

Usually this AND gate or its PROM equivalent goes in the interface hardware. We route a lead *from* the existing display-memory chip-select source *to* the tvt interface and call it CSI or *C*hip *S*elect *I*nput. After logical gating, we route a new lead *from* the tvt interface *to* the display memory and call it the *C*hip *S*elect *O*utput, or CSO.

Figure 3-24 shows how we add this new chip-select gating to your display memory. To review:

* The existing chip select going only to the memory CS inputs is cut. The source of this signal is called CSI.
* CSI is routed to the interface hardware and appears as a new output CSO. CSO is activated low either when the computer or the tvt wants use of the display memory.
* CSO is routed to the display memory.
* No change is made to the logic driving the output buffers.

Note particularly that the logic going to the output buffers stays the way it was. These bus drivers get activated only when the computer wants to read this particular memory. Chart 3-2 summarizes key upstream tap and chip-select interface rules.

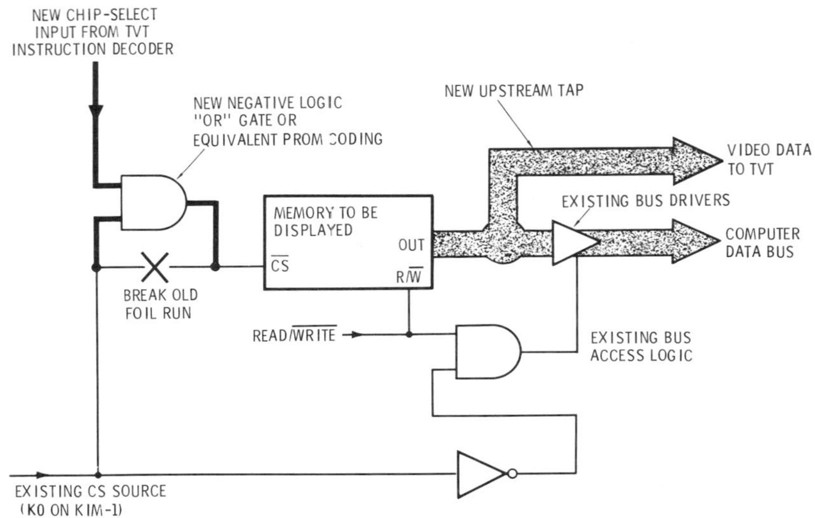

Fig. 3-24. Changes in chip-select circuitry needed to activate display memory during normal OR tvt Scan times.

Chart 3-2. Checklist for Upstream Tap and Chip-Select Interface Connections

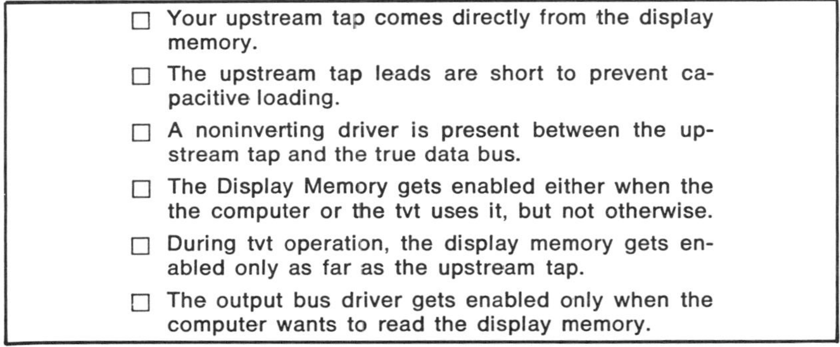

- ☐ Your upstream tap comes directly from the display memory.
- ☐ The upstream tap leads are short to prevent capacitive loading.
- ☐ A noninverting driver is present between the upstream tap and the true data bus.
- ☐ The Display Memory gets enabled either when the the computer or the tvt uses it, but not otherwise.
- ☐ During tvt operation, the display memory gets enabled only as far as the upstream tap.
- ☐ The output bus driver gets enabled only when the computer wants to read the display memory.

Decode Enable

The Decode Enable output (DEN) is an output from the tvt interface hardware. Its purpose is to stop anything else from using the data bus during Scan times. On the KIM-1, the Decode Enable goes high during Scan times to disable the K0 line of the KIM address decoder. This is an easy-to-reach point on the KIM.

On your particular system, you will somehow have to arrange to stop all other address enablings from happening during Scan times, starting with this DEN command. If your particular microcomputer uses a full decoding of all 65K address spaces for everything tacked onto your system, the DEN output will not be needed and can be ignored. The only time you must use DEN is if there is something else trying to use the data bus during tvt Scan times.

Changeover

Even with your Chip-Select line cut and all the extra connections made, your microcomputer will behave normally during non-tvt times, *as long as certain addresses are not called and as long as the interface hardware remains plugged in.*

The number of "no-no" addresses can be further minimized by using a tvt that can be enabled, or more elaborate tvt decoding. Usually, some extra logic will be involved to free these extra addresses. With the full transparency schemes of Chapter 5, we are

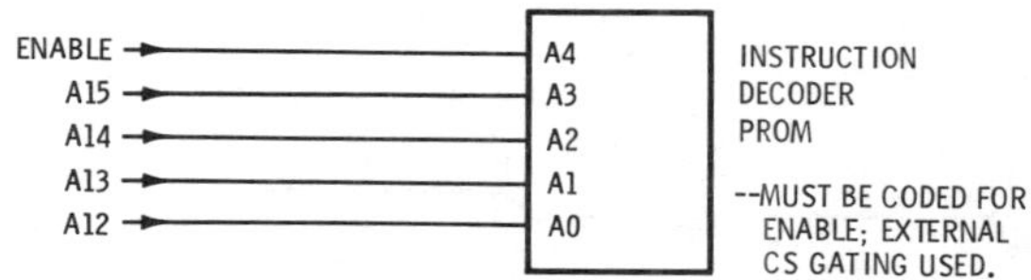

(A) Using decode PROM with tvt enable coding.

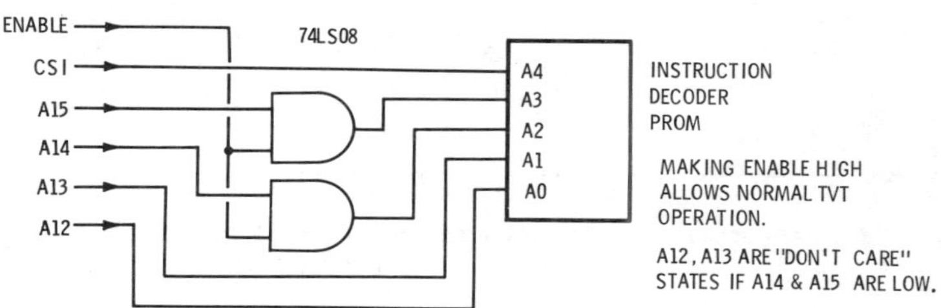

(B) Forcing a benign tvt decoding with and gates.

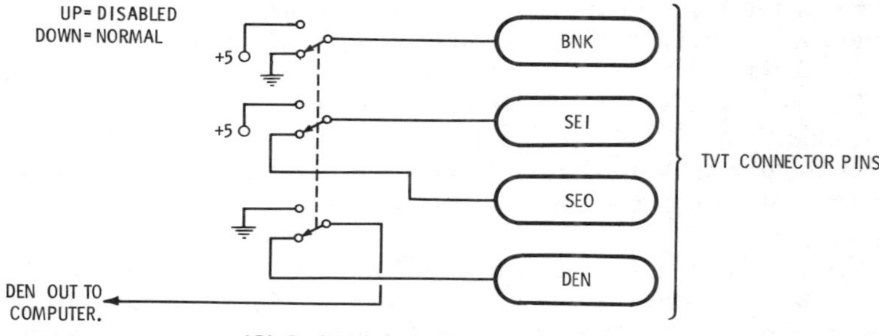

(C) Switching at the tvt connector.

Fig. 3-25. Three ways to disable your tvt during nondisplay times.

able to activate the tvt only during active Scan lines and do other computation during other times.

Fig. 3-25 shows three ways to disable your tvt circuit during non-tvt times. In Fig. 3-25A, we use an instruction decoder with an internally decoded enable command. In Fig. 3-25B we use an external gate to "force feed" the instruction decoder into a "use the computer normally" state. In Fig. 3-25C, external switching is added to the tvt connector.

If you want to be able to remove the tvt interface from your computer, or if you want to be able to use everything that came with the computer with no restrictions on addresses, you will have to add simple switching to activate or deactivate the tvt. Fig. 3-26 shows one possible changeover switch.

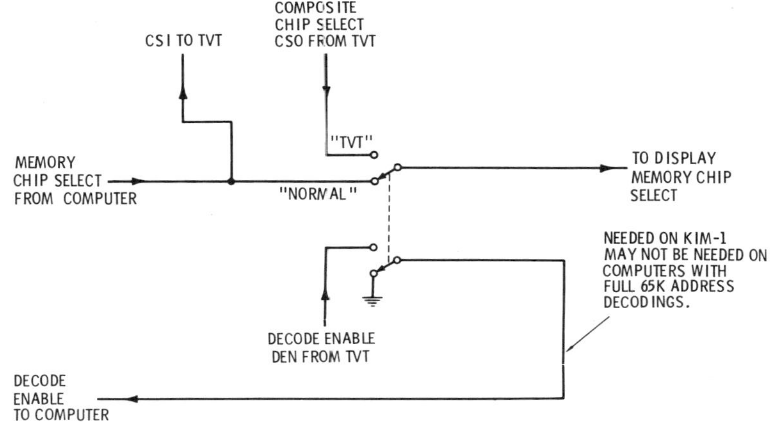

Fig. 3-26. Changeover switch may be needed if an interfaced microcomputer is to run normally with tvt unplugged.

Your TVT-NORMAL switch has to do two things. It must route CSI through the tvt to arrive as CSO at the display memory during tvt times. Otherwise, it directly connects CSI to CSO, effectively "repairing" the cut foil on the Chip-Select line.

The second switching contact has to route the decode enable from the tvt to the microcomputer during tvt times and has to permanently activate the decode enable during non-tvt times. This second switching may not be needed on systems with full 65K address decoding.

In the case of a KIM-1, a dpdt changeover switch can be added between the main board and the tvt connector. This switch gives you a choice of NORMAL or TVT operation. If you are using a second memory on your KIM, a second changeover switch must be used with a new connector. Remember that the upstream tap always has to come from the memory being displayed and CS Enabled.

Use of a changeover switch during a program may bomb the program, so *do your switching with the power off.* If you need switching under program control, use a tvt enable or an electronic switch "cold" driven from a debounced contact.

KIM-1 INTERFACE

Chart 3-3 lists all the connections needed for a KIM-1 and a KIM-2 interface. These connections are repeated in instruction form in Fig. 3-27 and 3-29 and as a pictorial in Fig. 3-28.

1. **Add a new 36-pin, single readout connector along the top of the KIM-1 above the crystal. Small "L" brackets can be added to use existing holes.**
2. **Make short and direct wire connections as described in Chart 3-3. Use a wiring pencil for all connections *except* +5 and GND, which should be short lengths of No. 18 wire.**

   Do not use ribbon cable or attempt extending the TVT 6 5/8.
3. **Break ONE foil run as shown, and add a dpdt changeover switch:**

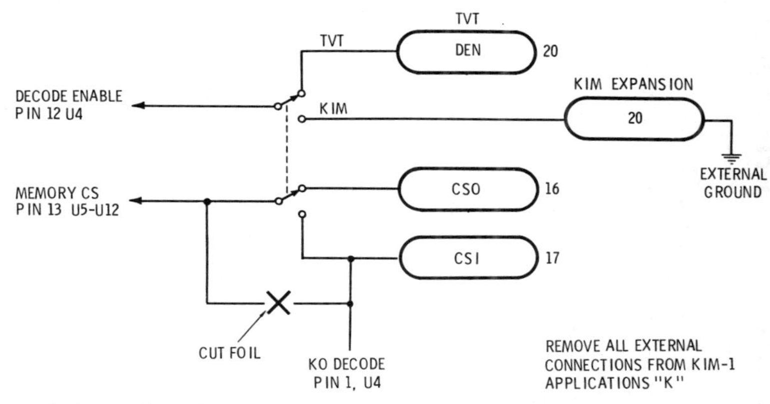

With the switch in the TVT position, operation is totally transparent so long as the TVT 6 5/8 is in its socket and addresses 6000-dFFF are not called.

Fig. 3-27. Modifying your KIM-1 for the TVT 6 5/8.

On the KIM-1 conversion, a 36-pin .156-in (3.96-mm) single-readout connector is placed along the top. All connections between connector and computer are made with a wiring pencil, with the exception of the supply and ground runs. Make these runs with

Chart 3-3. Connections Needed to Interface TVT 6 5/8 to KIM-1 or KIM-2

Pin	Ident	Function	Load	KIM-1 Connection	KIM-2 Connection
1*	GND	Ground return-heavy foil or wire	—	Expansion 22	Connector 1
2	BNK	Blanking input (ground)	1 TTL	TVT pin 1	TVT pin 1
3	HIN	Horizontal-sync input	1 TTL	TVT pin 20	TVT pin 20
4	VD7	Cursor or Graphics bit 8	varies	Pin 12 of U5	Pin 2 of U3
5	VD6	ASCII bit 7 from display memory	1 NMOS	Pin 12 of U6	Pin 6 of U3
6	VD5	ASCII bit 6 from display memory	1 NMOS	Pin 12 of U7	Pin 10 of U2
7	VD4	ASCII bit 5 from display memory	1 NMOS	Pin 12 of U8	Pin 2 of U2
8	VD3	ASCII bit 4 from display memory	1 NMOS	Pin 12 of U9	Pin 6 of U2
9	VD2	ASCII bit 3 from display memory	1 NMOS	Pin 12 of U10	Pin 10 of U1
10	VD1	ASCII bit 2 from display memory	1 NMOS	Pin 12 of U11	Pin 2 of U1
11	VDO	ASCII bit 1 from display memory	1 NMOS	Pin 12 of U12	Pin 6 of U1
12	A15	Address line 15	1 LSTTL	Expansion T	Connector U
13	A14	Address line 14	1 LSTTL	Expansion S	Connector T
14	A13	Address line 13	1 LSTTL	Expansion R	Connector S
15	A12	Address line 12	1 LSTTL	Expansion P	Connector R
16*	CSO	Chip Select TO display memory	TTL Out	Pin 13 U5-U12	Pin 2 of U6
17*	CSI	Chip Select FROM Enable Decoding	1 LSTTL	Pin 1 of U4	Pin 4 of U11
18	SEO	Scan Enable OUTPUT	TTL Out	TVT pin 19	TVT pin 19
19	SEI	Scan Enable INPUT	1 LSTTL	TVT pin 18	TVT pin 18
20*	DEN	Decode Enable TO KIM	TTL Out	Pin 12 of U4	Connector 3

21	VRF	Vertical Reference	TTL Out	no connection	no connection
22	A5	Address line 5	1 LSTTL	Expansion F	Connector H
23	A4	Address line 4	1 LSTTL	Expansion E	Connector F
24	A3	Address line 3	1 LSTTL	Expansion D	Connector E
25	A2	Address line 2	1 LSTTL	Expansion C	Connector D
26*	A1	Address line 1	1 LSTTL	Expansion B	Connector C
27	DB7	Data Bus 7	TTL TS OUT	Expansion 8	Connector 8
28	DB6	Data Bus 6	TTL TS OUT	Expansion 9	Connector 9
29	DB5	Data Bus 5	TTL TS OUT	Expansion 10	Connector 10
30	DB4	Data Bus 4	TTL TS OUT	Expansion 11	Connector 11
31	DB3	Data Bus 3	TTL TS OUT	Expansion 12	Connector 12
32	DB2	Data Bus 2	TTL TS OUT	Expansion 13	Connector 13
33	DB1	Data Bus 1	TTL TS OUT	Expansion 14	Connector 14
34	DB0	Data Bus 0	TTL TS OUT	Expansion 15	Connector 15
35*	VCL	Video Clock Ø2	1 LSTTL	Expansion U	Pin 4 of U10
36*	+5V	+5-volt supply	200 ma	Expansion 21	Connector V

Notes: (See * Above)

Pin 1—Ground should be heavy foil or No. 18 wire—all other connections are wire pencil short leads. *Do not use ribbon cables or attempt extension.*

Pin 16, 17—Chip-select line from decoding to display memory is broken by cutting foil and then replaced with a negative logic OR (positive AND) of the original chip select and the tvt chip select.

Pin 20—Decode Enable output goes low when tvt is NOT scanning; goes high otherwise. Decoding must be disabled during active Scans to allow Scan memory access to data bus.

Pin 26—Address line A0 is not used in tvt module as the Scan microinstruction indexes every *second* microsecond. A0 is used, however, in display memory addressing.

Pin 35—Video Clock must load character generator only when data output is stable and valid. Clock Ø2 on the KIM.

Pin 36—+5-volt power from computer must be noise free and well regulated. Heavy wire.

short pieces of heavy wire. A changeover switch goes near the crystal to let you select tvt or normal operation. One foil run is cut as shown.

The KIM-2 conversion is similar with the connector going along the far side of the memory card. If you are using some other 4K or 8K memory add-on instead of the KIM-2, the conversion details will stay about the same.

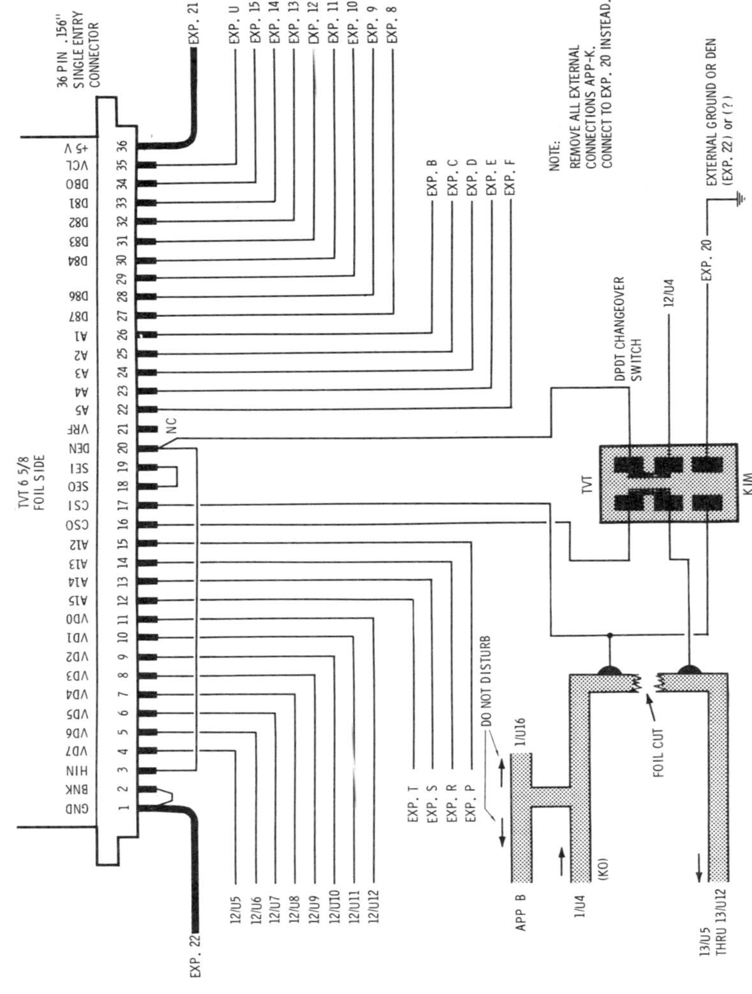

Fig. 3-28. Pictorial of KIM-1 to TVT 6 5/8 interface.

1. Add a new, 36-pin, single readout connector along the left edge of the card, the side away from the regulator. Small "L" brackets can use existing holes if one of the handle eyelets is replaced with a #6 screw.
2. Make short and direct wire connections as described in Chart 3-3. Use a wiring pencil for all connections *except* +5 and GND.
3. Break TWO foil leads as shown, and add a dpdt changeover switch:

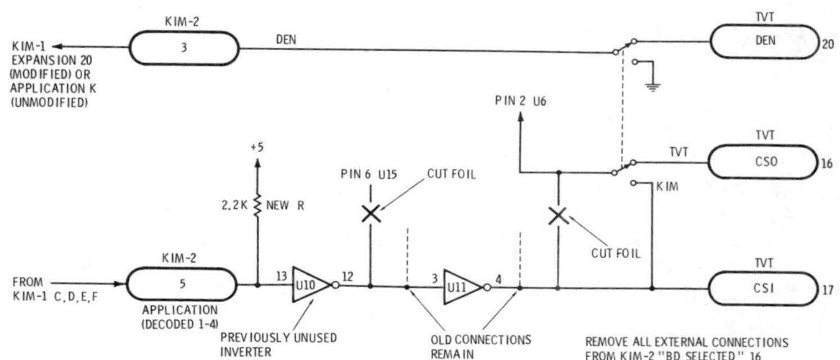

Note that we now have a new input pin on Connector 5 that is driven by KIM-1 decodings K1, 2, 3, and 4 in parallel from Application connector C, D, E, and F.

We also have a new output pin on Connector 3 that provides a ground for the KIM-1 Decode Enable. This is connected to Application Connector K on an *unmodified* KIM-1 and to Expansion Connector 20 or a KIM-1 modified per Fig. 3-27.

Note further that BD SELECTED output Connector 16 is not used.

These modifications cause your KIM-2 to respond to addresses 0400-13FF. The program address switches are no longer used.

Fig. 3-29. Modifying your KIM-2 for the TVT 6 5/8.

Always be sure to keep your upstream tap connections short and be sure to connect your upstream tap to the memory you are going to display. Note that your "bare" KIM-1 is usually limited to 512-character or smaller displays.

Other Micros

Chart 3-4 is a checklist that describes how to interface a processor-based video display to your particular microprocessor. As we have seen, interface to the KIM and other 6502 systems is very easy, and conversion to 6800 systems usually is about as easy.

What about the other microprocessors, particularly the 8080, Z-80, 1802 COSMAC, the 2650, the 8048, Bipolar beasts, and so on? The answer right now is "we simply have not tried it." Microprocessor-based video displays should, in theory, be useable with any micro

Chart 3-4. Checklist for Adapting Your Microprocessor-Based Video Display to Your Microprocessor (Most 6500, 6800, 8080, and Z-80 Systems Can Be Made to Meet These Needs)

- ☐ **Upstream Tap Must Be Separately Available From Data Bus.**
  —This means that a noninverting, separately enabled *external* driver must exist or be added between memory output and the computer true data bus.

- ☐ **During a Scan, the Display Memory Addresses Must Change Once Each Microsecond.**
  —This means the program counter must be able to cycle at a 1-MHz rate, or else something must be done at the display memory to cause the address lines to appear to change at this rate.

- ☐ **Display Memory Addresses Must All Be Present During a Scan.**
  —This means that in systems having multiplexed data and address lines, all lower address lines and at least some higher address lines must be stored for stable use. This also means addresses have to be latched and held during "floating" times, such as the "Status word" time on an 8080.

- ☐ **Each Character or Chunk Time Must Be a Constant 1 Microsecond.**
  —This may mean that the fetch and execute times must be the same on slower microprocessors.

- ☐ **Everything Else Must Be Disabled During a Scan.**
  —This means the Decode Enable output from the interface hardware has to be able to deactivate all other addressed locations.

- ☐ **The Display Memory Must Be Enabled Either From the Computer or the TVT Interface Circuit.**
  —This means that the normal CS line on the display memory must be broken and OR logic or its PROM equivalent must be added.

if you go to enough trouble. On the other hand, we hand picked the 6502 since it seemed the best suited to develop these techniques.

TELEVISION INTERFACE

All of your graphics Scan programs, all shorter-line alphanumeric programs, and a few long-line alphanumeric programs run with a display at normal or near-normal horizontal rates. If you have a rf modulator, a video monitor, or a fully converted tv set on hand, all you have to do is connect the Video output of your tvt to the Video input of the monitor, modulator, or modified (old way) television set.

You use a shielded cable. If you have control over the connectors, use a phono jack on the tvt end and a miniature phone plug at the display end. For premium display systems, use BNC connectors instead.

Fig. 3-30 shows the two output waveforms available from the TVT 6⅝. The Video output approximates EIA (Electronic Industries Association) standard video. White is a positive voltage of approximately 1 volt. Black is a positive voltage of approximately 0.25 volt, and sync tips are "blacker than black" at ground. A new "tv" output is also available. This offsets the waveform so the *white* level is at +4 volts. This +4 volts is the same bias voltage that many solid-state tv sets need at their first video stage input. The tv output greatly simplifies interface since the translating is already done for you.

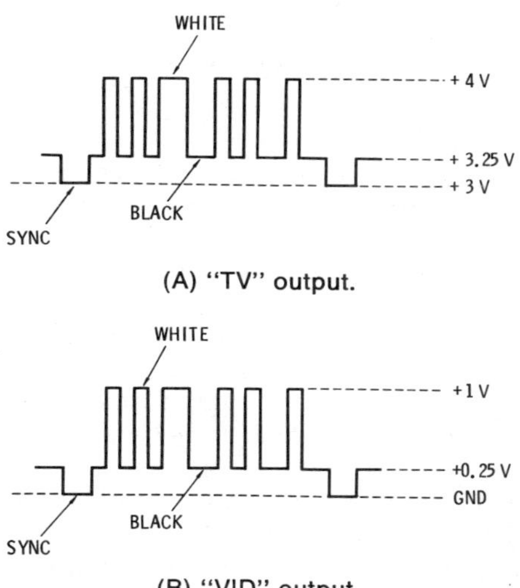

Fig. 3-30. Tvt output waveforms. "TV" output simplifies tv direct video interface. "VID" is for monitors.

Adding a TVT Input to Your Television Set

The conversion to be described next will let you use the television set normally or as a tvt display. Automatic video changeover is done with the headphone jack. Unplugging your tvt restores normal operation. *Note that what we are about to show you will only work with a tvt circuit that has a pretranslated tv output available.*

A checklist of the things in your tv set which you want for conversion is provided in Chart 3-5. Always start with this list and then select a suitable tv set. Do not just grab any old junker set and try to use it.

You will want a small screen black and white portable set, solid state, no tubes. Above all, **the set must have a power transformer and must not be a hot-chassis type.** A Sams PHOTOFACT Folder or other schematic MUST be on hand. (Obtain PHOTOFACT Folder

Chart 3-5. The Best Possible TV Set for Cheap Video Display Use Will Have These Features

- ☐ **Not a Hot Chassis; Uses Power Transformer**
- ☐ **Has Photofact or Other Schematic Available**
- ☐ Black and white
- ☐ Small screen
- ☐ Easy to work on
- ☐ Low horizontal supply voltage (40 volts or less)
- ☐ Has headphone jack
- ☐ Has horizontal yoke inductance between 100 and 350 microhenrys

from your local electronics parts distributor, or order direct from Howard W. Sams & Co. Inc.)

An already-there earphone jack will be a big help. And, if you are going to modify the width, things will be easiest if the horizontal deflection works off of a low-voltage supply, and the deflection horizontal inductance of the yoke is between 100 and 350 microhenrys.

The worst possible set to use is an old tube-type clunker. These use a different first video bias level than solid-state sets and rarely have enough sharpness or uniformity for a quality display. They are also a mess to work on.

The best possible set is one that has an optional battery pack that goes with it. While we usually will not need the battery, the design of this type set almost always uses a low horizontal deflection supply voltage and includes a power transformer and earphone jack; it often is extremely easy to work on and gives a sharp display as well.

Your actual conversion is very simple. You borrow the earphone jack and put it in the video line between the video detector and the first video stage so that plugging in the tvt switches you over automatically. Details are shown in Fig. 3-31 for a Sears, Roebuck & Company tv set.

You can do your conversion this way:

- ☐ With your schematic, first verify that you do NOT have a hot-chassis set by finding the power transformer. Now, find the input to the first video stage and make sure it needs an input bias level of +3 to +4.2 volts.

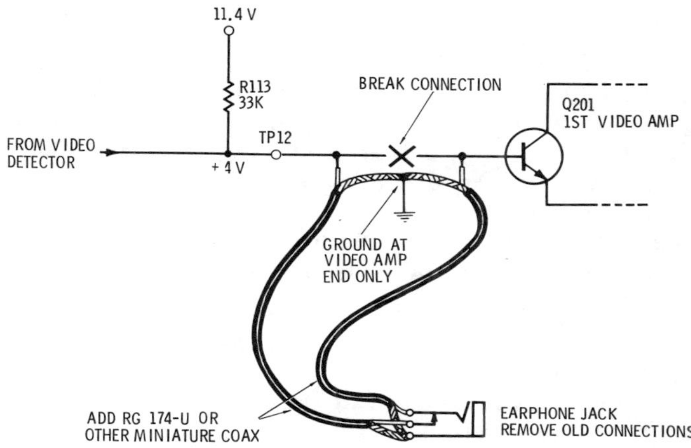

Fig. 3-31. Modifying a tv set for direct video input from "TV" output of cheap video system.

- ☐ Find the headphone jack and familiarize yourself with its circuitry. In particular, note the switching action that disconnects one lead when the jack is used.
- ☐ Remove all connections from the jack, including, if possible, any ground connection. Reconnect together any leads as needed to restore normal speaker operation. Check to make sure that the speaker still works after removing all jack connections.
- ☐ Prepare two pieces of shielded cable that will reach from the video detector to the phono jack and from the phono jack to the first video stage. Make these runs as short as possible, but provide enough room to work. RG-174U miniature coax is best, but any quality audio or CB shielded cable will do. Shielded cable ends are usually prepared by carefully poking a hole in the braid and pulling out the center conductor.
- ☐ Break the connection between the video detector and the first video stage by cutting foil as needed. *Make sure that any and all bias components stay on the video detector end of the cut.* A "bare" input to the first video stage base or IC input pin should be the only thing on one side of the cut.
- ☐ Connect your first shielded cable between the bare input to your first video stage and the phone jack contact that gets connected to the *center* of the miniature phone plug when the plug is inserted. Connect the ground of this cable to a shield or other ground point as close as possible to the first

video input stage. Connect the ground on the other end to the *frame* of the phone jack.

☐ Connect the second shielded cable to the video detector and biasing components. Connect the other end to the contact on the phone jack that gets *disconnected* when the plug is inserted. The ground of this cable goes to a shield or other ground near the video input on end and to the frame of the phone jack on the other, just like the other cable. *Avoid any other ground or chassis connections at the phone jack end.*

☐ Put the tv set back together and check it for normal operation. Plug a miniature phone plug into the phone jack. Change tuner to a blank channel. The screen should go blank with no background noise. Remove the jack, change channels and the program should return.

With any television interface, you will get best operation on an unused channel at minimum contrast levels and just enough brightness for a viewable display. Too much contrast cuts your video bandwidth and too much brightness blooms your spot size.

There might be a 2-megohm or so lightning protection resistor between the hot side of the power line and the chassis. If this is present, remove it unless you are still going to use the set on an outdoor antenna. The current through this resistor is not enough to give a dangerous shock, but it can produce a "liveness" or fuzzy sensation if the chassis or the computer is touched.

Removing the Sound Trap

A *sound trap* is a 4.5-MHz filter somewhere in the video path of the television set. This trap is used to keep audio from visibly interfering with the picture. If your set is to be used mostly as a cheap video display, you might want to remove the sound trap. This will increase the video bandwidth and improve the transient response.

Always study your schematic before altering any television set. The sound trap is often a series coil and capacitor to ground forming a series resonant circuit. Often you can simply lift one end of the capacitor to defeat the trap.

While series traps are the most common, there are many odd-ball variations on sound traps. Some Panasonic tv sets use a 4.5-MHz crystal; this is defeated by lifting the hot lead. A few sets may use a parallel resonant trap that the video has to go through to reach the output stage. These traps are defeated by shorting, rather than opening. Some cheap sets combine the sound pickoff with the sound trap; these can present problems. The best method on these is a try-it-and-see approach. If your modification improves the display, use it.

You can minimize the effect of a sound trap without modifying it simply by backing the slug almost all the way out. Normal tv operation is restored by readjusting for minimum visible audio interference in the picture.

Extending Hold Range

Should you want to use the 64- or 80-character lines or anything else that needs a reduced horizontal rate, you will have to run at lower than normal horizontal-Scan rates. This might be below the range of your horizontal-hold control that sets the horizontal-Scan frequency. You can check this detail without taking the set apart. Simply hold a scope probe somewhere near the left rear corner of the set by the high voltage cage and view the flyback pulse.

As you adjust your horizontal-hold control (on a blank channel) the pulse-to-pulse spacing should change. A 63.5-μs period is needed for normal horizontal operation and should be in the center of the hold-control range. On some sets a special square or hex alignment tool may be needed to adjust your hold control. These are available at tv parts supply houses at little cost.

For 80-character lines, you should be able to extend the hold control beyond 105 μs. If this is out of range, study your schematic and find the capacitor that determines the horizontal-hold frequency. Often this will be a capacitor that is directly across part of the horizontal-hold coil. Add a new mylar capacitor of one third the original value in parallel with this existing capacitor and recheck the hold-control range. Adjust the capacitor value if needed. After you get the low range plus a little bit more, be certain to check the high end to make sure you can still lock on ordinary program material at 63.5 μs.

Fig. 3-32 shows how to change this capacitor on two typical sets. Once again, be sure you are working on a small screen, black and white, portable, solid-state set without hot-chassis design.

Reducing Width

When you run at a reduced horizontal frequency, the width may go up. You will want a narrower display. You also might want to reduce width on a normal display, either to minimize overscan built into the tv set or to avoid spot defocusing that takes place at the screen edges.

We reduce set width by adding a small, homemade coil in series with the horizontal-yoke lead. Fig. 3-33 shows how this is done. The method we will show you works on small screen sets with a low horizontal-deflection supply voltage and having a horizontal-

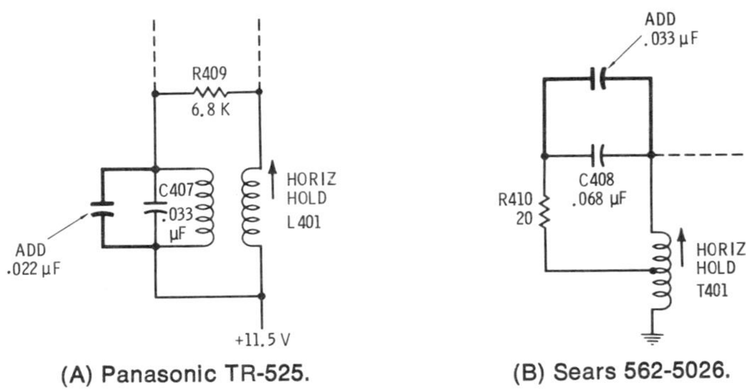

(A) Panasonic TR-525. (B) Sears 562-5026.

Fig. 3-32. Extending horizontal hold range for lower horizontal frequency operation.

yoke inductance of several hundred microhenrys.

If you have an existing width control or jumper, check it first to make sure it is on its minimum position. This usually won't help much.

For your initial trial, wind 50 turns of No. 22 enamel wire on a ½-in (1.27-cm) nylon form and put this in series with the horizontal-yoke lead. *Always remove tv set power when making yoke connec-*

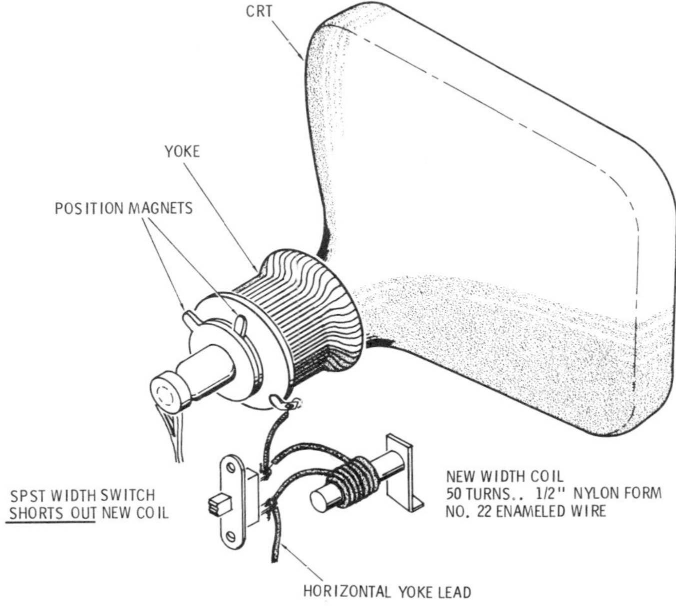

Fig. 3-33. Reducing tv set display width.

tions. Never power a tv set with an open yoke conection. And never reduce the width of a color tv set.

Have your tvt up and generating characters in the right format and have your hold locked before checking width. If the coil does the job, you are all set. If the width is still too wide, add turns. Remove turns if you have gone too far. Cutting the turns by 30% cuts the inductance in half. Increasing the turns by 40% doubles the inductance.

When you have the right number of turns, firmly mount the new width coil in some convenient place. Try to have the coil away from everything, more or less supported in mid air, but close to the yoke. If you get too close to the neck of the tube, you might get some field distortion that will give you a wavy or "S" shaped display. Repositioning should correct this.

Never use an iron core, a high-loss core material (e.g., wood), or fine wire for your new width coil. This must be a high Q coil to preserve linearity.

You can add a switch that *shorts out* your new width coil as needed to restore ordinary width. *Never open the yoke connections of a powered tv set.*

After you have reduced the width on your tv set, you will probably want to change the display height and positioning. Usually you will find a *vertical-height* control at the rear of the television set. A *vertical-linearity* control also should be nearby. These two controls strongly interact on most sets, so you have to adjust them both every time you change the display size. Linearity is properly set when all character rows are evenly spaced and the same height. These controls are usually screwdriver adjustable.

The positioning of the display is usually controlled by two small ring magnets on the crt neck behind the deflection yoke. These are rotated as needed to center your raster. Note that the positioning controls on your tvt can only move the live, unblanked portion of the display around with respect to the total raster. The raster itself can be moved only by readjusting these ring magnets.

Running at reduced width and reduced horizontal frequency at the same time should not be particularly rough on a small screen tv set that uses a low-voltage supply for horizontal deflection. If you get any obvious unhappiness such as bad linearity, high-voltage problems, etc., return to normal operation and sneak up on the problem.

Reduced horizontal operation can make the flyback sing at an audio rate. Depending on your set, this can range from just barely noticeable to absolutely "up the wall" intolerable. The singing is caused by the flyback transformer. Its normal pitch is high enough that most people cannot hear it, until you reduce the Scan frequency. You can minimize this singing by “glopping” parts of the flyback with silicon bathtub caulk. Be sure to use clear silicon rubber and avoid increasing winding capacitance or putting so much on that the flyback overheats. Extra circuit board supports and tightening everything will also help, as will covering up any new holes such as left off tuning knobs or anything similar. Internal sound deadening material can also help provided that it does not interfere with air circulation and is not extremely flammable.

Generally, you can minimize, but not eliminate, the singing. If the final result is still annoying, try a different brand television set, or run programs with a higher horizontal frequency.

You can get a fair idea ahead of time on this singing by simply lowering the horizontal frequency as far as possible and switching to an unused channel. The problem should not be as bad with sets that have the flyback inside a high-voltage cage.

CHAPTER 4

Building The TVT 6 5/8

The TVT 6⅝ is a typical example of what you can do with cheap video techniques. This is a single sided pc board as shown in Fig. 4-1A that holds six low cost integrated circuits. One or two additional ICs are added in the form of a small plug-in module. A closeup view of a plug-in module appears in Fig. 4-1B. The large socket in the center accepts an upper-case-only character generator or any of a number of plug-in modules for upper- and lower-case alphanumerics; color; or high-resolution graphics displays.

Chart 4-1 lists some of the many things you can do with this cheap

Chart 4-1. What Your TVT 6 5/8 Can Do

Alphanumeric Displays:

- 1 line of 8, 16, 32, or 40 characters
- 12 lines of 80 characters
- 16 lines of 32, 40, or 64 characters
- 24 lines of 80 characters
- 32 lines of 32, 40, or 64 characters
- PLUS . . . . most any other combination you can dream up

Graphics Displays:

- 128 × 128 and 256 × 256 black and white
- 48 × 64 and 96 × 128 color
- PLUS . . . . most any other combination you can dream up

Optional System Features:

- Full Transparency with high throughput
- Choice of ASCII characters or graphics chunks
- Scrolling Cursor with full editing
- Immediate access to screen memory at any time
- Works with 6502, 6800, and other micros
- Combined graphics and alphanumeric displays

(A) Video card.

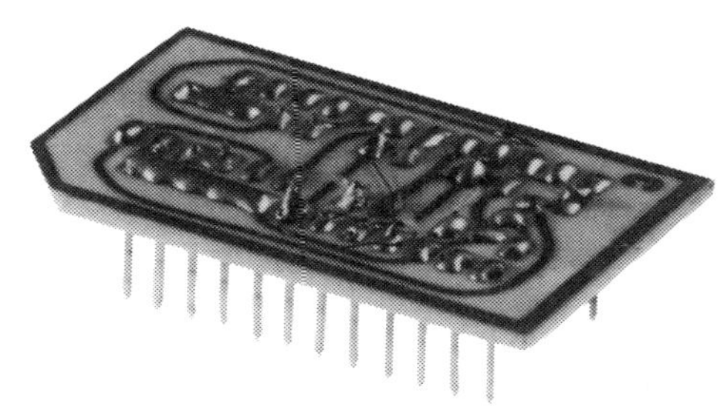

(B) Closeup of four-color graphics module.

Fig. 4-1. TVT 6 5/8 cheap video card and plug-in module.

video system. This is a third-generation design that picks up the best features of the TVT6 and TVT6L that earlier appeared in various issues of *Kilobaud* and *Popular Electronics.* New features added include the full graphics ability, transparency options, a simpler and cheaper overall circuit, and much more modest use of microcomputer address space.

In this chapter we will show you everything you need to build and use the TVT 6⅝ on your own. Your cost should be under $20 if you etch your own board and burn your own PROMS. If you prefer, assembled units, kits, circuit boards, and software tapes are commercially available. One source is PAIA Electronics, Box 14359, Oklahoma City, OK 73114. Other sources include several retail computer stores. You will also be shown how to check out and debug this board, again using the 6502 software and a KIM. Then, in the next chapter, we will look at how to pick up full transparency.

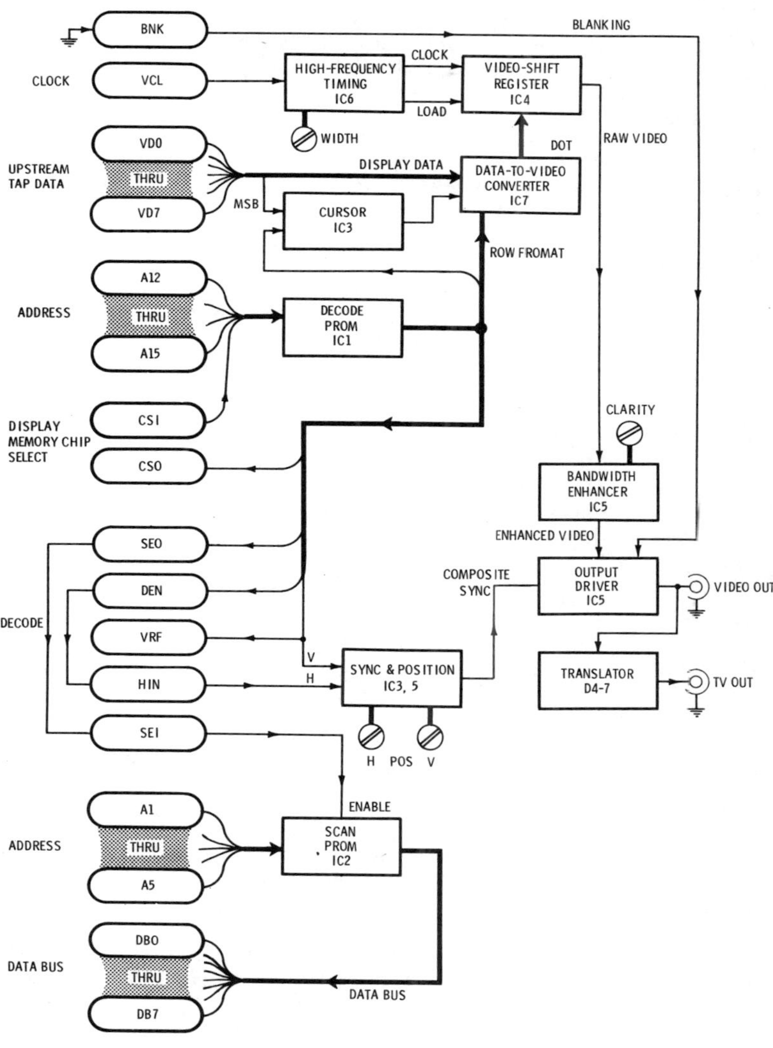

Fig. 4-2. Block diagram of TVT 6 5/8.

HOW IT WORKS

A block diagram of the TVT 6⅝ is shown in Fig. 4-2, followed by the schematic in Fig. 4-3 and a parts list in Chart 4-2.

Chart 4-2. TVT 6 5/8 Parts List

C1,3	470 pF disc ceramic capacitor
C2,6	270 pF polystyrene capacitor
C4	4700 pF polystyrene or mylar capacitor
C5	.01 μF mylar capacitor
C7	0.22 μF mylar capacitor
C8, 15-18	0.1 μF disc ceramic capacitor
C9	33 μF tantalum capacitor
C10	62 pF polystyrene capacitor
C11	150 pF polystyrene capacitor
C12	33 pF polystyrene capacitor
C13	1200 pF polystyrene or mylar capacitor
C14	3300 pF polystyrene or mylar capacitor
D1-8	1N4149 or equivalent silicon computer diode; D3 must be quality unit with low storage time
IC1	IM5610 or equivalent 32 × 8 TRI-STATE bipolar PROM, programmed to DECODE truth table selected
IC2	IM5610 or equivalent 32 × 8 TRI-STATE bipolar PROM, programmed to Scan truth table selected
IC3	4584 CMOS Hex Schmitt Trigger
IC4	74165 Parallel In, Serial Out Shift Register, TTL
IC5	7405 Hex open collector TTL inverter
IC6	74LS04 Hex LS TTL Inverter
IC7	Plug-in Module—see text and Figs. 4-10 through 4-14
J1,2	Side entry pc phono jack
R1,15	4.7K, 1/4 watt carbon resistor
R2	100K Upright pc trimmer, H POS
R3	500K Upright pc trimmer, V POS
R4,6	22K, 1/4 watt carbon resistor
R5,7	1.5K, 1/4 watt carbon resistor
R8	1K, 1/4 watt carbon resistor
R9	3.3 Megohm, 1/4 watt carbon resistor
R10	10K upright pc trimmer, CLARITY
R11	100 ohm, 1/4 watt carbon resistor
R12, 16	22 ohm, 1/4 watt carbon resistor
R13	150 ohm, 1/4 watt carbon resistor
R14	470 ohm, 1/4 watt carbon resistor
R17	250 ohm upright pc trimmer, WIDTH
S1-S4	Miniature spdt slide switches, 0.125 inch centers, Poly Paks EID3429 or equivalent
MISC.	Pc board, etched and drilled (see Figs. 4-5 through 4-7); bus strips for + and ground (see Figs. 4-8 and 4-9); data-to-video IC7 programming modules (see Figs. 4-10 through 4-14); jumper material; pc test point terminals (11); insulated sleeving; solder; 24-pin IC socket (1); 16-pin IC sockets (3); 14-pin IC sockets (3); Optional—36-pin 0.156″ single entry pc connector; Optional—output cable, shielded phono jack to miniature phone

Most of the circuit is based on the hardware details we looked at in the preceding chapter. A *Decode* PROM (IC1) is our control center that decides what the tvt is to do and when it is to do it. The *Decode* PROM controls our *Scan* PROM (IC2) which gives us a Scan microinstruction when activated.

A plug-in data-to-video module is used to pick alphanumeric or graphics display options. We will shortly be looking at details on four different modules. The input to our data-to-video module comes from the upstream tap in the display memory of the microprocessor.

Three lines are routed from the *Decode* PROM to the Data-to-Video converter. One is a *Row 1* command used for alphanumerics. One is a *Row 2* command for alphanumerics or a *Blanking* command for graphics. The final is a *Row 4* command for alphanumerics and an *A/B Select* command for graphics with split chunk formats.

Yet another data-to-video module input is derived from VD7 by way of a winking cursor generator. This Cursor command is blinked by oscillator IC3 and gated by diodes D1 and D2.

The plug-in module outputs to a video-shift register IC4. Loading and clocking of the video-shift register is handled by gated oscillator IC6. The coarse clock rate is set by the SLOW-FAST switch, while the fine rate is tuned with the WIDTH control. These rates are adjusted depending on the module in use.

The output of the video-shift register goes through a polarity selector S3 to pick normal (+) or inverted (−) video. The selected video is routed to the bandwidth enhancer in IC5 that works with R10 and C11. The CLARITY control predistorts the video to meet the needs of a limited tv video bandwidth.

Meanwhile, horizontal- (DEN) and vertical- (VR) sync outputs are routed to a positioning and delay circuit located in IC3 and IC5. Horizontal and vertical delayed-sync signals are combined at the R6, C6 junction to form composite sync.

The composite sync and the enhanced video are combined with IC5 and output as ordinary video at J1, with an approximate output impedance of 100 ohms. The diode and resistor offset network formed by D4 through D7 and R13 up-translate the video for our tv output which is referenced to a +4-volt white level. A remaining gate in IC5 is used to pick up a blanking input.

Besides the plug-in modules, the graphics options, and the more efficient use of address space, several obvious differences can be noted between the TVT 6⅝ and earlier designs. These are:

* The SCAN Enable lead from the instruction decoder PROM to the SCAN PROM is broken and now goes off board. *A jumper must be provided for 6502 or 6800 operation.*

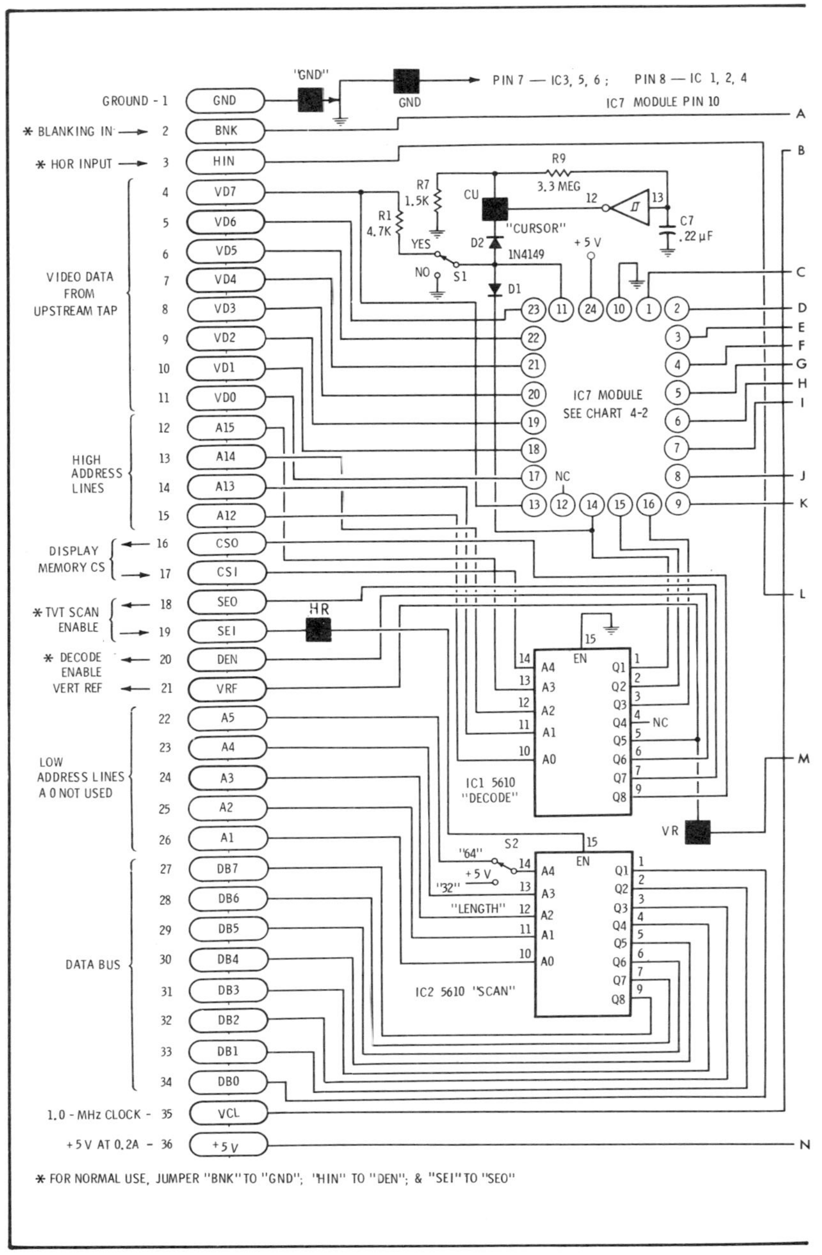

Fig. 4-3. Schematic

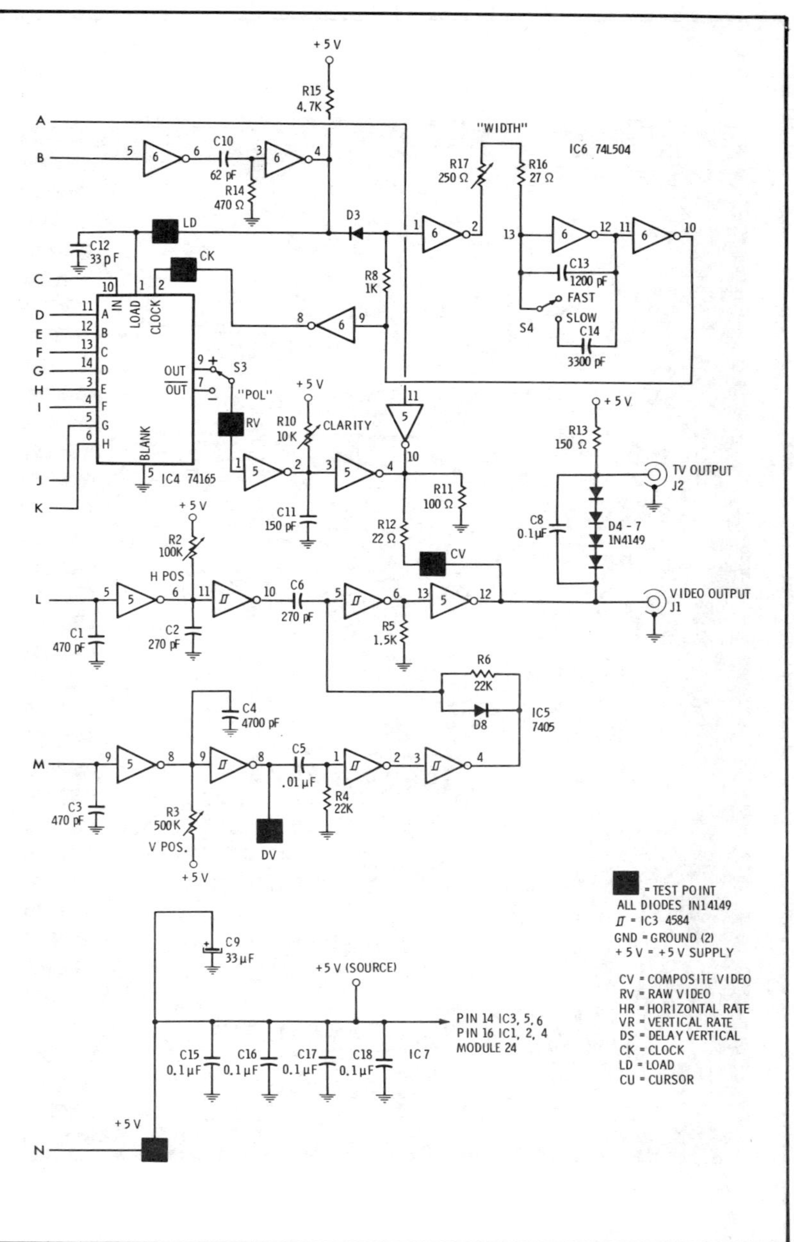

+5 V
R15
4.7K
A
B
C10
62 pF
R14
470 Ω
"WIDTH"
R17
250 Ω
R16
27 Ω
IC6 74LS04
D3
LD
C12
33 pF
CK
R8
1K
C13
1200 pF
FAST
SLOW
S4
C14
3300 pF
C
D
E
F
G
H
I
J
K
IN
LOAD
CLOCK
OUT
OUT
BLANK
IC4 74165
S3
"POL"
RV
+5 V
R10
10K
CLARITY
C11
150 pF
R11
100 Ω
R12
22 Ω
+5 V
R13
150 Ω
TV OUTPUT
J2
C8
0.1µF
D4 - 7
1N4149
+5 V
R2
100K
H POS
CV
L
C1
470 pF
C2
270 pF
C6
270 pF
R5
1.5K
VIDEO OUTPUT
J1
R6
22K
D8
IC5
7405
C4
4700 pF
M
C3
470 pF
C5
.01 µF
R4
22K
R3
500K
V POS.
+5 V
DV
= TEST POINT
ALL DIODES IN14149
= IC3 4584
GND = GROUND (2)
+5 V = +5 V SUPPLY
CV = COMPOSITE VIDEO
RV = RAW VIDEO
HR = HORIZONTAL RATE
VR = VERTICAL RATE
DS = DELAY VERTICAL
CK = CLOCK
LD = LOAD
CU = CURSOR
C9
33 µF
+5 V (SOURCE)
PIN 14 IC3, 5, 6
PIN 16 IC1, 2, 4
MODULE 24
C15
0.1µF
C16
0.1µF
C17
0.1µF
C18
0.1µF
IC7
+5 V
N

of TVT 6 5/8.

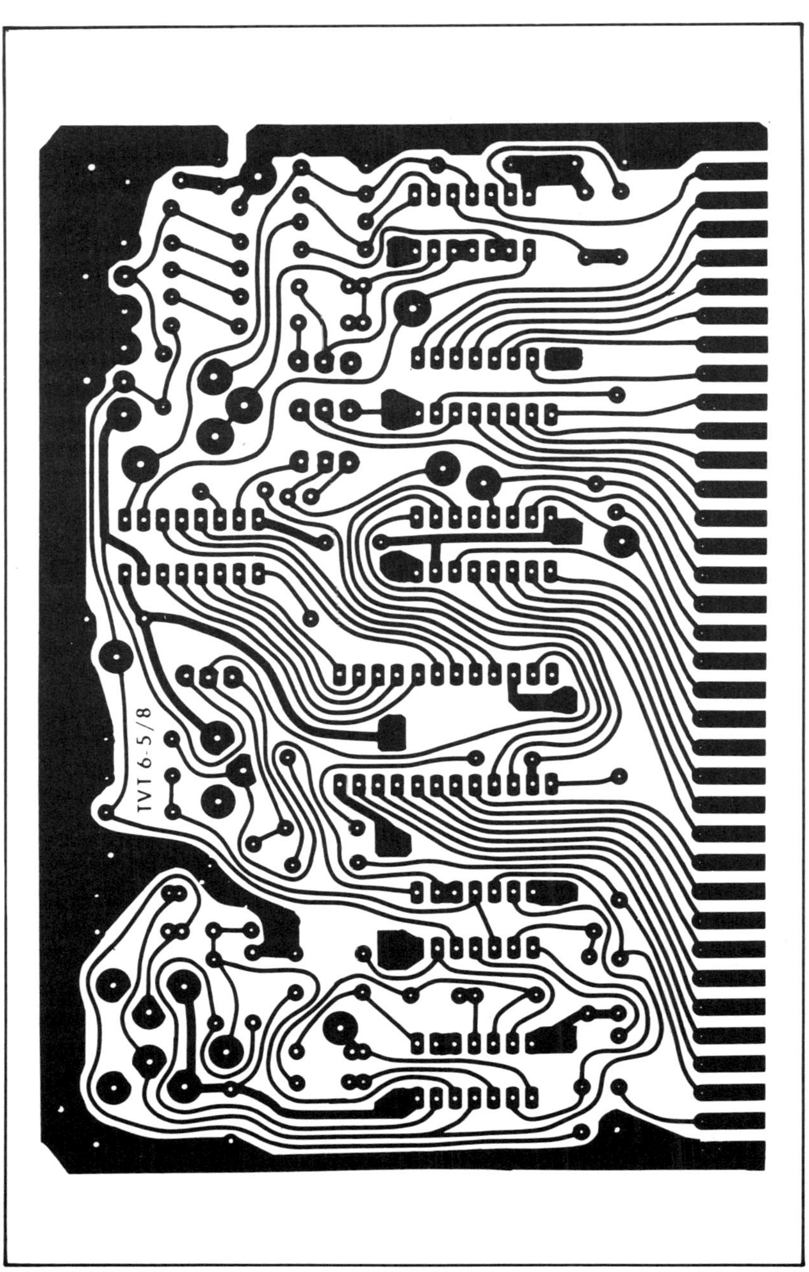

Fig. 4-4. Full size pc board pattern for TVT 6 5/8.

* The horizontal-sync input is also broken and now goes off board. This can let you run full transparency by filling in sync pulses from some other source. A *jumper must be provided between DEN and HIN for normal use.*

* An asynchronous blanking input is now available. This can be used to help transparency or simply to turn off the display. *The BNK input must be grounded for a visible display.*

Note particularly that the TVT 6⅝ is NOT pin compatible with earlier designs and earlier interface connections. This pin compatibility was traded off for improved operation, lower cost, and better transparency.

CONSTRUCTION DETAILS

A full size printed-circuit layout appears in Fig. 4-4 with its mechanical and drilling details in Fig. 4-5, and solder mask in Fig. 4-6. A single-sided layout with only ten jumpers is used. Components are arranged as shown in Fig. 4-7.

Two bus strips are used across the back of the circuit board for supply and ground connections. Fig. 4-8 shows the full-size patterns for these strips. These are made by filing, routing, or otherwise cutting pieces of 1/16-inch × 3/16-inch plated-brass strip. Ordinary 1/32-inch × 1/4-inch hobby-shop brass strip may be substituted. Fig.

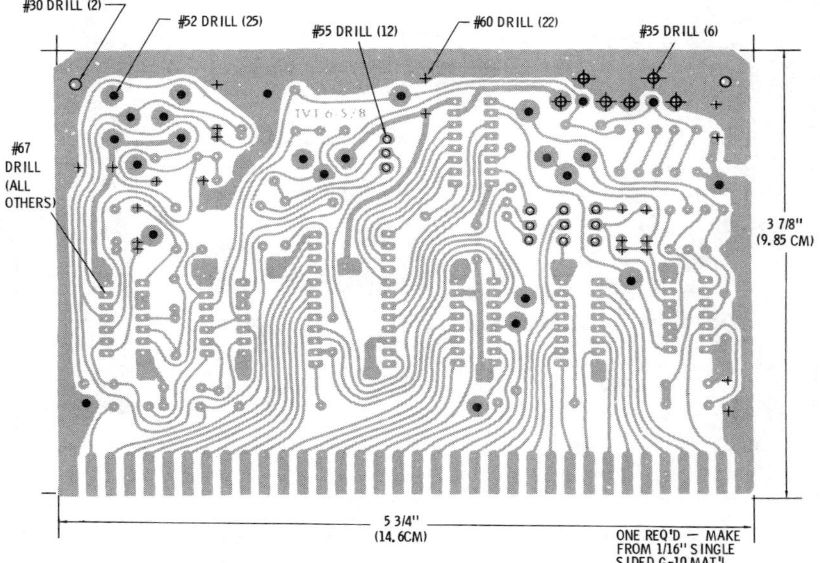

Fig. 4-5. Mechanical and drilling details for TVT 6 5/8.

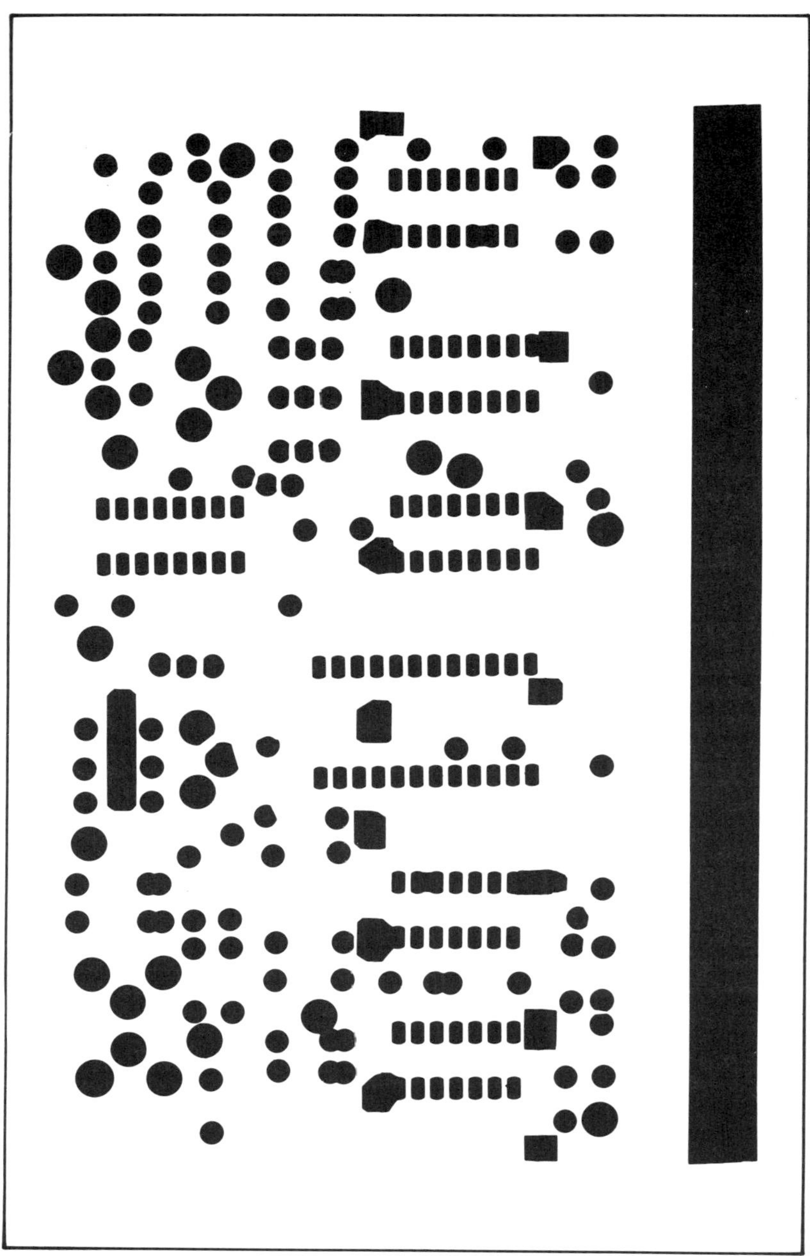

Fig. 4-6. Solder mask for TVT 6 5/8 (full size).

4-9 shows the locations of these strips on the foil side of the circuit board. Note that the ground strip does NOT contact the +5-volt foil run; that the +5-volt strip does NOT contact the ground foil; and that the +5-volt strip does NOT contact any pins on the Data-to-Video converter module or diode D8.

DATA-TO-VIDEO MODULES

The available pinouts to our data-to-video module are listed in Chart 4-3. A 24-pin IC socket is used as a connector. Inputs to the

Chart 4-3. Pinouts for the Data-to-Video Converter Modules

Pin	Function
1	Video Shift Register Serial Input
2	Video Shift Register Parallel Input A
3	Video Shift Register Parallel Input B
4	Video Shift Register Parallel Input C
5	Video Shift Register Parallel Input D
6	Video Shift Register Parallel Input E
7	Video Shift Register Parallel Input F
8	Video Shift Register Parallel Input G
9	Video Shift Register Parallel Input H
10	Ground
11	Winking Cursor input
12	No Connection- reserved
13	Video Data Input VD7
14	Row 1 select
15	Row 2 or Blanking Select
16	Row 4 or A/B select
17	Video Data Input VD0
18	Video Data Input VD1
19	Video Data Input VD2
20	Video Data Input VD3
21	Video Data Input VD4
22	Video Data Input VD5
23	Video Data Input VD6
24	+5-volt supply

module consist of eight video-data lines, three instruction decoder lines, and aCursor-control line. The outputs from the module go to the eight parallel inputs and the single serial input of a video-shift register. An unconnected pin, +5-volt supply, and ground completes the count.

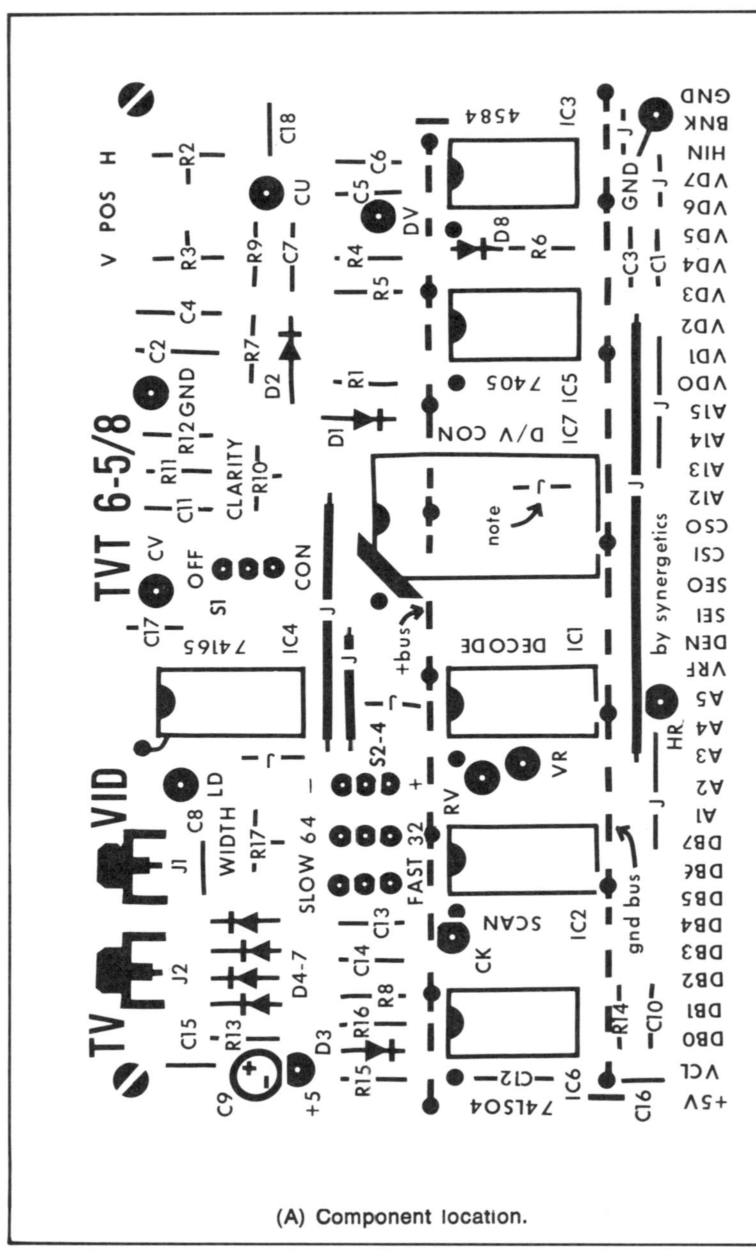

(A) Component location.

Fig. 4-7. Component location

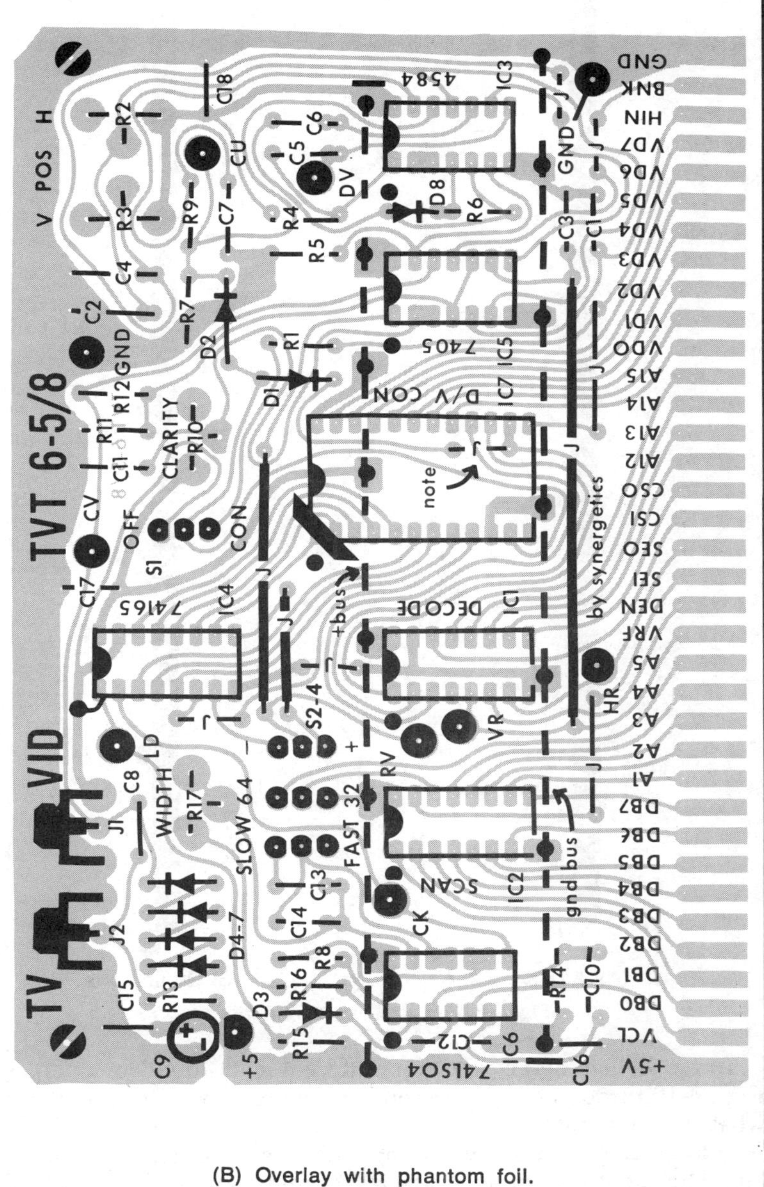

(B) Overlay with phantom foil.

for TVT 6 5/8.

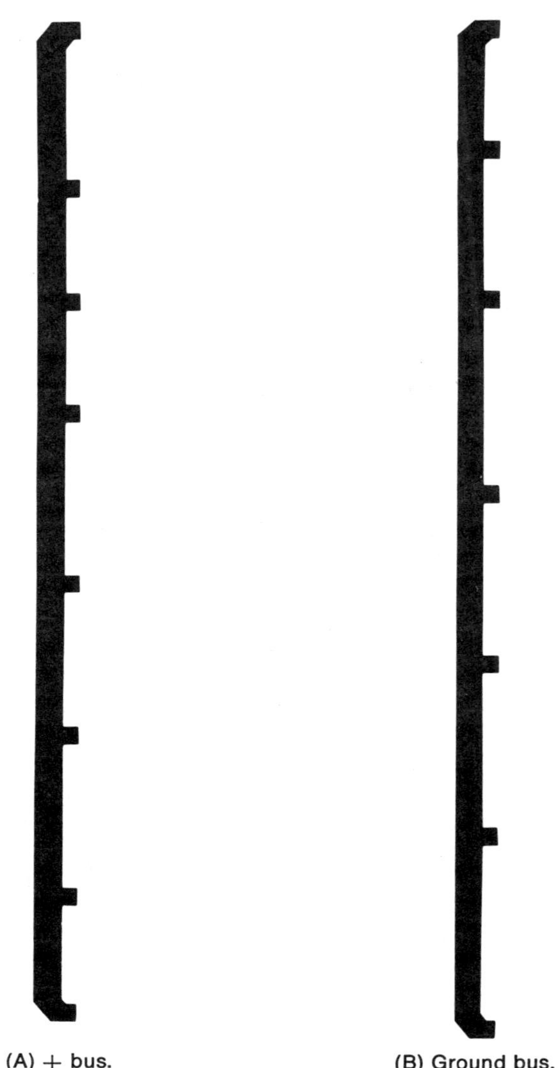

(A) + bus.

(B) Ground bus.

Fig. 4-8. Full size bus strip patterns.

You will find details on four different data-to-video modules in Figs. 4-10 through 4-13. The construction of these modules is somewhat unusual, but they are simple and inexpensive to build.

Module A provides upper- and lower-case alphanumeric characters. Module B is used for 256 × 256 graphics and is the only module that uses a second integrated circuit. Module C is used for 96 × 128

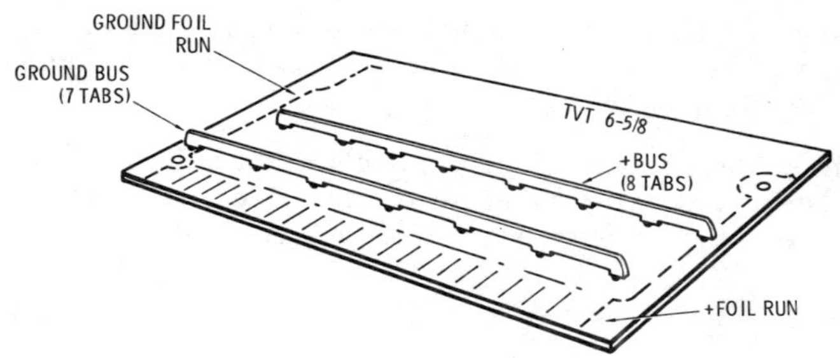

Fig. 4-9. Bus strips are located on the foil side as shown.

color graphics or 128 × 128 black and white graphics. Module C combines an integrated circuit LS TTL quad selector switch with a transistor blanking inverter.

Module D is not really a module—it is a plain old single supply 2513 character generator with a jumper wire attached at five places. This is the most economical alphanumeric module and is upper case only.

Modules A, B, and C plug in with their ICs "upside down," that is, the pins are pointing *away* from the main circuit board. Module D plugs in the usual way. This strange convention is used to make all the modules as pin compatible as possible while keeping a low profile. Jumpers are used in all four modules to enable us to use a single-sided pc board layout.

STEP BY STEP ASSEMBLY

The upcoming step-by-step assembly instructions assume you have on hand a fully-etched, drilled, and solder-masked pc board, along with two ready-to-install bus strips. We will further assume you are using the 658-KD8 ("Kim Decode—8-dot character") PROM of Fig. 3-5 for IC1 and that you are using the 658-KS64 ("Kim Scan—64 characters") PROM of Fig. 3-8 for IC2. You should have on hand a modified KIM-1, following the interface details of the previous chapter, a modified tv set or other way of accepting and displaying video, and a triggered-sweep scope for debugging.

If you are using a commercial kit to build your TVT 6⅝, be sure to check for any updates or corrections on the instructions that follow.

Your TVT 6⅝ board assembly can go like this:

- ☐ Carefully inspect the board for opens, solder bridges, mask, or overlay problems, etc. . . . Try tinning one of the large round areas on the board. If there is any problem with easy solder adhesion, carefully clean all areas to be soldered with an ordinary pink eraser. Avoid handling the board as it will make soldering more difficult.

☐ Insert the optional 11 pc terminals in the following locations. The terminals are staked to the foil side using an automatic center punch. They are then soldered after staking:

				☐ CU
☐ GND	☐ HR	☐ VR	☐ RV	☐ +5
☐ GND	☐ CK	☐ LD	☐ DV	☐ CV

☐ Add three jumpers using insulated sleeving to the component side of the board and solder in place:
- ☐ Jumper below IC4 (long)
- ☐ Jumper below IC4 (short)
- ☐ Jumper above "HR" test point

☐ Add seven bare jumpers to the component side of the board and solder in place:
- ☐ Jumper to the left of "HR"
- ☐ Jumper to the left of "C1"
- ☐ Jumper to the right of "C1"
- ☐ Jumper to the right of "C3"
- ☐ Jumper *inside* IC7 callout. Make sure this jumper is flat against the board.
- ☐ Vertical jumper between IC1 and IC4
- ☐ Vertical jumper below "LD" test point

☐ Add a 24-pin socket at IC7. If the socket has polarity marks on it, orient the socket to match the printing on the board. Bend all leads flat against the board. On this socket, keep the solder joints as flat as possible.

☐ Add three 16-pin sockets at the following locations, again watching polarity if the socket is so marked:

☐ IC1 ☐ IC2 ☐ IC4

☐ Similarly, add three 14-pin sockets at the following locations:

☐ IC3 ☐ IC5 ☐ IC6

☐ Place a 1N4148 or similar silicon computer diode at D8, being careful to observe polarity. Be sure to cut the leads on this particular diode very close to the foil.

☐ Add six more 1N4148 or similar diodes at the following locations, again observing polarity:

☐ D1	☐ D4	☐ D6
☐ D2	☐ D5	☐ D7
☐ D3		

☐ Tin all the points the ground bus is to contact. Then carefully remove as much of this new solder as possible, using a solder syringe or solder capillary braid. Then carefully tin both ends of the seven-tab ground bus.

☐ Refer to Fig. 4-9 for the location of the ground bus. It goes nearest the connector. Make sure the ground bus is flat against the board and perfectly vertical and centered from end to end on the pads it has to contact. Tack the bus in place at the ends only.

☐ Check to make certain that your ground bus starts at the ground end, contacts seven places total, but does NOT extend to the +5-V line.

☐ Solder the ground bus on both sides at each of seven places. Alternate sides of the bus on your first soldering pass to keep the bus from twisting or bending. Check the solder at all pads.

☐ Similarly prepare the pads for the eight-tab + bus by first tinning and then removing solder. Tin both ends of the + bus and tack in place as shown in Fig. 4-9.

☐ Check to be certain that the + bus starts at the +5-V foil run, contacts eight places total, and touches nothing else, ESPECIALLY ANY PINS ON IC7, OR DIODE D8.

☐ Solder the + bus to all eight pads on both sides of the bus. Check the solder at all pads.

☐ Once again, carefully inspect both the + bus and the ground bus for contacting only where they are supposed to go.

☐ Add resistors in the following sequence:
- ☐ R15 4.7K, yellow-purple-red
- ☐ R16 22 ohms, red-red-black
- ☐ R8 1K, black-brown-red
- ☐ R14 470 ohms, yellow-purple-brown
- ☐ R13 150 ohms, brown-green-brown
- ☐ R1 4.7K, yellow-purple-red
- ☐ R5 1.5K, brown-green-red
- ☐ R6 22K, red-red-orange
- ☐ R4 22K, red-red-orange
- ☐ R9 3.3 Meg, orange-orange-green
- ☐ R7 1.5K, brown-green-red
- ☐ R12 22 ohms, red-red-black
- ☐ R11 100 ohms, black-brown-brown

Solder the resistors in place.

☐ Add 0.1-μF disc ceramic capacitors at the following locations:
  ☐ C8 ☐ C17
  ☐ C15 ☐ C18
  ☐ C16

☐ Add a 33-μF tantalum capacitor at C9, observing polarity.

☐ Add two 470-pF disc capacitors at the following locations:
  ☐ C1
  ☐ C3

☐ Add a 0.015-μF mylar capacitor at C5

☐ Add a 4700-pF mylar capacitor at C4

☐ Add a 1200-pF polystyrene or mylar capacitor at C14

☐ Add a 3300-pF polystyrene or mylar capacitor at C13
☐ Add a 62-pF polystyrene capacitor at C10, near IC6

☐ Add a 33-pF polystyrene capacitor at C12
☐ Add a 150-pF polystyrene capacitor at C11

☐ Add two 270-pF polystyrene capacitors at these locations:
  ☐ C2
  ☐ C6

☐ Add two phono jacks at J1 and J2. Be sure the jacks are flush with the board before soldering in place.

☐ Add four spdt slide switches to the following locations:
  ☐ SLOW/FAST
  ☐ 64/32
  ☐ +/−
  ☐ CON/OFF

☐ Add WIDTH control R17, 250-ohm trimmer pot (might be coded R251)

☐ Add CLARITY control R10, 10-K trimmer pot (might be coded R103)

☐ Add V POS control R3, 500-K trimmer pot (might be coded R504)

☐ Add H POS control R2, 100-K trimmer pot (might be coded R104)

☐ Carefully inspect the board for
  ☐ Everything properly soldered
  ☐ Anything missing
  ☐ Bus to board clearances
  ☐ Diode polarity
  ☐ Electrolytic polarity

☐ Do NOT install the integrated circuits at this time.

☐ This completes assembly of your TVT 6⅝. Proceed to module construction.

MODULE CONSTRUCTION

MODULE "A": Module "A" is an upper- and lower-case alphanumeric module, detailed in Fig. 4-10.

☐ Carefully inspect the circuit board for opens, solder bridges, etc. Try tinning one of the runs on the board. If there is any problem with easy solder adhesion, carefully clean all areas to be soldered with an ordinary pink eraser. Avoid handling the board as it will make soldering more difficult.

☐ Set your pc board bare side up with the notch in the upper left-hand corner. Insert a 0.1-μF disc ceramic capacitor in the two middle, left-most holes. Solder the capacitor in place. Save the excess leads.

☐ Use the excess leads from the previous step to provide a jumper in the two middle, right-most holes.

☐ Now provide a second jumper immediately to the left of the one installed previously.

☐ Add an 18-pin integrated-circuit socket in the remaining holes between the capacitor and jumper. If the socket has orientation marks on it, place these toward the capacitor.

☐ Insert a pin strip above the socket. The long end of the pins and the spacer go on the bare side; the short pin side goes to the foil and is soldered. Be sure this strip is flat before soldering.

☐ Add a pin strip to the 12 remaining holes at the bottom. Be sure this strip is flat before soldering.

☐ Carefully study Fig. 4-10D and add the following wire pencil connections on the *FOIL SIDE:*

- ☐ IC pin 12 to module pin 4
- ☐ IC pin 13 to module pin 5
- ☐ IC pin 15 to module pin 7
- ☐ IC pin 16 to module pin 8

Be sure you understand the numbering before you start. On the foil side, the connector pins run *counterclockwise;* the 18-pin IC count runs *clockwise;* and end jumper or capacitor pads are not counted.

☐ Check the previous step. Your four connections should be a "cross within a cross" that reverses the sequence of five side-by-side pad pairs.

Upper—and Lower—Case

Parts List
1—MCM6674 Character Generator (Motorola)
1—18-pin low-profile IC socket
1—0.1-μF disc ceramic capacitor
2—12-pin strips (AMP 1-640098-2)
1—circuit board "A"
2—jumpers made from capacitor leads
4—jumpers made with wiring pencil
—solder

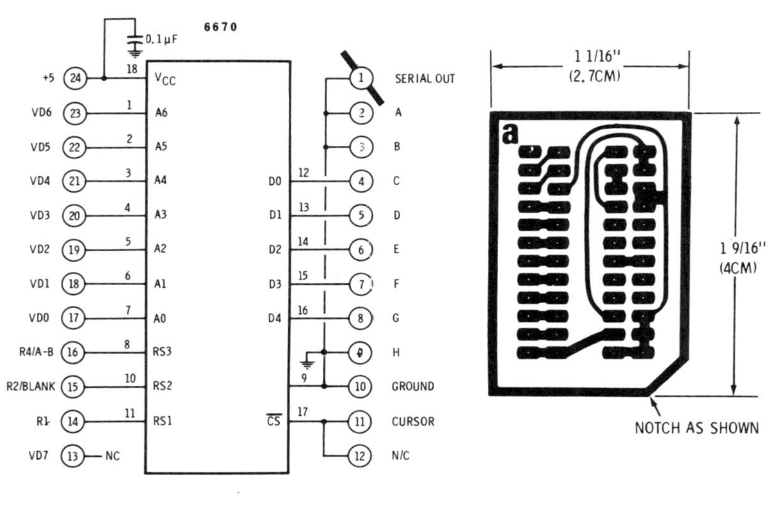

(A) Schematic. (B) Foil pattern.

Fig. 4-10. Module A

Alphanumeric Module

How It Works

ASCII code is input on pins VD0 through VD6. Row 1, 2, and 4 commands are input from instruction decoder. Winking cursor CS command is input from cursor gate when switch selected. Dot matrix code is output to video-shift–register leads C, D, E, F, and G. Ground is hard-wired to video-shift–register leads A, B, H, and the video-shift–register serial input. Input VD7 is not used.

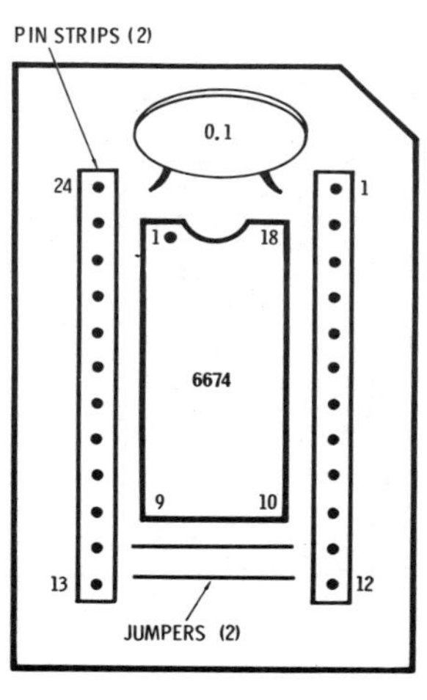

(C) Pin side.

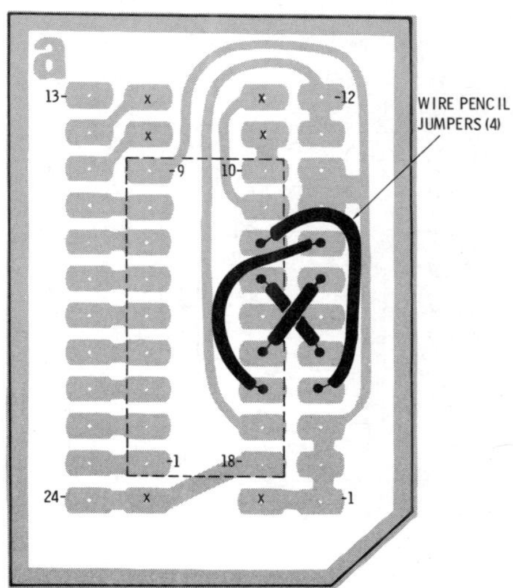

(D) Foil side.

Normal Settings: Cursor ON; FAST clock; WIDTH set to SEVEN pulses.

construction details.

256 X 256 Black and White

Parts List
2—74LS08 Quad AND Gate, LS TTL
1—0.1-μF disc ceramic capacitor
1—circuit board "B"
2—12-pin strips, AMP #1-640098-2
2—insulated sleeving, 1/2"
1—jumper wire, 3"
—solder

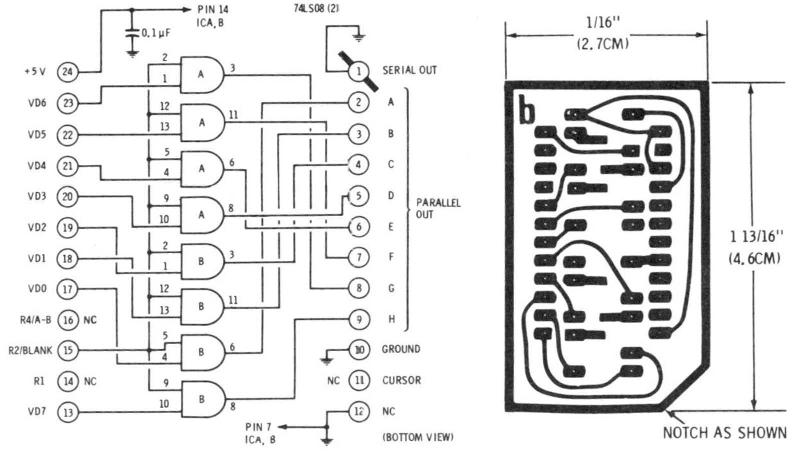

(A) Schematic.

(B) Foil pattern.

Fig. 4-11. Module B

Graphics Module

B

How It Works

Eight-bit chunk code is input on pins VD0 through VD7. Row 2 command from instruction decoder PROM used as a blanking input. Input code is passed out to video-shift–register inputs A through H when blanking is high. Blank (all zeros) code passed to video-shift–register when blank input is low. Cursor is not used. Video-shift–register serial input is hard-wired to ground.

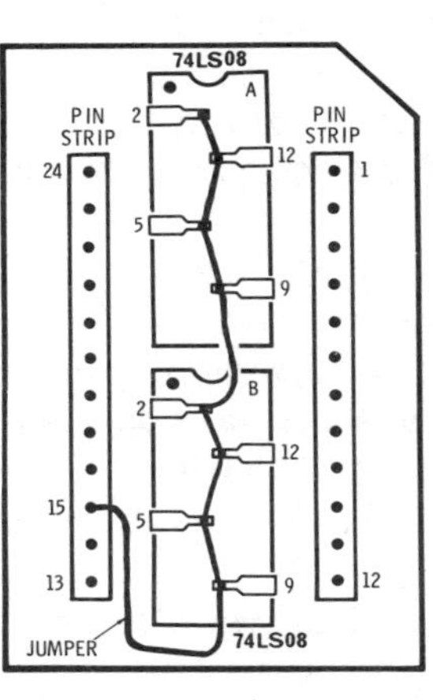

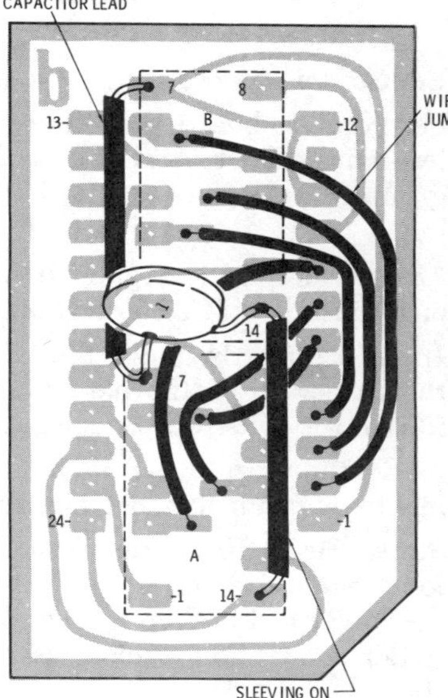

(C) Pin side.

Normal Settings: Cursor OFF; FAST clock; WIDTH set to EIGHT pulses.

construction details.

☐ Insert an MC6674 Character generator IC placing the dot and notch at the capacitor end.

☐ Store your completed Module A in the protective foam supplied with the character generator. *Always return your module to this foam when not in use.*

This completes assembly of your Module "A."

MODULE "B": Module B is a 256 × 256 graphics module, detailed in Fig. 4-11.

☐ Carefully inspect the circuit board for opens, solder bridges, etc. Try tinning one of the runs on the board. If there is any problem with easy solder adhesion, carefully clean all areas to be soldered with an ordinary pink eraser. Avoid handling the board as it will make soldering more difficult.

☐ Take a 74LS08 Quad AND gate and bend the following pins up and over the back of the integrated circuit:

- ☐ Pin 2 ☐ Pin 9
- ☐ Pin 5 ☐ Pin 12

☐ Repeat this process with the second 74LS08 Quad AND Gate.

☐ Set your pc board bare side up with the notch in the upper left-hand corner. Add one of the AND Gates to the left center group of holes, so that the notch and dot goes to the extreme left.

☐ Add the second AND gate so its notch and dot abut the previously installed IC. Solder both ICs in place.

☐ Insert a pin strip above the ICs. The long end of the pins and the spacer go on the bare side; the short pin side goes to the foil and is soldered. Be sure this strip is flat before soldering.

☐ Add a pin strip to the remaining 12 holes at the bottom, again making certain it is flat before soldering.

☐ Study Fig. 4-10C. Prepare a 2-inch bare wire. Form a small loop in one end and solder this to module pin 15, the third from the lower right when the notch is in the upper left. Make this solder connection as close as possible to the spacer on the pin strip.

☐ Route the other end of this wire to the eight pins folded over the top of the AND gates. Arrange things for neat and flat appearance, and then solder this wire to *all eight* folded up pins.

☐ Carefully study Fig. 4-11D and add the following six wire pencil connections on the FOIL SIDE:

- ☐ "A" IC pin 3 to module pin 8
- ☐ "A" IC pin 6 to module pin 6

- ☐ "A" IC pin 11 to module pin 7
- ☐ "B" IC pin 3 to module pin 4
- ☐ "B" IC pin 6 to module pin 2
- ☐ "B" IC pin 11 to module pin 3

Be sure you understand the numbering before you start. On the foil side, the connector pins run *counterclockwise*, while the 14-pin IC counts individually run *clockwise*.

☐ Check the previous step. Your six connections and one foil run should reverse the sequence of seven side-by-side pad pairs.

☐ Bend two loops near the body of a 0.1-μF disc ceramic capacitor. Note that pin 7 of the right-hand gate has no connections and needs to be connected to ground. Note that the left-hand gate has no connection to pin 14 and needs a connection to +5 V. Solder the capacitor between the presently unconnected pins 7 and 14 as close to the capacitor body as you can. *Do not cut the leads.*

☐ Add a ⅝-inch piece of insulated sleeving to both capacitor leads.

☐ Lay the lower pin 14 lead flat against the board and solder it to the end pin 14 of the other integrated circuit. This lead should go to the lower left, parallel to the pad rows. Trim any remaining lead beyond this second connection.

☐ Lay the upper pin 7 lead flat against the board and solder it to the end pin 7 of the other integrated circuit. This lead should go to the upper right, parallel to the pad rows. Trim any remaining lead beyond this second connection.

☐ Store this completed module in protective foam. The foam is not needed for static protection on this particular module, but helps keep the pins from bending.

This completes your Module "B."

MODULE "C": Module C is a 96 × 128 color graphics or a 128 × 128 black and white graphics module detailed in Fig. 4-12.

☐ Carefuly inspect, test tin, and clean the circuit board as you did for the two previous modules.

☐ Set your pc board bare side up with the notch in the upper left-hand corner. Add a 2.2-K, red-red-red resistor to the center holes in the extreme left side.

☐ Add a 0.1-μF disc ceramic capacitor immediately to the right of the resistor. Leave enough lead length between the base of the capacitor and the board so that you can fold the capacitor

96 X 128 Color

Parts List
1—74LS157 Quad Selector, LS TTL
1—2N4400 or equivalent silicon NPN switching transistor
1—1K, 1/4 watt resistor
1—2.2K, 1/4 watt resistor
1—0.1-μF ceramic disc capacitor
1—circuit board "C"
2—12-pin strips, AMP #1-640098-2
4—Insulated wire jumpers
1—jumper made from component lead
—solder

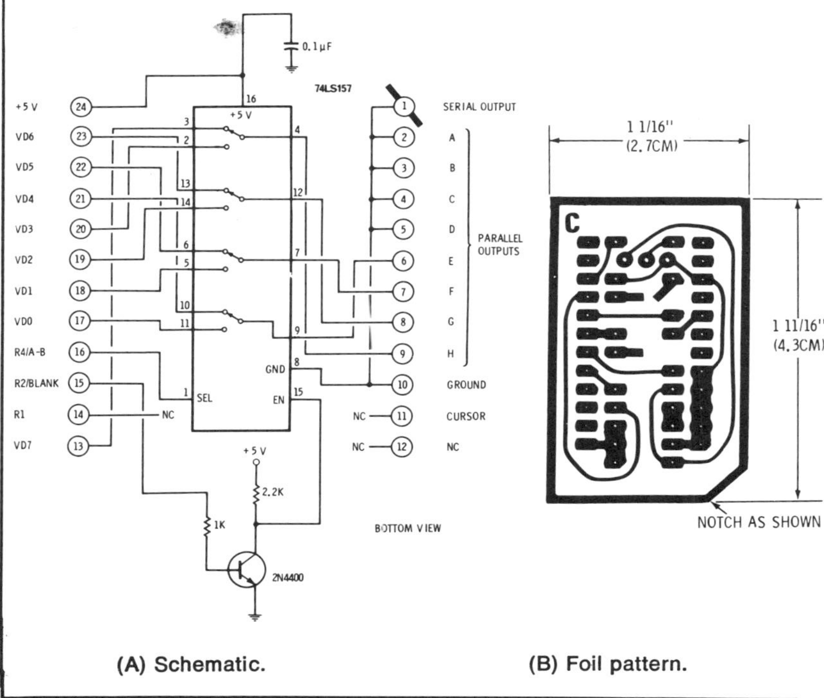

(A) Schematic.

(B) Foil pattern.

Fig. 4-12. Module C

Graphics Module

C

How It Works

Lower chunk code is input on pins VD0 through VD3. Upper chunk code is input on pins VD4 through VD7. A/B select code is input from instruction decoder as "Row 4" command. Blanking is input from instruction decoder as "Row 2" command, and inverted with transistor RTL inverter. Selected chunk half is routed to video-shift–register D,E,F, and G outputs when unblanked. Ground is hard-wired to video-shift–register serial input and parallel inputs A,B,C, and D. Cursor is not used.

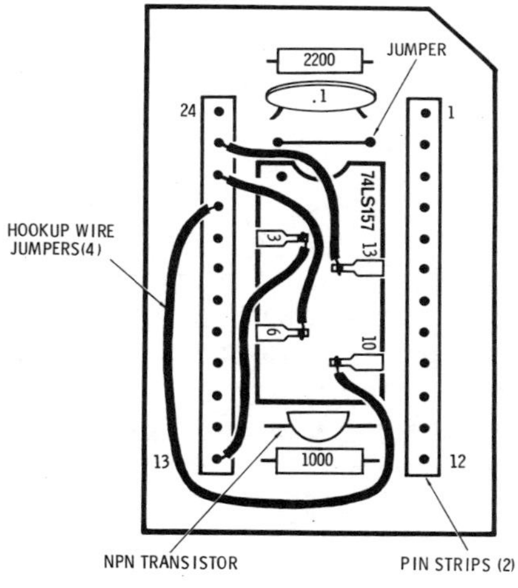

(C) Pin side.

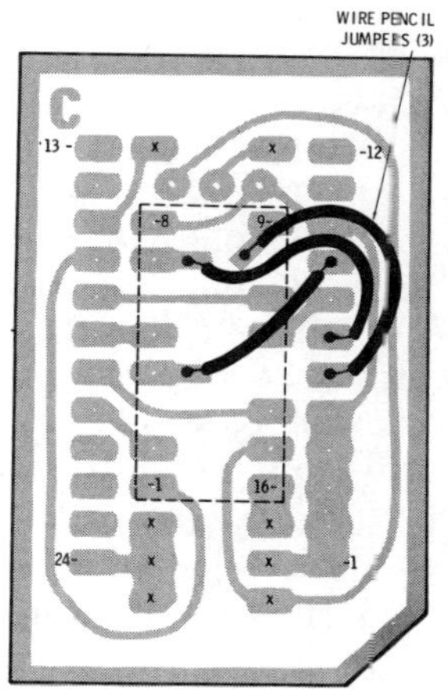

(D) Foil side.

Normal Settings: Cursor OFF; SLOW clock; WIDTH set to FOUR pulses for 128 × 128 black and white, or to THREE pulses for 96 × 128 color.

construction details.

over on top of the resistor and have it lie flat. (Note: if a miniature capacitor is used, ignore this detail. The pins should stick up well beyond the highest point on the capacitor.) *Save one of the capacitor leads after trimming.*

☐ Add a jumper immediately to the right of the capacitor using the lead saved above. At this point, the six left-most, center holes should be filled, looking from the bare side with the notch in the upper left.

☐ Take a 74LS157 Quad Selector 16-pin Integrated Circuit, and bend the following pins up over the top of the IC:

☐ Pin 3 ☐ Pin 10
☐ Pin 6 ☐ Pin 13

☐ Install this integrated circuit so that the dot and notch are nearest the jumper.

☐ Add a 12-pin strip to an outside row of holes. The short end goes to the foil side. Be sure pin strip is flat before soldering.

☐ Add a second pin strip in the remaining holes.

☐ Prepare four 1-inch–long pieces of solid, insulated hookup wire. Bend a small loop in *one* end of each wire.

☐ Carefully study Fig. 4-12C. Connect these four wires as follows:

☐ IC pin 3 to module pin 13
☐ IC pin 6 to module pin 22
☐ IC pin 10 to module pin 21
☐ IC pin 13 to module pin 23

Be sure to solder the module pins as close to the spacer as possible. Be sure you understand the numbering before you start. On the bare side, the connector pins run *clockwise,* while the 16-pin IC count runs *counterclockwise.*

☐ Add a 2N4400 or similar npn switching transistor to the three holes at the end of the integrated circuit. The flat side of the transistor goes toward the flat end of the IC.

☐ Add a 1-K resistor, brown-black-red, to the remaining two holes to the right of the transistor.

☐ Carefully inspect all solder connections on both sides of the module. Turn the module to the foil side with the notch in the upper right.

☐ Carefully study Fig. 4-12D. Add the following three wire pencil connections to the foil side:

☐ IC pin 9 to module pin 6
☐ IC pin 7 to module pin 7
☐ IC pin 4 to module pin 9

Once again, watch the pin numbering. On the foil side, the connector pins run *counterclockwise,* while the 16-pin IC count runs *clockwise.*

- ☐ Check the previous step. Your four connections and one foil run should reverse the sequence of five side-by-side pad pairs.
- ☐ Store your completed module in protective foam. While not needed for static protection on this particular module, the foam will prevent the pins from becoming bent or misaligned.

This completes assembly of Module "C."

MODULE "D": Module D is a Lower-Case–only alphanumeric module detailed in Fig. 4-13. No circuit board is used with this module.

- ☐ Secure a piece of protective foam to a piece of wood, your bench, or otherwise nail it down so that it will not move.
- ☐ Insert a 2513 character generator into this piece of foam. Tin leads 1, 2, 3, 9, and 10.
- ☐ Make a wiring pencil connection between pins 1, 2, 3, 9, and 10.
- ☐ Check to be certain the wire does not contact any other pins, particularly pins 4 and 8.
- ☐ Return the 2513 to protective foam for storage.

This completes the assembly of Module "D."

DEBUG AND CHECKOUT

A cheap video system uses hardware and software working together to produce a final display. If something does not seem right, this could be a hardware problem, a software problem, or an operator problem.

Hardware problems can be something wrong with the computer, with the computer interface, with the tvt card, with the modules, or with the tv interface.

Software problems can be an actual coding error, a mismatch between what the software and hardware is trying to do, or a program that is misconfigured by having the wrong format, incorrect starting address, memory locations in the wrong slots, and so on.

Operator problems are the most common. These include misadjusted switches and controls, programs that have bombed or otherwise are not doing what you think they are, flags and IRQ vectors set wrong, running software and hardware that is not compatible, and so on.

If you have any problem with a cheap video system, remember it could be hardware, software, operation, or some combination of the

Upper Case Only

Parts List
1—2513 character generator (General Instruments) (*MUST* be single supply type)
1—jumper wire from wiring pencil
—solder

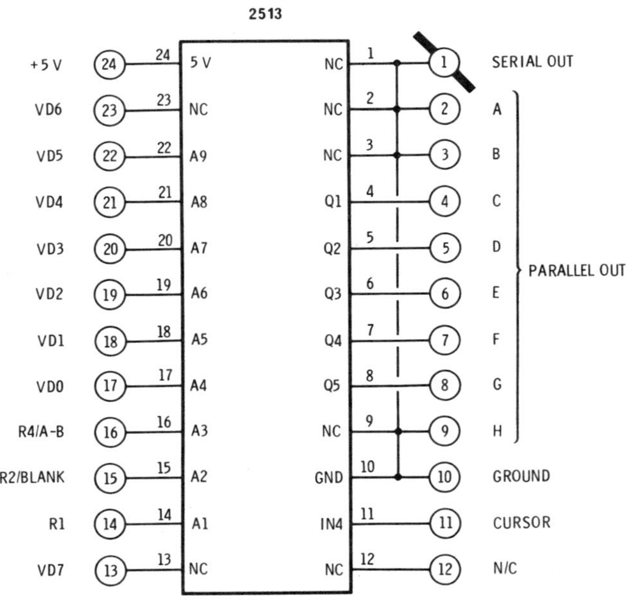

(A) Schematic.

Fig. 4-13. Module D

Alphanumeric Module

D

How It Works

ASCII code is input on pins VD0 through VD6. Row 1, 2, and 4 commands are input from instruction decoder PROM. Winking cursor CS command is input from cursor gate when switch selected. Dot matrix code is output to video-shift–register leads C, D, E, F, and G. Ground is hard-wired to video-shift–register leads A, B, H, and the video-shift–register serial input. ASCII code inputs VD6 and VD7 are not used.

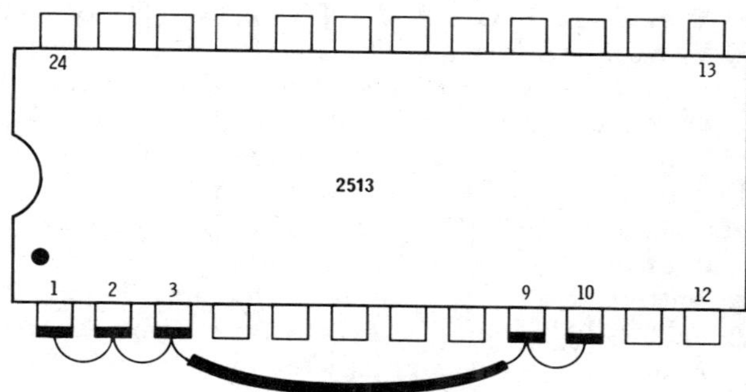

(B) Jumper detail.

Normal Settings: Cursor ON; FAST clock; WIDTH set to SIX pulses.

construction details.

three. *Always assume you have an operator problem first,* but do not ever discount a hardware or software solution completely, no matter how obvious the source of the problem is. Remember that computers are dumber than people but smarter than programmers.

The debug and checkout that follows assumes you are running on a KIM-1 or a KIM-1 with expanded memory. We will further assume you have a ready-to-go video monitor or converted tv set, and that your KIM interface is complete and presumably working.

While it is not essential, a good triggered-sweep oscilloscope will be handy, particularly if hardware problems crop up.

Above all, *be sure to get your TVT 6⅝ and its modules up and working and thoroughly checked out before applying it to any system other than a KIM.* If you do not have a KIM system, use a ready-to-go assembled TVT 6⅝ or have someone else (perhaps a local computer club member) check your board out for you.

When you debug *any* cheap video system, always start with the simplest possible tests and work from there. Always start with the utility 16 × 32 upper case alphanumeric mode before trying anything fancy. Always get your actual display software up and working before worrying about Cursors or loaders.

In the debug and checkout list that follows, **NEVER GO BEYOND A PARTICULAR DEBUG STEP UNLESS YOU ARE CERTAIN EVERYTHING UP TO THAT POINT IS WORKING PROPERLY.** Avoid adding or removing ICs in a powered circuit. Always reload or otherwise verify your programs and your flags and vectors in each step immediately before trial. On a KIM, always check the obvious things such as staying in your binary mode (00F1-00), having your NMI ready for the operating system (00FA 00 1C); and having your IRQ vector (00Fd low; 00FE high) where you want it to go. It pays to further disable your interrupt line physically with a switch to prevent interrupts before they are needed. Accidentally bumping a keyboard can bomb everything you have done if your software is not ready for an interrupt.

Your TVT 6⅝ checkout can go like this:

- ☐ With the changeover switch in the KIM position and the tvt unplugged, try running a simple program. If the program will not run, look for solder shorts on the display memory upstream tap or incorrect switch wiring. Switch to the tvt position. Your program should bomb and refuse to operate.
- ☐ Plug in your still empty tvt card. Switch to TVT. Center all controls. Have switches set to "Fast", "+", "32", "Off". Add *only* the IC1 Decode PROM 658-KD8. Repower the computer and attempt to run the following program:

Test Program A

```
┌0000 EA
└0001 4C 00 00          Normal loop
```

Single stepping the program should alternate between 0000 and 0001. Should the computer not run normally, something is happening to your CSI and CSO so that chip selects are not passing through properly, or something is wrong with your DEN, perhaps the decode enable line.

If test program A runs, try running a complicated, existing program of your own. Operation should be normal and transparent.

☐ Now add your Scan PROM at IC2, using PROM 658-KS64. Rerun test program A. Everything should remain normal. If the test program will not run, look for IC1 incorrectly grabbing the data bus.

☐ Check memory location 6000. It should be an A0. IF IT IS NOT, STOP IMMEDIATELY AND FIND OUT WHY. One obvious thing to watch is a mixup on the PROMs.

☐ Check the next 256 memory locations. You should get twenty-nine more A0's, followed by two 60's, followed by thirty more A0's, followed by two 60's, all the way up. Should you get funny spacing, check your address lines going to the Decode PROM for possible errors or poor soldering. Do not go beyond this point unless you can call a sequence of thirty A0's followed by two 60's continuously anywhere between 6000 and dFFF. With the switch in the "64" position, check for sixty-two A0's followed by two 60's.

☐ Load the following program:

Test Program B

```
0000 JSR  20  00  60     KIM calling a 32-character Scan;
0003 JMP  4C  00  00       Scan returning control to KIM.
```

Single step the program with the switch at "32." You should go from 0000 to 6000 to 6002, and then advance by two's to 601E. After 601E you should go to 0003, then 0001, and then the sequence should repeat. If this program works, the KIM is capable of calling a Scan from the tvt and the tvt is capable of returning control to the KIM at the end of the SCAN command. DO NOT GO BEYOND THIS POINT UNTIL TEST PROGRAM B WILL RUN.

☐ Insert IC3, IC5, and IC6 and verify that test program B will still run. You will have to reload your program and vectors every time you reapply power. If there is any change, look for a backwards or wrong socketed IC or some similar problem. IC3, 5, and 6 should have no apparent effect at this time.

☐ Load the Program of Chart 4-4, a 16×32 interlaced alphanumeric Scan. Verify all program locations after loading. Verify your binary mode and NMI vectors. Save the program on tape if you do not have a copy at this time.

☐ Check to be sure the TVT switch is still in the 32 position. With SST OFF, hit reset. Then go to address 17A6. Run the program. Stop the program. The program should stop and light the display, with the display reading some address between 1780 and 17d3, or some address between 6000 and dFFF. Hit GO, then STOP alternately. The program should always return you to the keyboard and always be in the bounds of 1780-17d3 or 6000-dFFF. If your program will not do this, single step it until you find the problem. Note that you can shorten all the blank Scan trips by waiting until the second or third blanking Scan stops at 6000. Then you load a one in the X register by 00F5 01. Then you return to 6000 and continue single stepping as needed until the problem is solved.
DO NOT GO BEYOND THIS POINT UNTIL YOU GET PROPER PROGRAM OPERATION.

☐ Center with the V POS control. Now, using a triggered-sweep scope, look for a 1-millisecond pulse at test point DV in Fig. 4-3. The POSITION control should change the width of this pulse from 0.2 to 1.5 milliseconds or so. Recenter with the control.

☐ Now for a crucial test. With the program shown in Fig. 2-10 running and checking test point DV, switch your scope to LINE sync. This pulse should break loose and wander around VERY slowly. Set the time base of the scope so that a second pulse is seen only when the present pulse moves off one or the other end of the screen. It should take 40 seconds or more for a pulse to leave the screen. If you pass this test, your tvt is properly controlling your KIM and your Scan program is apparently working correctly, hitting a magic number for 60 Hz vertical.

☐ Center with the H POS control. Recenter the control. Check pin 10 of IC3 for a 63-μs rectangular pulse. The low time should be adjustable from 2 to 20 μs with the H POS control. Recenter with the control.

☐ Check for a composite sync signal 1 volt high at test point CV. The sync tips should go near ground. Check for a similar signal referenced to +4 volts at the tv output jack.

- [ ] Connect a monitor to the VID output or a properly converted tv set to the tv output. Reload and rerun the Scan program. You should get a clean and stable blank raster, locked both horizontally and vertically. Retouch the hold controls if needed. As a final check, misadjust the VERTICAL-HOLD control of the tv until you can briefly produce a stationary thin black bar in the middle of the raster.

- [ ] With or without any program running, check the LD test point of Fig. 4-3 with your scope. You should get a normally high waveform that goes low for 35 nanoseconds each microsecond. If you get something else, first check your 10:1 scope probe ground connection and calibration. This is the Load pulse for your video shift register and must be available and clean before you go on.

- [ ] With the sync of your scope locked on Load, check the waveform at CK. With the switch in the Fast position, you should be able to get eight, seven, or six clock pulses per load pulse as you vary the WIDTH control. These pulses should be adjustable for a stable, clean display. If you seem to have trouble getting eight clean pulses, reduce capacitor C14, perhaps by 200 pF. If you cannot get six clean pulses, increase C14 as needed, but not so much that you cannot get eight clean pulses as well. Normally, you should have more than enough range with the supplied capacitor to cover six, seven, and eight clock pulses.

- [ ] Now switch to Slow, and adjust your WIDTH control. You should get three or four clean pulses per load pulse. If you cannot get four pulses, reduce C13; if you cannot get three pulses increase C13; this should almost never be needed. Return to Fast and adjust the WIDTH control to seven clean clock pulses. Center the WIDTH control in the middle of the seven clock pulse stable area.

- [ ] Switch to CON and check test point CU of Fig. 4-3 for a 3-Hz square wave. This is your winking cursor oscillator.

- [ ] Use a wire to topside jumper pins 7 and 8 to 10 on the D/V converter socket IC7. Plug in IC4. Switch to "—." Reload and rerun the program from Fig. 2-10. You should get a display of thin vertical stripes. Adjust the CLARITY control. These stripes should get thinner or thicker. A complete dropout near one *extreme* end of the CLARITY control is normal. If you have no stripes, look for shift-register loading and clocking problems. If you cannot control the stripes, look for Clarity-Control circuit problems.

- [ ] Insert module "D" in slot IC7 after removing the jumpers. Be sure the notch lines up with pin 1 of the 2513 character generator. Reload and rerun the program from Fig. 2-10. Switches should be set at "32", "Fast", "+", and "Off". You should get a random character display. Adjust CONTRAST and BRIGHTNESS and your POSITION controls until you get a display with which you are completely happy. If slight sugar appears on the characters, adjust the WIDTH control as needed. Try other positions of the WIDTH control. Try various CLARITY control settings. The best usually just closes the display of a "M" or a "W". DO NOT GO ON UNTIL YOU HAVE A DISPLAY WITH WHICH YOU ARE COMPLETELY AND ABSOLUTELY HAPPY.
- [ ] Briefly switch to CON. Your screen should wildly wink several hundred cursor boxes at you. You get all those Cursors since you have a random character load. Any time VD7 is a one, a Cursor results. They will disappear when you write a proper Cursor program. Switch to OFF.
- [ ] Now load the following slots, starting with 0200:

```
0200  57 45 4C 43 4F 4d 45 20 54 4F 20 54 48 45 20 43
0210  48 45 41 50 20 56 49 44 45 4F 20 57 4F 52 4C 44
0220  20 20 20 20 20 20 20 20 20 20 20 20 20 20 20 20
0230  20 20 20 20 20 20 20 20 20 20 20 20 20 20 20 20
```

  Run the program shown in Fig. 2-10. You should have a secret message displayed on the top line, followed by a line of blanks. If you do not get a message, look for upstream tap problems or VD-line mixups or opens.
- [ ] Change to module "A," and rerun the Fig. 2-10 program and the test data of the previous step. You should get the same display as above. Now, go through the above program and every time you see a most significant "5", make it a 7. Every time you see a most significant "4", make it a 6. But leave 0200 at 57. Rerun the Fig. 2-10 program. Your message should be lower case, starting with a capital.
- [ ] This completes the alphanumeric portion of the checkout. Your interconnections, tvt card, and modules A and B are apparently working. From here, you should try your cursor programs and then go on to your final format.
- [ ] Insert module "B" and check for normal computer operation. Now load the program shown in Fig. 2-18 (256 × 256 graphics) and run it. Check first for run-stop normal operation in the bounds of the 1780 scratchpad and high addresses 6000-dFFF. Then check for a stationary DV signal on line sync. You should get a display of random dots. Switch to FAST and adjust the

WIDTH control to get eight dots per load. Change from + to − to invert the display. Use near-minimum CLARITY control values for − displays.

☐ Load the following data at locations as shown:
0200 00 00
0220 80 00
0240 40 00
0260 20 00
0280 10 00
02A0 08 00
02C0 04 00
02E0 02 00
0300 01 00
0320 00 00
You should get a display of eight slanting lines besides the random display you had before. The WIDTH control lets you pick six, seven, or eight dots per slant. Set it to eight stable dots with no sugar.

☐ The reason you get things repeated eight times over in the previous test is that your program wants 8K of memory and you are only giving it 1K, so it is repeating itself eight times. To properly use Module B, you will have to have at least 4K of useable RAM for a 128 × 256 display or 8K of RAM for a 256 × 256 display.

☐ If you have extended RAM in your KIM, check it out at this time, using the connector and changeover switch that goes to the upstream tap of the memory selected for display use. Remember to switch only *one* changeover switch to tvt operation at any time. If there are two switches (one on the bare KIM; one on the extension memory); make sure both of them are in the KIM position for normal computer use, and only one of them is in the tvt position for display use. The tvt must, of course, be plugged into the selected upstream tap.

☐ If you have at least 3K of RAM available starting at memory location 0400, load and run the "Special Fonts" test program of Chart 4-4. Note that this is a display memory *data* listing; you also still have to load and run the Scan program of Fig. 2-18 to get a display. The *data* decides what goes on the screen; the *Scan program* puts it there.

☐ Remove module B and insert module C. Load and run the program of Fig. 2-16. Have switches set to "Slow", "+", "Off", and "32". You should get a random display of somewhat coarser proportions than you did with the previous module.

Chart 4-4. Data for the "Special Fonts" Typography Display of Fig. 1-6

Use TVT 6⅝ and Module B — Format—40 × 256
Use Scan Program of Fig. 2-16 — Display Space—0600-0AFF

0600	00	00	00	0F	80	00	00	00	00	00	00	01	C0	00	00	1F
0610	80	00	00	00	7C	00	00	00	00	03	00	00	00	00	00	00
0620	00	00	00	1F	CC	00	00	00	00	00	00	01	C0	00	00	1F
0630	80	00	00	00	FE	00	00	00	00	03	00	00	00	00	00	00
0640	00	00	00	3F	EC	00	00	00	00	00	00	01	C0	00	00	1F
0650	80	00	00	00	FF	00	00	00	00	03	00	00	00	00	00	00
0660	00	00	00	7F	FC	00	00	00	00	00	00	01	C0	00	00	1F
0670	80	00	00	01	E3	00	00	00	00	03	00	00	00	00	00	00
0680	00	00	00	7F	FC	00	00	00	00	00	00	00	00	00	00	03
0690	80	00	00	01	C3	00	00	00	00	03	00	00	00	00	00	00
06A0	00	00	00	F8	FC	00	00	00	00	00	00	00	00	00	00	03
06b0	80	00	00	01	C0	00	00	00	00	03	00	00	00	00	00	00
06C0	00	00	00	F0	3C	00	00	00	00	00	00	00	00	00	00	03
06d0	80	00	00	01	C0	00	00	00	00	07	00	00	00	00	00	00
06E0	00	00	00	C0	0C	00	00	00	00	00	00	00	00	00	00	03
06F0	80	00	00	01	C0	00	00	00	00	07	00	00	00	00	00	00
0700	00	00	00	C0	0C	00	00	00	00	00	00	00	00	00	00	03
0710	80	00	00	01	C0	00	00	00	00	0F	00	00	00	00	00	00
0720	00	00	00	C0	0C	7E	38	00	78	00	78	0F	C0	0F	00	03
0730	80	00	00	0F	F8	0F	00	F0	C0	3F	E0	07	98	00	00	00
0740	00	00	00	E0	0C	7E	7C	00	FC	00	FC	0F	C0	1F	80	03
0750	80	00	00	0F	F8	1F	80	F3	E0	3F	E0	1F	d8	00	00	00
0760	00	00	00	70	0C	7E	FE	01	FE	01	FE	0F	C0	3F	E0	03
0770	80	00	00	0F	F8	3F	C0	F7	F0	3F	E0	3F	F8	00	00	00
0780	00	00	00	38	00	7E	FE	01	FE	01	FE	0F	C0	7F	E0	03
0790	80	00	00	0F	F8	3F	C0	F7	F0	3F	E0	7F	F8	00	00	00
07A0	00	00	00	1C	00	07	CF	03	CF	03	CF	01	C0	F8	F0	03
07b0	80	00	00	01	C0	79	E0	3E	78	07	00	7C	F8	00	00	00
07C0	00	00	00	07	00	07	87	03	87	03	87	01	C0	F0	70	03
07d0	80	00	00	01	C0	F0	E0	3C	38	07	00	78	38	00	00	00
07E0	00	00	00	03	80	07	03	87	03	87	03	81	C0	E0	30	30
07F0	80	00	00	01	C0	E0	70	38	1C	07	00	70	18	00	00	00
0800	00	00	00	00	E0	07	03	87	03	87	03	81	C0	00	30	03
0810	80	00	00	01	C0	E0	70	38	1C	07	00	30	18	00	00	00
0820	00	00	00	00	70	06	01	86	01	86	03	81	C0	00	30	03
0830	80	00	00	01	C0	C0	30	30	0C	07	00	3C	00	00	00	00
0840	00	00	00	00	38	06	01	86	01	86	00	01	C0	00	70	03
0850	80	00	00	01	C0	C0	30	30	0C	07	00	1E	00	00	00	00
0860	00	00	00	00	1C	06	01	87	FF	86	00	01	C0	01	F0	03
0870	80	00	00	01	C0	C0	30	30	0C	07	00	07	80	00	00	00
0880	00	00	00	00	1C	06	01	87	FF	86	00	01	C0	07	b0	03
0890	80	00	00	01	C0	C0	30	30	0C	07	00	01	E0	00	00	00
08A0	00	00	00	C0	0E	06	01	86	00	06	00	01	C0	1E	30	03
08b0	80	00	00	01	C0	C0	30	30	0C	07	00	00	70	00	00	00

```
08C0  00 00 00 E0 06 06 01 86 00 06 00 01 C0 38 30 03
08d0  80 00 00 01 C0 C0 30 30 0C 07 00 00 38 00 00 00
08E0  00 00 00 F0 06 06 01 86 03 86 03 81 C0 70 30 03
08F0  80 00 00 01 C0 C0 30 30 0C 07 00 60 1C 00 00 00

0900  00 00 00 F0 06 07 03 87 03 87 03 81 C0 E0 30 03
0910  80 00 00 01 C0 E0 70 30 0C 07 0C 60 1C 00 00 00
0920  00 00 00 F8 0E 07 03 87 03 87 03 81 C0 E0 73 03
0930  80 00 00 01 C0 E0 70 30 0C 07 0C 70 1C 00 00 00

0940  00 00 00 FC 1E 07 87 03 87 03 87 01 C0 E0 73 03
0950  80 00 00 01 C0 70 E0 30 0C 07 0C 78 3C 00 00 00
0960  00 00 00 FF FE 07 CF 03 CF 03 CF 01 C0 F0 db 03
0970  80 00 00 01 C0 79 E0 30 0C 07 9C 7C 7C 00 00 00

0980  00 00 00 FF FC 06 FE 01 FE 01 FE 0F F8 FF dF 1F
0990  F0 00 00 0F F8 3F C0 FC 3F 07 FC 7F F8 00 00 00
09A0  00 00 00 dF FC 06 FE 01 FE 01 FE 0F F8 7F 9F 1F
09b0  F0 00 00 0F F8 3F C0 FC 3F 03 F8 6F F8 00 00 00

09C0  00 00 00 CF F8 06 7C 00 FC 00 FC 0F F8 3F 0E 1F
09d0  F0 00 00 0F F8 1F 80 FC 3F 03 F0 67 F0 00 00 00
09E0  00 00 00 C7 E0 06 38 00 78 00 78 0F F8 1F 06 1F
09F0  F0 00 00 0F F8 0F 00 FC 3F 01 E0 63 C0 00 00 00

0A00  00 00 00 00 00 06 00 00 00 00 00 00 00 00 00 00
0A10  00 00 00 00 00 00 00 00 00 00 00 00 00 00 00 00
0A20  00 00 00 00 00 06 00 00 00 00 00 00 00 00 00 00
0A30  00 00 00 00 00 00 00 00 00 00 00 00 00 00 00 00

0A40  00 00 00 00 00 06 00 00 00 00 00 00 00 00 00 00
0A50  00 00 00 00 00 00 00 00 00 00 00 00 00 00 00 00
0A60  00 00 00 00 00 06 00 00 00 00 00 00 00 00 00 00
0A70  00 00 00 00 00 00 00 00 00 00 00 00 00 00 00 00

0A80  00 00 00 00 00 7F C0 00 00 00 00 00 00 00 00 00
0A90  00 00 00 00 00 00 00 00 00 00 00 00 00 00 00 00
0AA0  00 00 00 00 00 7F C0 00 00 00 00 00 00 00 00 00
0Ab0  00 00 00 00 00 00 00 00 00 00 00 00 00 00 00 00

0AC0  00 00 00 00 00 7F C0 00 00 00 00 00 00 00 00 00
0Ad0  00 00 00 00 00 00 00 00 00 00 00 00 00 00 00 00
0AE0  00 00 00 00 00 7F C0 00 00 00 00 00 00 00 00 00
0AF0  00 00 00 00 00 00 00 00 00 00 00 00 00 00 00 00
```

☐ Load the following data (this assumes you are back on a bare KIM; if not, find a suitable starting address)

0200 77 00 77 77 07 70 77 77 00

You should get a batch of bars that repeats twice in your display. The proper color setting is to set your WIDTH control so that you get a short "equals" followed by a long equals that extends *continuously* on the right end.

After this equals ends, a new "upside down" one should start. This gives you three clocks per chunk. Reset your WIDTH control so that stable black bars appear, and you are ready to run on 128 × 128 black-and-white graphics.

☐ If you have extended memory available, at least 2K starting at location 0600, load and run the color chessboard of Chart 4-5. You will have to use a color modulator for a full-color display. Once again, Chart 4-5 is *data*. You have to run the Scan *program* of Fig. 2-16 with it to get a display.

Chart 4-5. Data for the Chessboard Background of Fig. 1-5

Use TVT 6⅝ and Module C — Format: 96 × 96 color
Use Scan Program of Fig. 2-18 — Display Space: 0600- 0bFF
Board is programmed to color "00"

0600	76	70	70	73	00	00	00	00	76	70	70	73	00	00	00	00
0610	76	70	70	73	00	00	00	00	76	70	70	73	00	00	00	00
0620	44	00	00	11	00	00	00	00	44	00	00	11	00	00	00	00
0630	44	00	00	11	00	00	00	00	44	00	00	11	00	00	00	00
0640	44	00	00	11	00	00	00	00	44	00	00	11	00	00	00	00
0650	44	00	00	11	00	00	00	00	44	00	00	11	00	00	00	00
0660	44	00	00	11	00	00	00	00	44	00	00	11	00	00	00	00
0670	44	00	00	11	00	00	00	00	44	00	00	11	00	00	00	00
0680	44	00	00	11	00	00	00	00	44	00	00	11	00	00	00	00
0690	44	00	00	11	00	00	00	00	44	00	00	11	00	00	00	00
06A0	67	07	07	37	00	00	00	00	67	07	07	37	00	00	00	00
06b0	67	07	07	37	00	00	00	00	67	07	07	37	00	00	00	00
06C0	00	00	00	00	76	70	70	73	00	00	00	00	76	70	70	73
06d0	00	00	00	00	76	70	70	73	00	00	00	00	76	70	70	73
06E0	00	00	00	00	44	00	00	11	00	00	00	00	44	00	00	11
06F0	00	00	00	00	44	00	00	11	00	00	00	00	44	00	00	11
0700	00	00	00	00	44	00	00	11	00	00	00	00	44	00	00	11
0710	00	00	00	00	44	00	00	11	00	00	00	00	44	00	00	11
0720	00	00	00	00	44	00	00	11	00	00	00	00	44	00	00	11
0730	00	00	00	00	44	00	00	11	00	00	00	00	44	00	00	11
0740	00	00	00	00	44	00	00	11	00	00	00	00	44	00	00	11
0750	00	00	00	00	44	00	00	11	00	00	00	00	44	00	00	11
0760	00	00	00	00	67	07	07	37	00	00	00	00	67	07	07	37
0770	00	00	00	00	67	07	07	37	00	00	00	00	67	07	07	37

0780-08FF Repeat above code
0900-0A7F Repeat above code
0A80-0bFF Repeat above code

☐ Add chessmen to your display as desired by hand loading as shown in Fig. 4-14 and Chart 4-6. You will eventually want to write a software loader to do this for you.

☐ This completes the preliminary checkout of your TVT 6⅝ and the four available modules.

Number your chessboard this way:

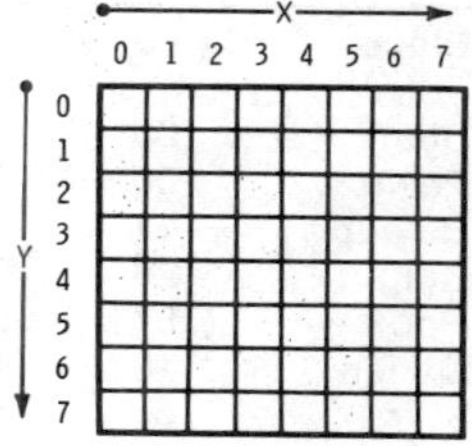

Let X be the number of squares right from upper left. (0-7)

Let Y be the number of squares down from upper left. (0-7)

Let S be the starting address needed to load a chess piece.

If your display memory starts at 6000, your S will equal

S = 0621 + (4 * X) + (CO * Y)

in HEXADECIMAL. For instance, the third square to the right has an X value of "2." The fifth square down has a Y value of "4." To find S, we take 0621 and add 4 to it twice and add C0 to it four times, or

S = 0621 + (4 * 2) + (CO * 4) = 0929

Your chess piece consists of eight memory words. These words go in a 2 × 4 chunk matrix that calls 48 dots, resulting in a 6 × 8 symbol. If S is your starting address, the symbol chunk locations are:

S	S + 1
S + 20	S + 21
S + 40	S + 41
S + 60	S + 61

with each chunk arranged as

VD6	VD5	VD4
VD2	VD1	VD0

Color is set by VD7 (most significant bit) and VD3 (least significant bit) for a choice of four colors plus black.

Fig. 4-14. Calling chess pieces from a file.

MODIFICATIONS

Usually, you will change software to get your TVT 6⅝ to do different things. You also have quite a few hardware options. Many of these options are listed in Chart 4-7. The next chapter details the most important option of full transparency.

Your SLOW-FAST switch and the WIDTH control are normally set visually for the right number of clocks per microsecond. Seven or eight clocks are usually best for combined upper- and lower-case (Module B) alphanumerics, while six or seven will look best with upper-case–only (Module D) displays. For graphics displays, the clock must, of course, be properly set to the selected 3, 4, or 8

Chart 4-6. Data for Chess Piece File

Piece	S+00	S+01	S+20	S+21	S+40	S+41	S+60	S+61
Blank	00	00	00	00	00	00	00	00
Pawn	00	00	11	44	13	46	76	73
Bishop	11	44	77	77	11	44	17	47
Knight	26	00	23	07	32	62	27	27
Rook	57	57	33	66	33	66	37	67
Queen	13	46	75	75	74	71	76	73
King	57	57	75	75	67	37	73	76

For color 00, add nothing to above
For color 01, add 08 to above
For color 10, add 80 to above
For color 11, add 88 to above

Chart 4-7. Some Hardware Use Options for Your TVT 6 5/8

Blanking—You blank the display by making the BNK input positive. For a normal display, ground BNK. Blanking is useful for improving transparency or any other time you want the display off.

Horizontal Fill In—Your horizontal-sync timing pulses can come from another source by breaking the DEN to HIN connector jumper and routing new horizontal-sync pulses to HIN. Position delay starts from the + *to ground* transition of a signal input to HIN. This is useful for fully transparent operation when horizontal-sync pulses are supplied from somewhere else during vertical blanking times.

Vertical Lock—The VRF pin outputs a 1-μs pulse at the undelayed start of each frame. This signal is useful for line-locking system timing and for delaying character entry until the start of the blank vertical time.

Video Polarity—Video polarity is selected with the +, — switch. The CLARITY control only works in the + position and should be set to its near minimum value if you are running with inverted video. (See Fig. 4-17).

Scan Enable—Breaking the SEO to SEI line disables any scanning. To prevent scanning, keep SEI high. This is useful as a tvt enable means.

External CS Gating—The display memory CS gating can be moved out of the instruction PROM. To do this using an instruction PROM having internal CS gating, connect CSI to +5V and relable CSO to CSOT, the Chip Select output *from* your tvt. CSOT goes low when the tvt wants use of the upstream tap.

Dual Mode—You can run graphics and alphanumerics on alternate fields by combining modules into one super module. Your field changeover can be done with a flip-flop that is clocked with the VRF signal. To initialize your flip-flop, note that CG Row 1 high output is never used in the *graphics* mode. If this coincidence occurs, reset the flip-flop to the alphanumeric state.

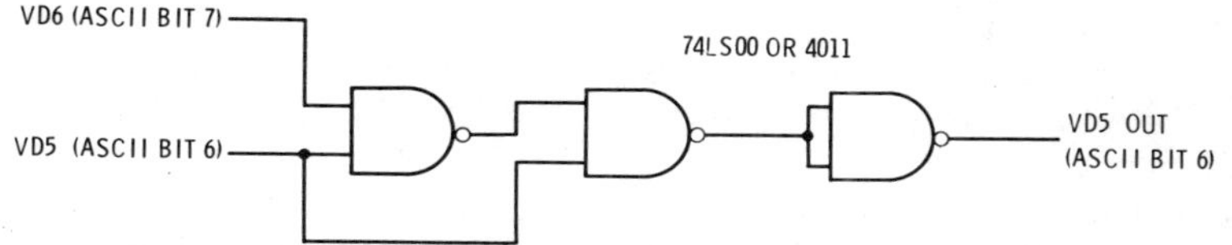

Fig. 4-15. Logical gating needed to display combined upper- and lower-case characters as upper case only.

clocks per chunk selected. Otherwise part of your display will be missing or may have "bulldozer tracks" running through it. If there is any sugar or other display instability, readjust your WIDTH control and set it to the middle of the stable area.

Your "32-64" switch is set in the "32" position for most graphics and 32-character lines. Set it to the "64" position for practically anything else.

Your winking Cursor rate is set by R9 and C7. Increasing either of these will lower the wink frequency and vice versa.

A 74LS165 shift register can be used instead of the 74165 to de-

The inputs to your SCAN PROM are labeled A1, A2, A3, A4, and A5. These are the connections you use on a nonrepacked 6502 cheap video system. *Address connections may change for other uses.* Here are three typical examples:

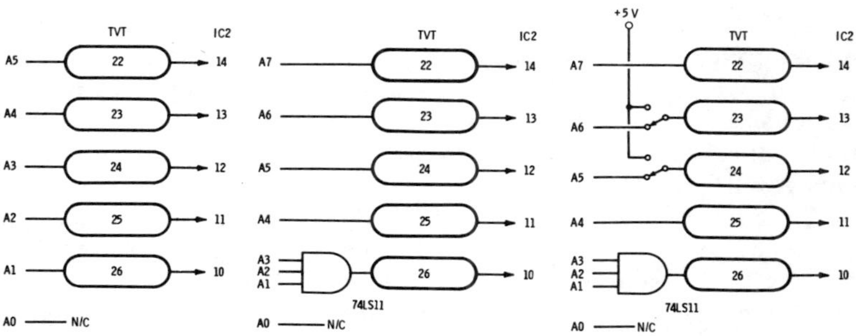

(a) 6500, 6800 no repacking

(b) 6500, 6800 repacked

(c) 6500, 6800 either way

Connection (c) is often the best choice, but needs a gate plus two switches and it is limited to multiples of *eight* characters or chunks per line.

Fig. 4-16. Scan PROM address options.

crease the supply current, but you may need five to eight 4.7-K pullup resistors on the inputs for proper Cursor operation.

Note that we have two different places to blank our display. The blanking on modules B and C is synchronous with the characters and blanks whole characters or chunks. Since the video shift register takes 1 μs to output a character or chunk *after* it is received, there is a 1-μs *blanking skew* difference between blanking at Module B or C and blanking on the BNK input. Use the BNK input for general-purpose "paint the display black" uses; use module blanking to blank specific whole characters.

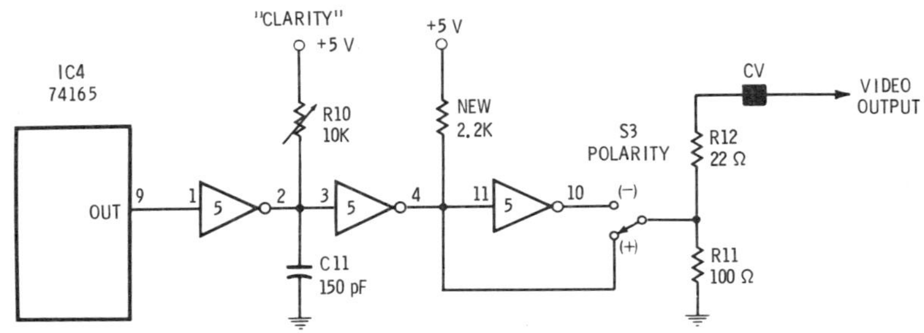

Fig. 4-17. Alternate clarity circuit works on normal or inverted video.

If you attempt to use an upper-case–only character generator on mixed upper- and lower-case data, all the lower-case characters will be read wrong. Normally, you should match the input coding with the character generator in use. Fig. 4-15 shows you simple gating that will convert upper- and lower-case ASCII code into upper-case–only ASCII code.

The address inputs to your Scan PROM change as you change to memory repacking or switch to a different computer system. These options are shown in Fig. 4-16. *Be sure that your Scan PROM, your intended mode of operation, and your computer connections are compatible.*

The original CLARITY control used for video-bandwidth enhancement only works with normal "+" (white characters on a black screen) video. Fig. 4-17 shows an alternate circuit that works with either normal or inverted "−" (black characters on a white screen) video. Inverted operation is a handy way to totally eliminate any flicker on double-stuffed displays. The one extra gate needed for this modification is borrowed from the blanking circuit. Blanking is either lost or picked up with a new gate or an added npn transistor.

Some typical waveforms for the 16 × 32 interlaced display are shown in Fig. 4-18. The waveforms are present only when the Scan program is working properly, so they are not too useful as a debugging tool. These waveforms will change wildly as you change Scan software and will disappear entirely during nonscan times.

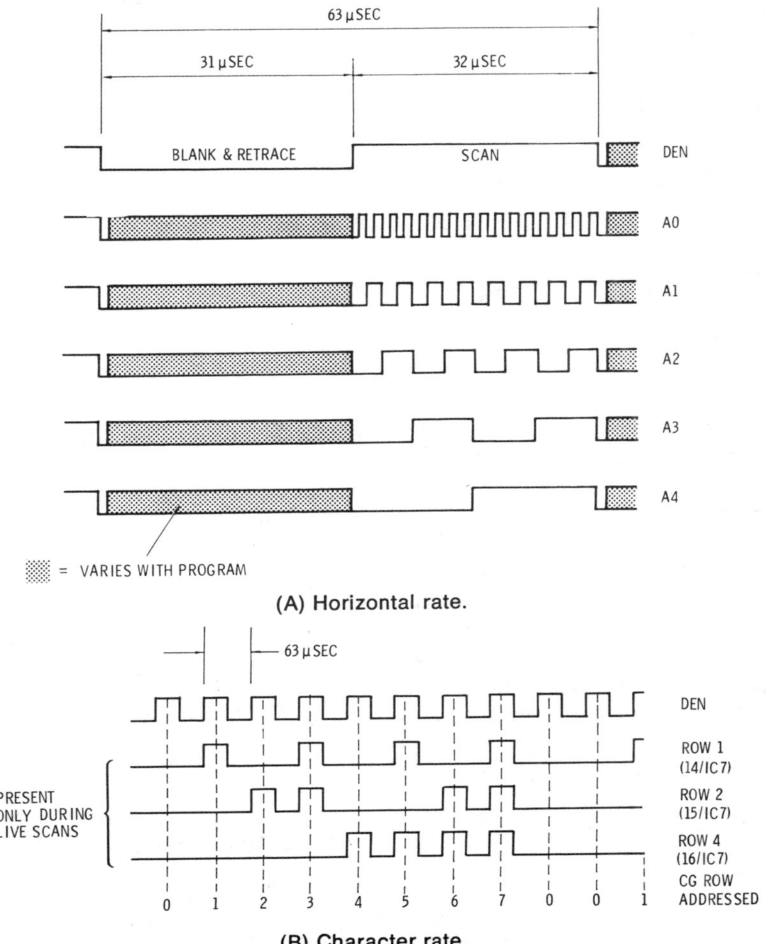

(A) Horizontal rate.

(B) Character rate.

Fig. 4-18. 16 × 32 Scan waveforms.

CHAPTER **5**

Transparency

If you have a *transparent* cheap video display system, you can let the microprocessor do other things at the same time you are displaying, or at least seem to do so. Transparency looks good, but more importantly, it lets you run a BASIC program and a continuous display together, or a graphics game display and its move calculations at the same time. To a transparent display, other computer goings-on will be invisible, without any breaks or tearing in the picture.

Transparency is obviously going to be tricky, since the tv seems to need continuous sync and video signals. So far, our cheap video circuits have apparently needed 100% of the available computer time during a display. We might suspect that the "more" we want in the way of transparency, the more it is going to cost us in circuitry, software, throughput, and design time.

SOME TRANSPARENCY PRINCIPLES

Most digital instruments only light a single display numeral at any particular time. This is called *multiplexing*. It is done to simplify circuitry and cut down on the number of display leads. Only one numeral is lit at a time, but the numerals are scanned in sequence faster than the eye can follow. You end up with the *illusion* of a continuous display. If we demanded a "perfect" display that was lit all the time, it would cost a lot more—and nobody would be able to tell the difference anyway.

The same concept goes for video displays. Namely, *we do not need true transparency. Anything that gives us an acceptable illusion of transparency will do the job for us.* This idea tells us to do other things while the screen is black. A particularly handy time is the long vertical-blanking interval.

A second transparency principle tells us that *seldom happening events are not nearly as bad as those that happen often.* So, if we make the more glaringly obvious computer goings-on transparent, we can probably ignore many of the rest and nobody will notice.

A third handle on transparency tells us to *watch just how we hurt the display.* Interruptions that disrupt the vertical timing so badly that the tv has to relock its vertical hold will be the worst of all to live with. Interruptions that last exactly one or two horizontal lines or exactly a full field usually will not be as bad. Recovery from a horizontal error takes a small fraction of a millisecond. This may look bad, but it turns out to be easy to fix. On the other hand, recovery from a vertical-sync error can take a tenth of a second or more, and *always* will look far worse and be much more difficult to fix. Thus, you have to be far more careful with longer interruptions to your SCAN programs. A vertical-sync pulse that is late (and stays late) by half a horizontal line will not be noticeable. One that misses by a line will appear as a slight bump, and anything more will be painfully obvious.

A fourth clue to transparency tells us to *lock any interruptions to the display scanning.* You can do this simply by *delaying* the interruption until convenient, or by *integrating* the interruption. Integration is done by including what used to be an interruption activity as part of the Scan program.

Principle number five tells us to "*paint it black.*" Anything that completely *blanks* the screen is far less bad than interruptions that tear up the screen. It is much easier to spot something lit and out of place than just temporarily missing.

These simple rules are all we need for the usual service type programs—those that enter characters, handle the Cursor, Scan a companion keyboard, and so forth. But if we are going to run something heavy at the same time—like a BASIC program, or the move computations for a game display— we may have to get both sneakier and fancier in what we do in the way of transparency.

So, rule number six tells us to *fill in sync signals from somewhere else when the computer is busy.* Somewhere else could be a simple binary counter, a programmable divider, a software-controlled timer, a line-locked phase-lock loop, or a television vertical chip.

And, our final transparency rule is the sledgehammer concept. *If all else fails, throw in another microprocessor chip.* They are cheap, simple, and easy to use these days.

Let's see just how these transparency ideas can be applied to systems that work. We will look at several routes to transparency more or less in an order of increasing hassle.

IGNORE IT

In most real-world micro uses, display tearing and interruption sounds *much* worse than it really turns out to be. This is especially true if the display is for your personal use or if very low display cost and complexity is important to you.

This "let her rip" philosophy also gives you a free "the computer is busy" signal that tells you what your other programs happen to be up to.

So, simplest of all is to *forget completely about transparency until you are absolutely sure you need it.* A good rule is to develop your display first without anything special in the way of transparency, and then include the absolute minimum in the way of additions to get something with which you or your users are happy.

Almost always, your final result can be far simpler than you may first think possible. Always try alternating your compute and display modes (just like the KIM-1 now does with its operating system) first; perhaps that is all you will need.

TIME IT

If you make a short interruption exactly equal the number of microseconds in one or two horizontal lines, there will be a minimum screen disturbance. This can be more than enough time to enter several characters, scan a keyboard, move a Cursor, change a game

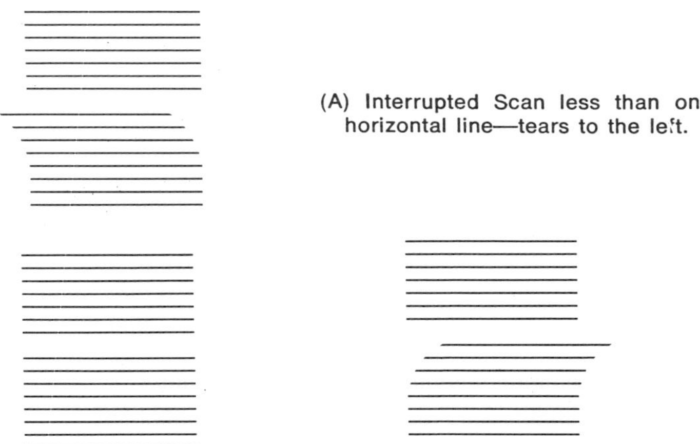

(A) Interrupted Scan less than one horizontal line—tears to the left.

(B) Interrupted Scan equals one horizontal line—slight vertical "bump."

(C) Interrupted Scan more than one horizontal line—tears to the right.

Fig. 5-1. Scan interruptions of exactly one horizontal line have almost no effect on display.

symbol, or do other relatively simple things. By taking exactly one or two horizontal lines, there will be no horizontal tearing and only a very slight vertical jog will result.

Fig. 5-1 shows the effect of three short interruptions. In Fig. 5-1A, our interruption takes less than one horizontal line and tears to the left. In Fig. 5-1B, we take exactly one horizontal line and get no tearing. In Fig. 5-1C, we have overdone things and taken longer than a single horizontal line, which tears to the right.

The closer you get to exactly one line, the smaller the amount of tearing. If you try to match three or more horizontal lines, the amount of vertical jog gets too high.

Longer interruptions will give you more objectionable screen motions. If you can make your program interruption last exactly one field, you can eliminate vertical tearing, but some time will be needed to regain horizontal lock. Scrolling programs, screen reads, and erase to end of screen lend themselves to exactly one field time.

LOCK IT

An exactly timed interruption can be much further improved by synchronizing it so that it starts at some convenient point in the Scan. If you start a one line horizontal interruption during the horizontal retrace time, you will get a whole line dropped out, rather than a random pair of lines that start and stop during a live Scan.

The best time to start an interruption is on the undelayed vertical-sync command. This causes most of the interruption and much of the recovery time to happen while the screen is blank.

Locking an interruption is a powerful and simple way to gain transparency. Its basic limitations are that you have to add an external flip-flop, and that you are limited to 60 interrupts per second maximum. Note that this is much faster than you can type, and that one interruption can be used to add or remove several characters.

Figure 5-2 shows how to lock an interrupt from a keyboard to a TVT 6⅝ working with a KIM-1. The keypressed pulse sets the flip-flop, which is reset by the undelayed vertical-sync pulse from the instruction decoder. The falling edge of the flip-flop is used to interrupt the Scan program. Interruption always takes place immediately after the undelayed vertical-sync pulse, during the black retrace time of the screen.

LOCK IT AND SHORTEN THE NEXT FIELD

Once we have locked our interruption to the vertical sync, there is an even neater trick we can pull to gain more transparency. And, all it costs are two software words.

These two words are DEX. If you know your interruption is going to take approximately two horizontal lines, you simply knock two lines off the total number of blank Scan lines to be used this time around during retrace. This either eliminates the vertical bump completely or else makes it so small you will not notice it.

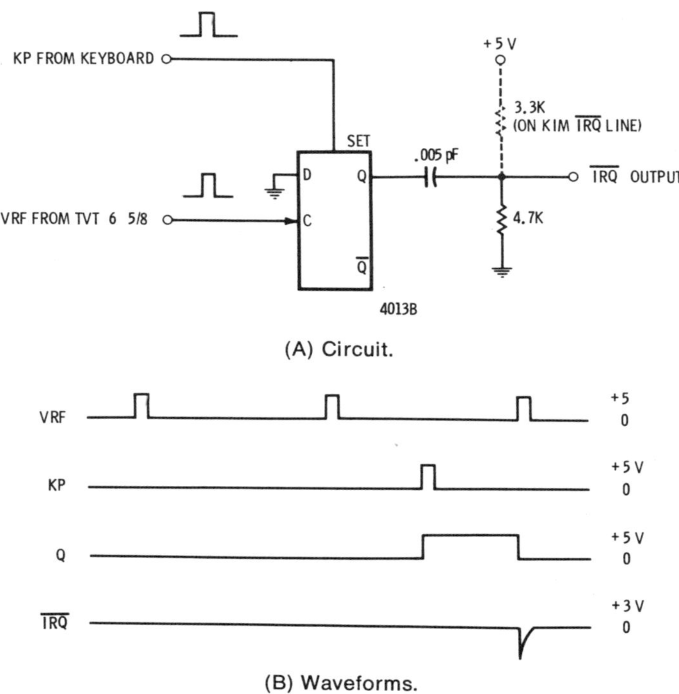

(A) Circuit.

(B) Waveforms.

Fig. 5-2. Delaying character entry or other interrupts until start of vertical blanking time greatly helps transparency.

Our scrolling Cursor program of Fig. 2-20 already has this "knock two lines off" capability built into it in the pair of DEX commands at steps 014C and 014d. If an interruption does NOT take place, the normal number of vertical blank Scans are used. If an interruption does take place, the interruption is delayed until the vertical-blanking time, after the number of Scans needed has been loaded into the X register. Most of the Cursor program interruptions take up approximately two horizontal lines. These two extra lines are removed from the upcoming blank Scans by decrementing the X register twice.

For this technique to work, your interrupt MUST be synchronized to the vertical-sync pulse of the interface hardware. Your Scan program also must load the number of retrace lines to be used BEFORE the vertical-sync command.

To recap how retrace shortening works, when there is no interrupt, the normal number of vertical-blank Scans is used. When there is a character-entry interrupt, the interrupt time takes about two horizontal Scans and then knocks off two horizontal Scans from the Scan program, making things come out even.

If you want to go to the trouble, you can make everything come out *exactly* even for each and every Cursor motion. One way to do this is to equalize each route through your Cursor program so that it takes identical time to execute. A much simpler approach would have you start a software timer and measure how long the interruption took; your main Scan length would then be corrected with some DEX commands and a short blank subroutine. But all this hassle is rarely needed. If you get a perfect match on the most common loop through the Cursor program (single character entry), most everything else is close enough that you will never notice.

PAINT IT BLACK

A screen that goes totally blank for a brief time is not nearly as bad as one that tears. It is much easier to spot something that is bright and obviously wrong, however brief, than something that

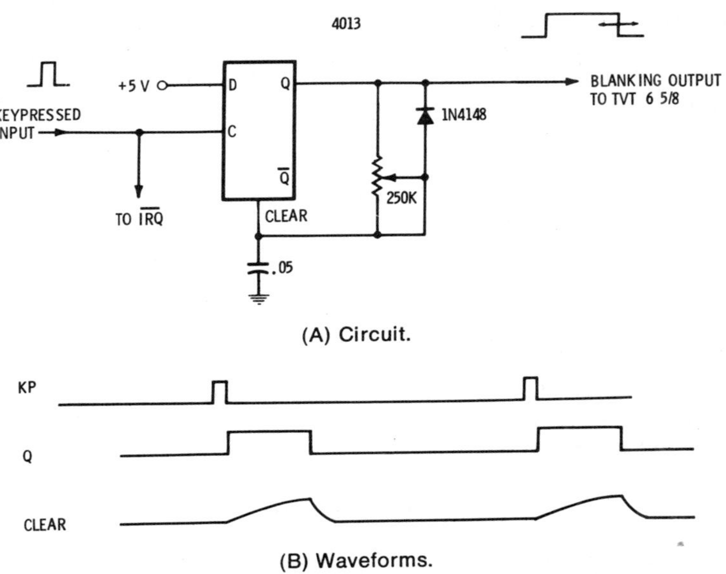

(A) Circuit.

(B) Waveforms.

Fig. 5-3. Blanking display after interruption also helps transparency.

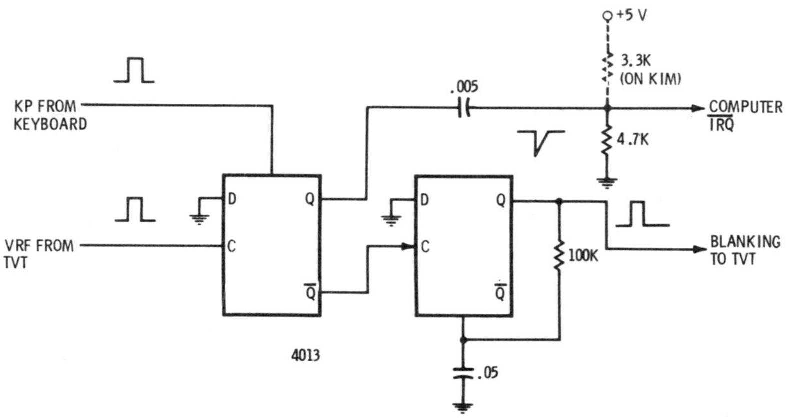

Fig. 5-4. Combined blanking and delay circuit.

is black and just not there. Blanking can also be used to make all disturbances identical so that they look like they belong.

The TVT 6⅝ has a blanking input, pin 2 BNK. This input is normally grounded. If you make it positive, the screen goes black for the length of time the BNK input is high.

A simple blanking generator is shown in Fig. 5-3. This uses a CMOS Type D flip-flop as a triggerable monostable component. The blank time is adjustable. Blanking times of a few character rows are almost invisible and eliminate most, if not all, horizontal tearing.

Blanking, locking, and shortening are easily combined as shown in Fig. 5-4. This circuit uses both halves of a 4013 CMOS Type D flip-flop and needs the two extra code words in your Cursor program—not a bad price to pay to gain nearly complete transparency of an interrupting Cursor program.

This particular circuit fixes the entire Cursor except for three long-time operations—Erase, Erase to End of Screen, and Scroll up. Erase is free—it quickly removes characters from the screen, tearing up a blank or nearly blank display, so it presents no problem. Erase to End of Screen creates more of a disturbance, but it also gives us some blanking and is rare enough that you don't have to worry about it. The Scrolling Cursor is more of a problem. We will note in passing that the Cursor tearing during a scroll can be dramatically improved by making the Cursor scroll take exactly one vertical interval.

INTEGRATE IT

In an *integrated* Scan program, you build everything else you want to do with your computer *into* the Scan program. You do the other things during your vertical-retrace time. Since everything else gets done during blank time and since there can be continuous timing without interruption, you can end up with a totally transparent display.

An integrated program works well for things like cursors and editors, as well as scanning and debouncing a companion ASCII keyboard. Some motions for simpler game graphics are also possible. It also frees the computer interrupt structure for other uses.

There are several hassles involved. Your Scan program will be longer and more complex. Your programs will be harder to change. Design and debug also will take longer. The other things the computer is to do must be stuffed into a few milliseconds reoccurring 60 times a second. Integrated programs are totally unsuited for games with complex graphics or where you are running a display and BASIC or another higher-level language together.

Just combining everything into one program does not guarantee transparency. You have to make the tv timing continuous, at least for the more often used program functions.

There are two ways to make sure your timing is continuous for transparency. One is to make certain each and every major path through the "something else" software takes exactly the same time. Another route is to start a software timer and measure how long the "something else" routine took. After measuring the time, you can then equalize the remaining Scan program by shortening one blank Scan and lopping off as many others as you have to.

The each-and-every path is usable for simple Cursors and keyboard Scans, but you will want the timer route anytime you need a full performance Cursor or run any other program that has several different or variable execution times.

As an example of an integrated program, let's build a simple 16 × 32 interlaced alphanumeric display that has a built-in transparent Cursor that allows us to sequentially enter characters, carriage return, or screen erase. We will use the each-and-every method for transparency since there are only four routes through the Cursor program. These routes are do nothing, enter, return, and clear.

Since we are no longer interrupt driven, we cannot use the interrupt line for a keypressed indication. Instead, we use the dual flip-flop circuit of Fig. 5-5. An external keypressed command toggles the first flip-flop. Every time a field is complete, an "entry test" pulse transfers the contents of the first flip-flop onto the second. The first flip-flop is also set at the same time. Our second flip-flop in turn holds and passes on a "0" to parallel input PA7 if a character is to be entered and a "1" if no character is to be entered.

Besides freeing the interrupt structure for other uses, this two flip-flop synchronizer gives us a full handshaking interface that minimizes any of the times when a character could be ignored or double entered.

Our integrated program is shown in Fig. 5-6. To keep things simple, we have kept the program in two pieces. The Scan part of our program is our old program of Fig. 2-10, the 16 × 32 utility interlaced Scan. This program is patched in two places, as shown, to jump to the Curse part of the program shortly after the start of the vertical-blanking interval.

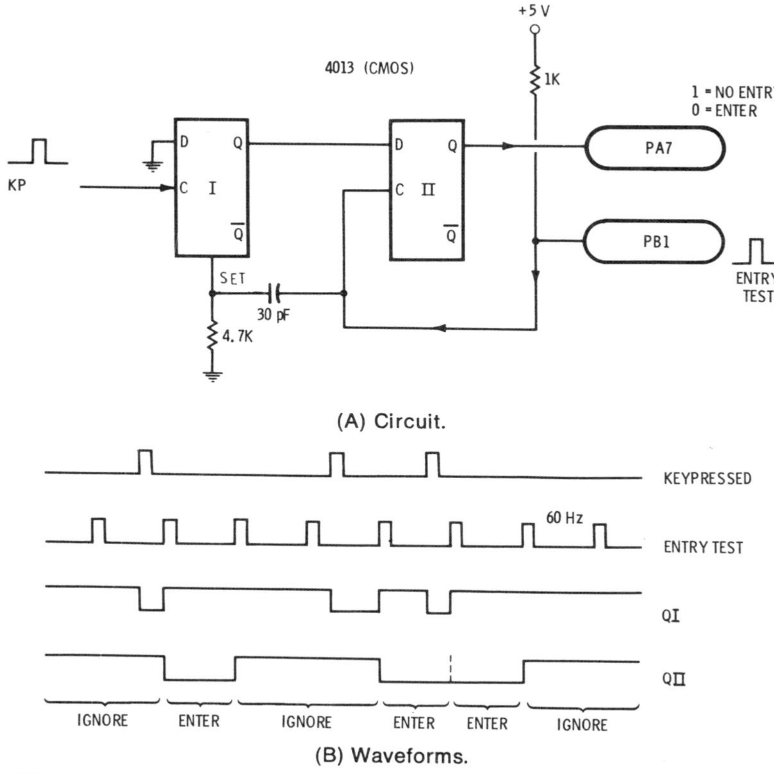

(A) Circuit.

(B) Waveforms.

Fig. 5-5. Keypressed handshaking interface for integrated Scan programs.

Shortly after the vertical-blanking time starts, our Curse program starting at 0100 outputs a pulse to our handshaking flip-flops to test if a new key has been pressed. The program then tests for the four possible conditions of do nothing, enter, return, and clear. The do-nothing is based on a most significant parallel input bit (A7) of "1," and returns us directly to the Scan program, taking up just enough time to properly space the horizontal-sync times.

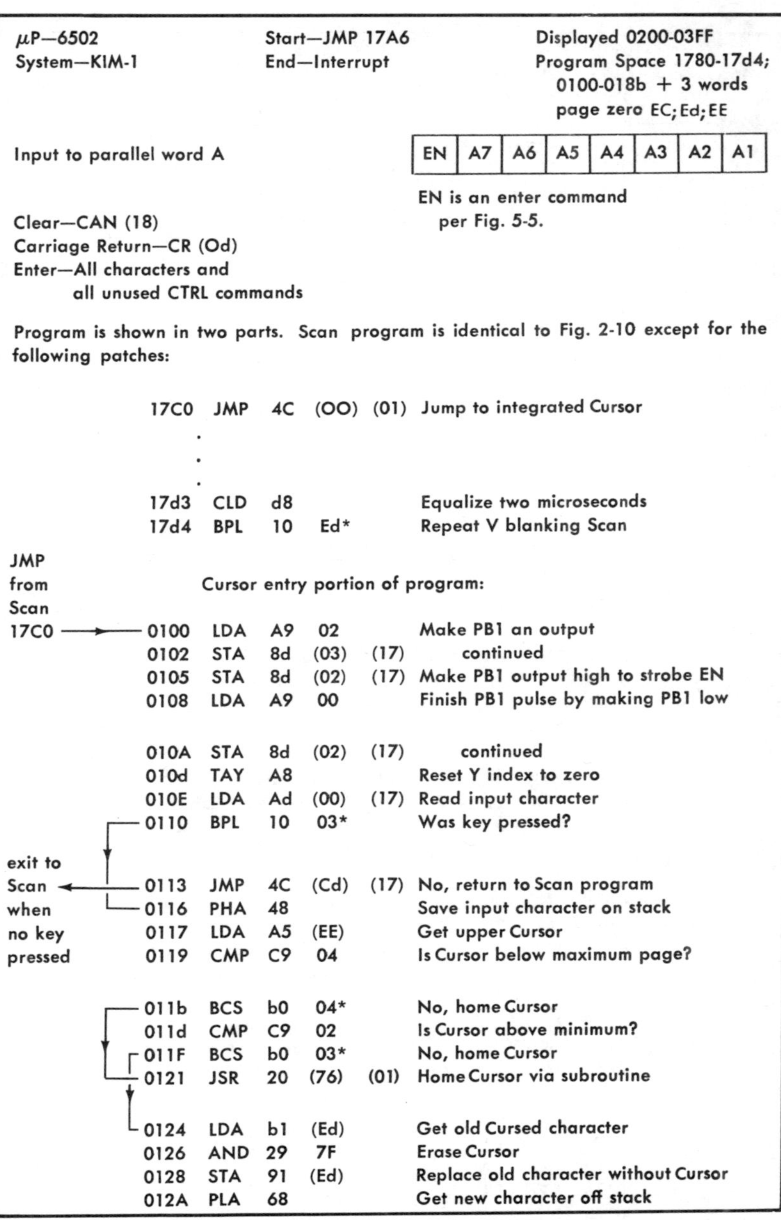

μP—6502
System—KIM-1

Start—JMP 17A6
End—Interrupt

Displayed 0200-03FF
Program Space 1780-17d4;
0100-018b + 3 words
page zero EC; Ed; EE

Input to parallel word A

EN	A7	A6	A5	A4	A3	A2	A1

EN is an enter command per Fig. 5-5.

Clear—CAN (18)
Carriage Return—CR (Od)
Enter—All characters and all unused CTRL commands

Program is shown in two parts. Scan program is identical to Fig. 2-10 except for the following patches:

```
17C0  JMP  4C  (OO)  (01)  Jump to integrated Cursor
        .
        .
        .
17d3  CLD  d8              Equalize two microseconds
17d4  BPL  10  Ed*         Repeat V blanking Scan
```

JMP from Scan 17C0 → Cursor entry portion of program:

```
0100  LDA  A9  02          Make PB1 an output
0102  STA  8d  (03)  (17)      continued
0105  STA  8d  (02)  (17)  Make PB1 output high to strobe EN
0108  LDA  A9  00          Finish PB1 pulse by making PB1 low

010A  STA  8d  (02)  (17)      continued
010d  TAY  A8              Reset Y index to zero
010E  LDA  Ad  (00)  (17)  Read input character
0110  BPL  10  03*         Was key pressed?

0113  JMP  4C  (Cd)  (17)  No, return to Scan program
0116  PHA  48              Save input character on stack
0117  LDA  A5  (EE)        Get upper Cursor
0119  CMP  C9  04          Is Cursor below maximum page?

011b  BCS  b0  04*         No, home Cursor
011d  CMP  C9  02          Is Cursor above minimum?
011F  BCS  b0  03*         No, home Cursor
0121  JSR  20  (76)  (01)  Home Cursor via subroutine

0124  LDA  b1  (Ed)        Get old Cursed character
0126  AND  29  7F          Erase Cursor
0128  STA  91  (Ed)        Replace old character without Cursor
012A  PLA  68              Get new character off stack
```

(exit to Scan when no key pressed ← 0113)

Fig. 5-6. Program for 16-line, 32 character per line, interlaced TVT 6 5/8 Raster Scan with integrated minimum Cursor.

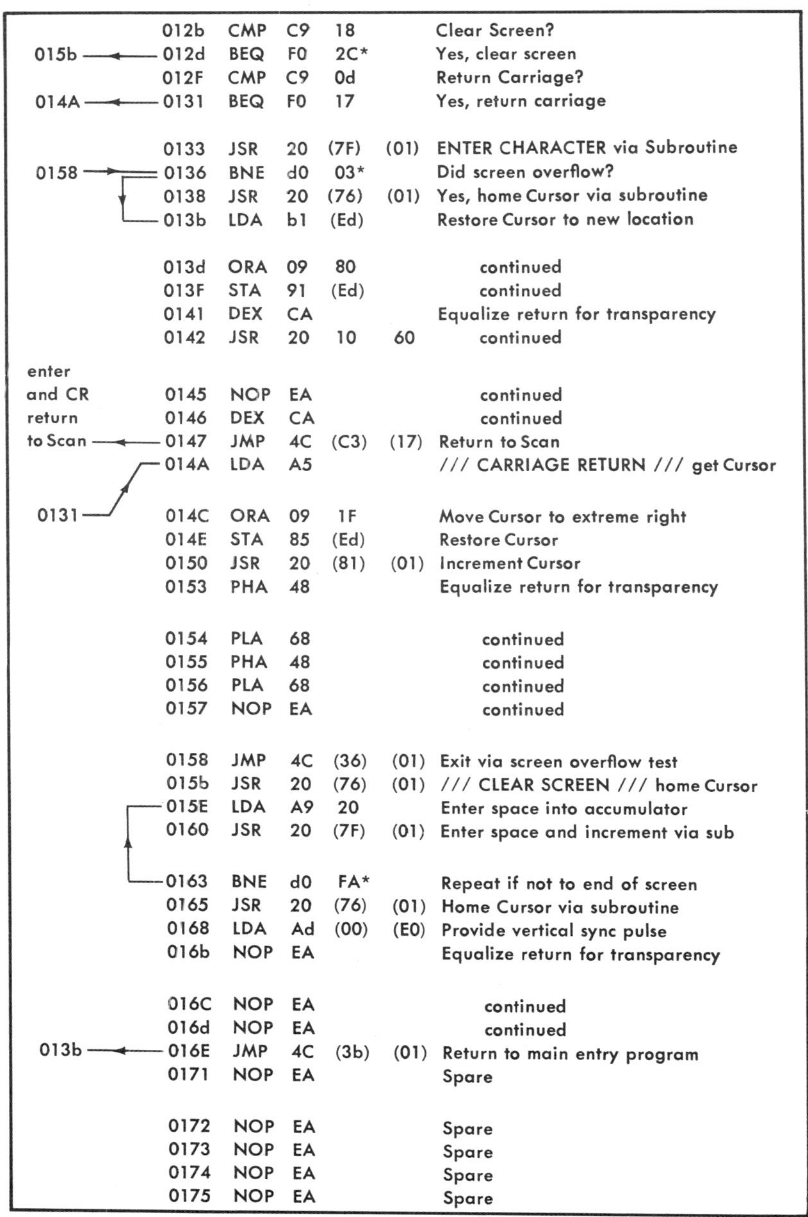

```
                 012b  CMP  C9  18               Clear Screen?
015b  <-------   012d  BEQ  F0  2C*              Yes, clear screen
                 012F  CMP  C9  0d               Return Carriage?
014A  <-------   0131  BEQ  F0  17               Yes, return carriage

                 0133  JSR  20  (7F)   (01)      ENTER CHARACTER via Subroutine
0158  ------->   0136  BNE  d0  03*              Did screen overflow?
                 0138  JSR  20  (76)   (01)      Yes, home Cursor via subroutine
                 013b  LDA  b1  (Ed)             Restore Cursor to new location

                 013d  ORA  09  80                    continued
                 013F  STA  91  (Ed)                  continued
                 0141  DEX  CA                   Equalize return for transparency
                 0142  JSR  20  10     60             continued
enter
and CR           0145  NOP  EA                        continued
return           0146  DEX  CA                        continued
to Scan <-----   0147  JMP  4C  (C3)   (17)      Return to Scan
                 014A  LDA  A5                   /// CARRIAGE RETURN /// get Cursor

0131  ------->   014C  ORA  09  1F               Move Cursor to extreme right
                 014E  STA  85  (Ed)             Restore Cursor
                 0150  JSR  20  (81)   (01)      Increment Cursor
                 0153  PHA  48                   Equalize return for transparency

                 0154  PLA  68                        continued
                 0155  PHA  48                        continued
                 0156  PLA  68                        continued
                 0157  NOP  EA                        continued

                 0158  JMP  4C  (36)   (01)      Exit via screen overflow test
                 015b  JSR  20  (76)   (01)      /// CLEAR SCREEN /// home Cursor
                 015E  LDA  A9  20               Enter space into accumulator
                 0160  JSR  20  (7F)   (01)      Enter space and increment via sub

                 0163  BNE  d0  FA*              Repeat if not to end of screen
                 0165  JSR  20  (76)   (01)      Home Cursor via subroutine
                 0168  LDA  Ad  (00)   (E0)      Provide vertical sync pulse
                 016b  NOP  EA                   Equalize return for transparency

                 016C  NOP  EA                        continued
                 016d  NOP  EA                        continued
013b  <-------   016E  JMP  4C  (3b)   (01)      Return to main entry program
                 0171  NOP  EA                   Spare

                 0172  NOP  EA                   Spare
                 0173  NOP  EA                   Spare
                 0174  NOP  EA                   Spare
                 0175  NOP  EA                   Spare
```

Fig. 5-6 *Continued.* Program for 16-line, 32 character per line,

```
   0176  LDA  A9  00      SUBROUTINE—/// HOME CURSOR ////
   0178  STA  85  (Ed)    Set lower Cursor to 00
   017A  LDA  A9  02      Set upper Cursor to 02
   017C  STA  85  (EE)        continued

   017E  RTS  60          Return
   017F  STA  91  (Ed)    SUB—// ENTER AND INCREMENT //
   0181  INC  E6  (Ed)    Increment lower address
┌─ 0183  BNE  d0  06*     Did page overflow?
│
▼  0185  INC  E6  (EE)    Increment upper address
   0187  LDA  A9  04      Load page above display maximum
   0189  CMP  C5  (EE)    Test for screen overflow
└─ 018b  RTS  60          Return
```

NOTES:

Refer to notes at end of Fig. 2-10.

Cursor Address is stored at 00Ed low and 00EE high.

Available remaining stack length is approximately 100 words.

* Denotes a relative branch that is program length sensitive.

( ) Denotes an absolute address that is program location sensitive.

Continued on next page.

interlaced TVT 6 5/8 Raster Scan with integrated minimum Cursor.

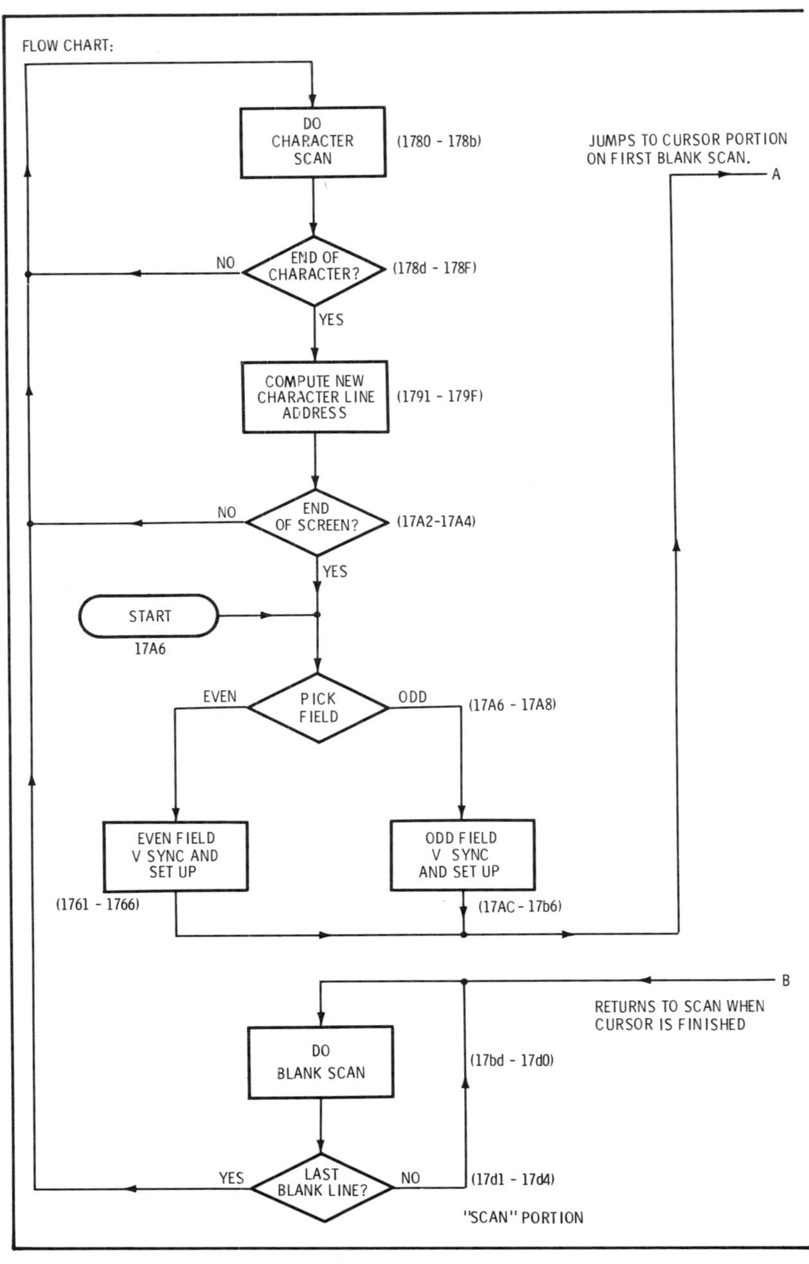

Fig. 5-6 *Continued.* Program for 16-line, 32 character per line,

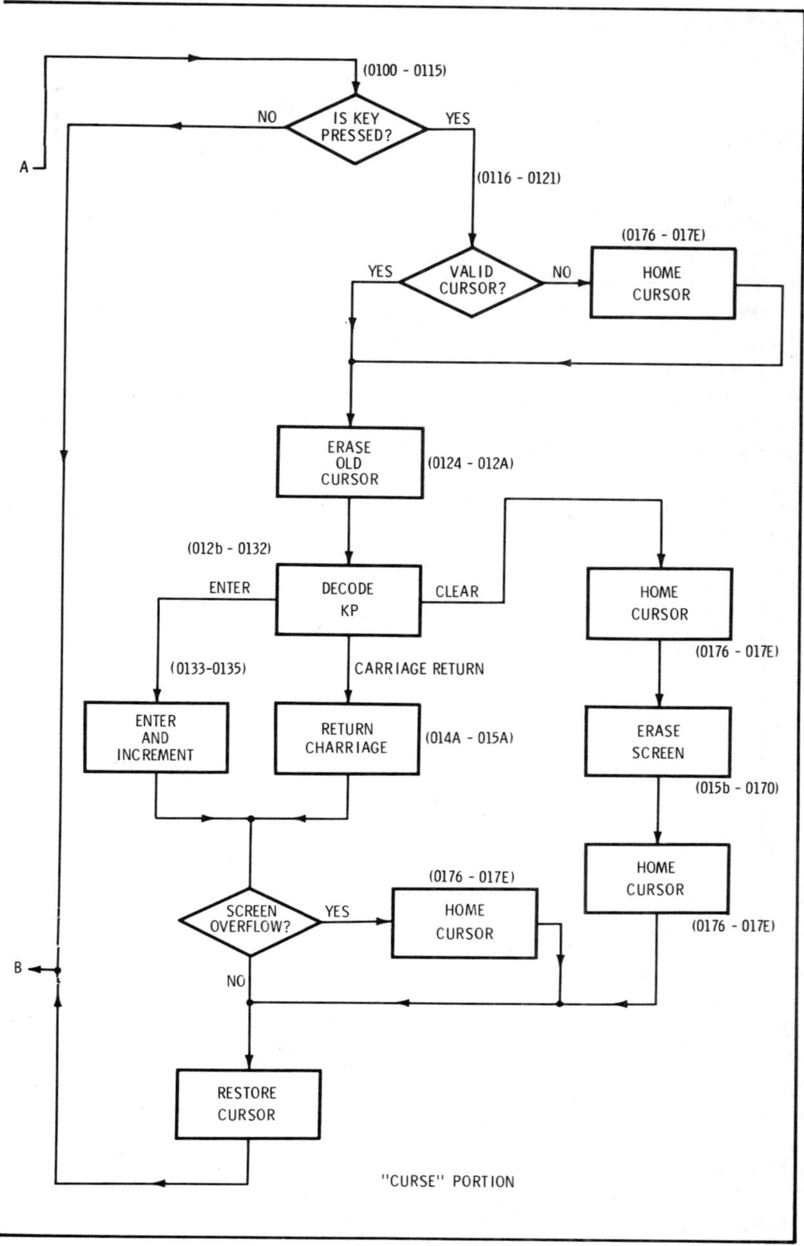

interlaced TVT 6 5/8 Raster Scan with integrated minimum Cursor.

The keypressed commands of enter, carriage return, and clear are done pretty much the same way we did with the Scrolling Cursor program of Fig. 2-20. The only differences are that we add extra equalization time as needed to get everything to take the right amount of time.

"Enter" and "Carriage Return" take slightly more than one horizontal time, so we add equalization to come up to a whole number of Scan lines, and then knock two lines out of the blank Scans to make things come out even. On a "Clear" command, we take an *entire* field to complete clearing since we have to repeat enter a space 512 consecutive times. At the end of this "used" field, we throw in a new *vertical*-sync pulse to hold vertical lock and then go on to the Scan program.

The coding in this program is a little sloppy. You should be able to make it much more efficient. At the same time, we get "perfect" invisible equalization of the display, but you may find a few background glitches that are annoying on a reverse-video (black on white) display. These can be fixed with a little extra work on your part.

Your Turn:

Combine both program halves into a single integrated Scan and Cursor program. Make the coding more efficient and further improve the transparency. Then add coding that will let you transparently Scan a companion ASCII keyboard. Do not use an external keyboard encoder.

As you will see when you use this program, absolutely perfect equalization of all the paths through the program is not often needed. This is particularly true for seldom happening things like extra code that is picked up because of a page overflow, and so on.

Since your Cursor *is* part of the Scan program, the amount of equalization needed will change as you change the number of microseconds of horizontal-Scan time.

Should you want to integrate a more complicated Cursor or other program, consider measuring how long the other activities take with a timer and then correct for it rather than keeping track of each and every possible path through the software.

FILL IN THE SYNC PULSES

Integrated Scan programs are nice for totally transparent Cursors, keyboard scanning, I/O, and similar support tasks. But, if we want to run a display along with a higher-level language such as Extended BASIC, or if we have very involved game motion calculations, integrating the two programs together either will not work at all or else will be "mind blowingly" complex. Something fancier is needed if we are going to get full transparency with heavier programs.

One solution to total transparency is called the *counter method,* otherwise known as *sync fill-in.* We note our usual tvt Scan program is not up to very much during the entire vertical-blanking interval. All the Scan program does during this time is provide horizontal-sync pulses and keep track of the total lines in the field. If we can find some other ways to do these two simple tasks, the entire blanking time can be released for other uses. Obvious "other ways" include a counter or a software timer.

A good approach is to reverse the roles of tvt scanning and the main program from what we have done so far. We let our main program *be* the main program, running all the time, and *interrupted by* the tvt scanning. The main program gets interrupted 60 times a second. During an interrupt, the Scan program provides us with the live portion only of a field. After the live portion of the field is complete, some source of continuing horizontal-sync pulses and

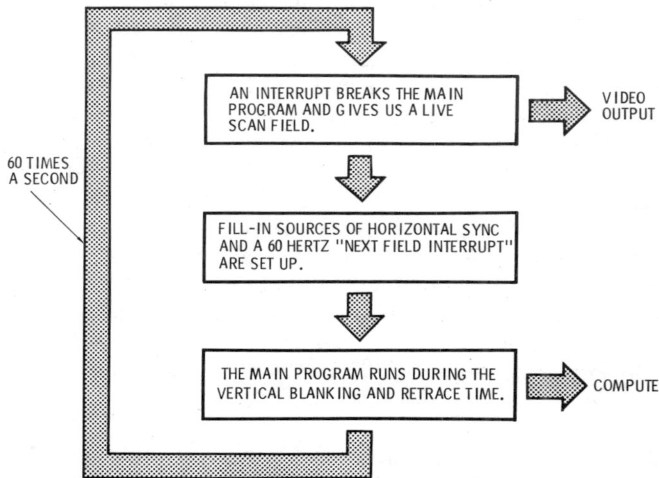

Fig. 5-7. Sync fill-in in method gives total transparency by letting main program run during display vertical blanking time.

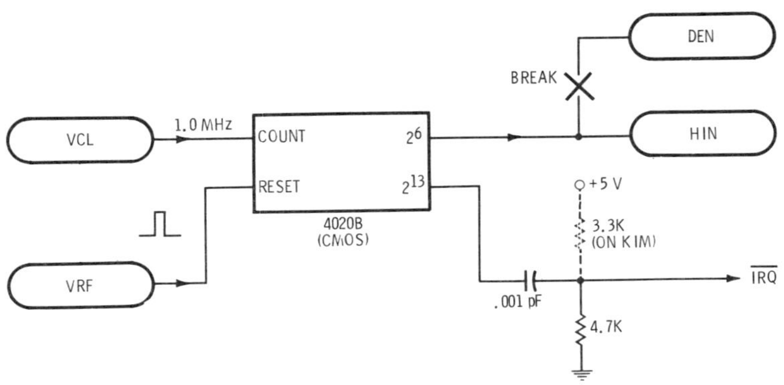

Fig. 5-8. Counter to add to TVT 6 5/8 for transparent sync Fill-In.

start-the-next-field timing is located. The interrupt is then released and the main program continues.

The sync fill-in method is similar to the interrupting of a running program by a front-panel monitor, as is commonly done in many microcomputers. Fig. 5-7 sums up what we have to do for the sync fill-in method to work.

We can add a single, long binary counter to our TVT 6⅝ to pick up fully transparent, sync fill-in operation. Details of the new counter are shown in Fig. 5-8. Our new counter is driven by the 1-MHz system clock. Once every 64 μs, a horizontal-sync pulse is output. Once every 128 horizontal lines *after reset*, an interrupting pulse is output. By resetting the counter at the end of each field with the VRF command, we automatically set up 128 blanking lines during which the main program runs normally.

Details of a 14 × 32 Scan software program that works well with the counter method are shown in Fig. 5-9. Since our counter calls for a 64-μs line, the software is adjusted to provide the same length. Except for one very obscure and sticky detail, the Scan program is very simple and straightforward. We start out by saving all the registers on the stack so the main program can resume normal operation later. Then we do some equalization. Then we initialize the starting addresses and the number of lines to be scanned. We then do the usual character row Scans. After the last line, we do some more equalization, output a vertical-sync pulse and reset our counter, restore the registers and return to the main program.

The obscure and sticky detail was slid over with the word "equalization" in the above description. If we could be sure that an interrupt always took place the instant we told it to, there would be no problem at all. But, that is not the way interrupts work. Interrupts

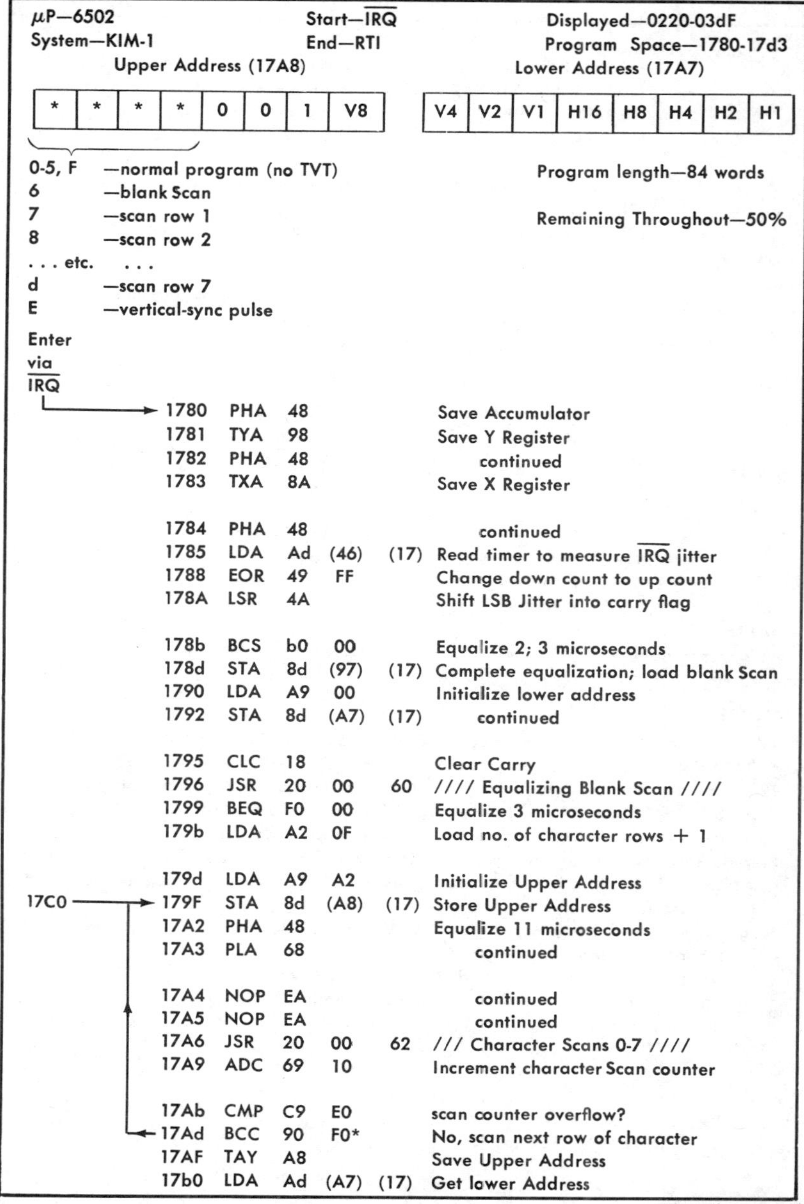

μP—6502
System—KIM-1
Start—$\overline{IRQ}$
End—RTI
Displayed—0220-03dF
Program Space—1780-17d3

Upper Address (17A8)

*	*	*	*	0	0	1	V8

Lower Address (17A7)

V4	V2	V1	H16	H8	H4	H2	H1

0-5, F —normal program (no TVT)
6 —blank Scan
7 —scan row 1
8 —scan row 2
. . . etc. . . .
d —scan row 7
E —vertical-sync pulse

Program length—84 words

Remaining Throughout—50%

Enter via $\overline{IRQ}$

```
→ 1780  PHA  48                 Save Accumulator
  1781  TYA  98                 Save Y Register
  1782  PHA  48                     continued
  1783  TXA  8A                 Save X Register

  1784  PHA  48                     continued
  1785  LDA  Ad  (46)   (17)    Read timer to measure IRQ jitter
  1788  EOR  49  FF             Change down count to up count
  178A  LSR  4A                 Shift LSB Jitter into carry flag

  178b  BCS  b0  00             Equalize 2; 3 microseconds
  178d  STA  8d  (97)   (17)    Complete equalization; load blank Scan
  1790  LDA  A9  00             Initialize lower address
  1792  STA  8d  (A7)   (17)        continued

  1795  CLC  18                 Clear Carry
  1796  JSR  20  00     60      //// Equalizing Blank Scan ////
  1799  BEQ  F0  00             Equalize 3 microseconds
  179b  LDA  A2  0F             Load no. of character rows + 1

  179d  LDA  A9  A2             Initialize Upper Address
17C0 → 179F  STA  8d  (A8)   (17)    Store Upper Address
  17A2  PHA  48                 Equalize 11 microseconds
  17A3  PLA  68                     continued

  17A4  NOP  EA                     continued
  17A5  NOP  EA                     continued
  17A6  JSR  20  00     62      /// Character Scans 0-7 ////
  17A9  ADC  69  10             Increment character Scan counter

  17Ab  CMP  C9  E0             scan counter overflow?
← 17Ad  BCC  90  F0*            No, scan next row of character
  17AF  TAY  A8                 Save Upper Address
  17b0  LDA  Ad  (A7)   (17)    Get lower Address
```

Continued on next page.

Fig. 5-9. Transparent 14 × 32 Scan program for TVT 6 5/8 using counter method for sync fill-in.

```
              17b3  ADC  69  1F          Increment Lower Address; save carry
              17b5  STA  8d  (A7) (17)   Restore Lower Address
              17b8  TYA  98              Get upper address
              17b9  ADC  69  90          Add Carry; reset upper address

              17bb  JSR  20  00   62     ///// Blank Scan 8 /////
              17bE  CLC  18              Clear Carry
              17bF  DEX  CA              End of screen?
179F <------- 17C0  BNE  d0  dd*         No, do a new character row

              17C2  LDA  A9  38          Set Timer to measure IRQ jitter
              17C4  STA  8d  (44) (17)       continued
              17C7  LDA  Ad  00   E0     Output Vertical-Sync Pulse
              17CA  PLA  68              Restore X Register

              17Cb  TAX  AA                  continued
              17CC  PLA  68              Restore Y Register
              17Cd  TAY  A8                  continued
              17CE  PLA  68              Restore Accumulator

              17CF  PHA  48              Equalize 14 microseconds
              17d0  PLA  68                  continued
              17d1  PHA  48                  continued
              17d2  PLA  68                  continued
exit to
main <------- 17d3  RTI  40              Return from Interrupt
program
```

NOTES:

TVT 6 5/8 must be connected and both the Scan (658-KS8) and Decode (658-KD64) PROMs must be in circuit for program to run. TVT 6 5/8 must be in "32" position.

This program runs by interrupting another one. For a default main program use 0100 EA EA 4C 00 01. Counter of Fig. 5-8 must also be in use.

Load 20 in locations 0200-021F to blank top equalization lines.

Step 17A6 goes to where the upper address stored in 17A8 and the lower address stored in 17A7 tells it to. Values in these slots continuously change throughout the program.

Program horizontal frequency 15,625 Hz; Vertical 59.98 Hz; 64 μs per line, 260.5 lines total, no interlace. 50-second hum bar.

( ) Denotes an absolute address that is program location sensitive.

* Denotes a relative branch that is program length sensitive.

Fig. 5-9. Transparent 14 × 32 Scan

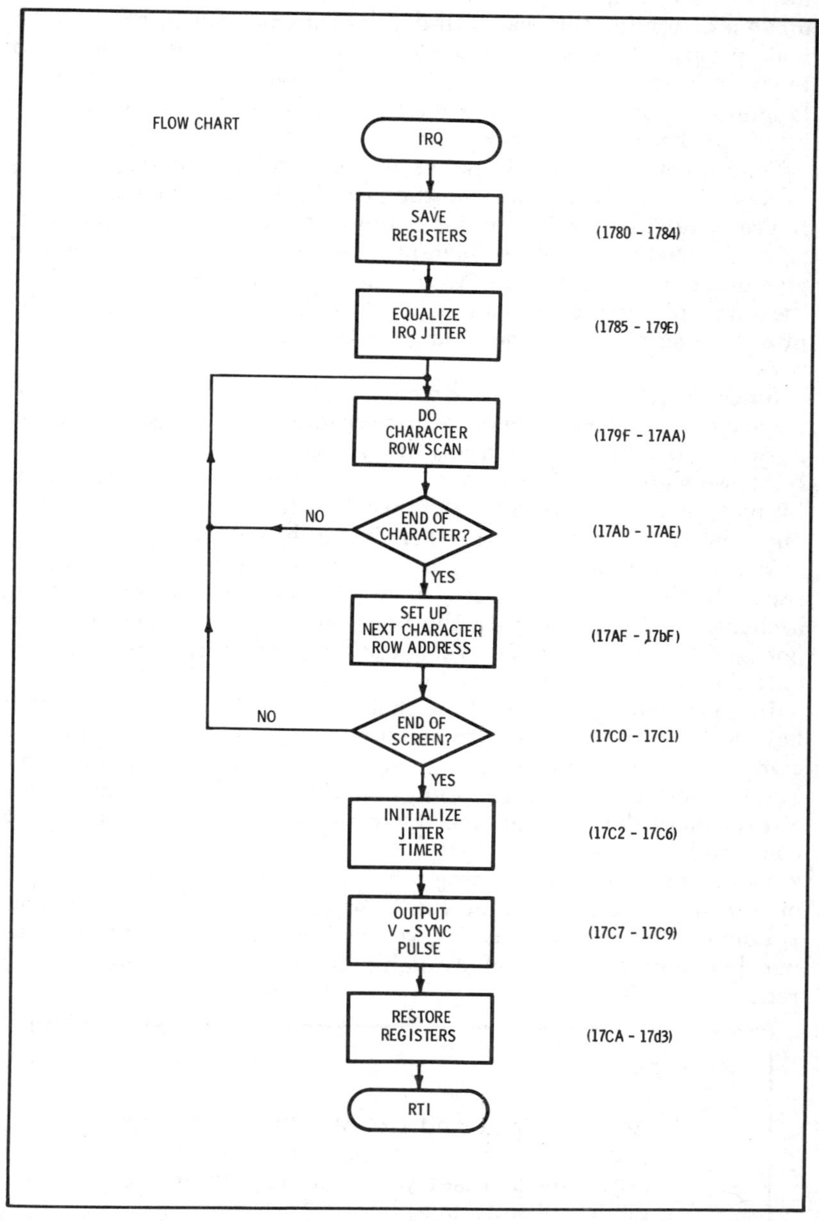

program for TVT 6 5/8 using counter method for sync fill-in.

always wait until the present instruction is carried out. Depending on your computer, this wait will depend on whatever instruction the main program happens to be working on, and can range from one to ten or more microseconds. If we ignore this, we will get several overlapping displays, randomly jittering around as the actual time-to-interrupt dictates.

So, a precise method of finding out how long an interrupt took is needed. In the KIM-1, we use the "free" software timer buried in the cassette circuitry. We initialize this timer at the end of one field. *After* the next interrupt, we measure the time in the timer. This will give us a number that relates to the number of microseconds of jitter the interrupting process caused us. We then go on to correct the jitter by lengthening or shortening the time before the first character row.

Since the KIM timer is a down counter, this is the opposite of what we need. So, we complement the time reading at 1788, converting the answer into a string of numbers that increases with increasing time. Next, we shift everything right one bit, putting the least significant bit into the carry. A BCS 00 will take 2 μs for a zero and 3 μs for a one. This takes part of the problem and solves it for us.

We then take the remaining value and use it as a lower address to start a blank Scan. Each unit change in blank Scan address gives us a change of 2 μs, nicely dividing out the "times two multiply" we got with the right shift. The value initially loaded into the timer not only does our equalization, but also gives us a position control.

In your own system, anything that works can be used. What you have to do is find some way to measure how long after you told your computer to interrupt that it actually did so, and then use this number to shorten or lengthen things so that the first character row always takes the same number of microseconds after the interrupt command is given.

Our counter and its Scan program is an extremely elegant example of how simple it is to pick up full transparency in a tvt system. This is admittedly a special case as we are limited to Scans with 64 μs per line and 128 lines of available transparency during vertical retrace.

> *Your Turn:*
>
> Add Interlace and Double Stuffing to this Scan program. Note that you will need a new way to reset your counter when you go to full interlace.

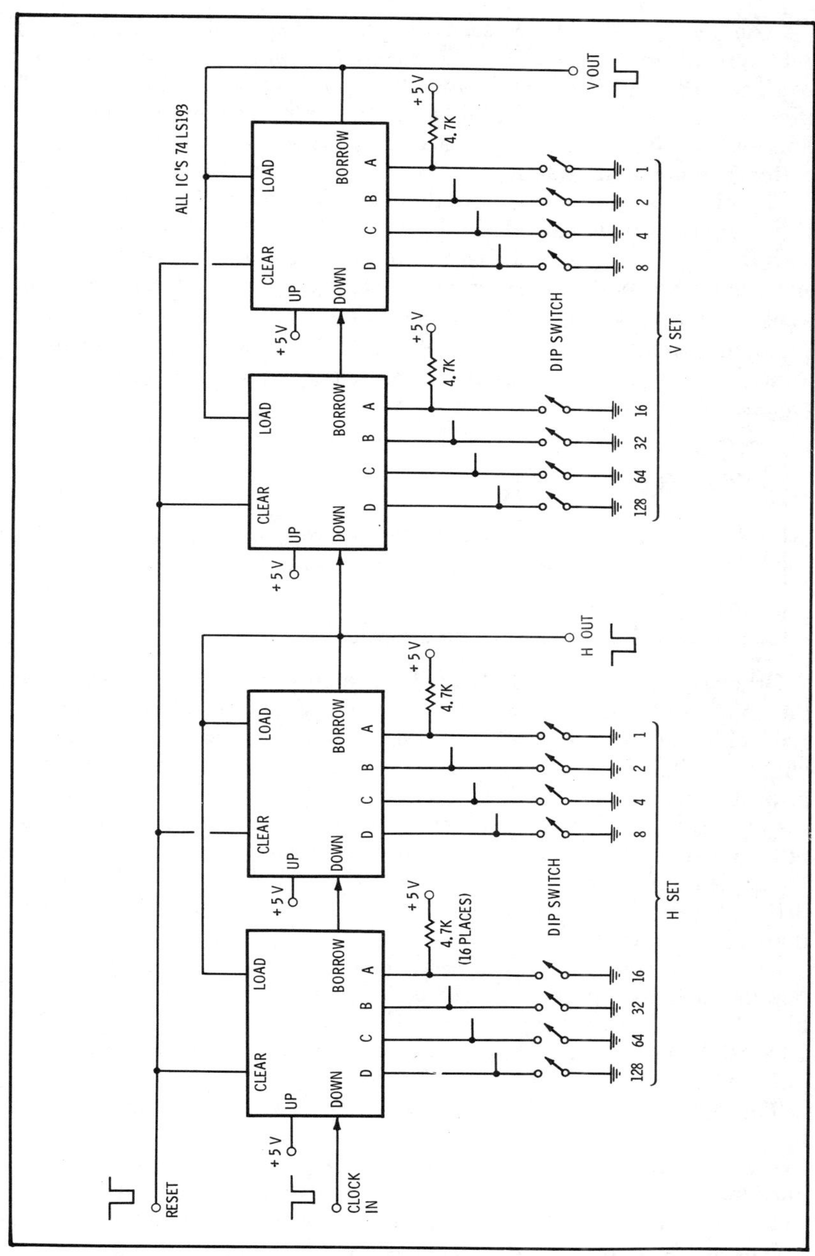

Fig. 5-10. Programmable counter useful for tvt development.

In general, you have lots of options toward total transparency with sync fill-in. By going to a divide-by-N counter for the H source, you can get any line length you want. A traditional, but not cost effective, divide-by-H and divide-by-V counter appears in Fig. 5-10. This will be fine to get you started, but you will want something better in your final system.

The obvious, crying-to-be-used source for the 60-Hz interrupt is, of course, the power line. This also will give you a stationary display with the resulting line lock. To use the power line, a phase measurement must be made to speed up or slow down the microprocessor clock so that lock can be held. Another route is to add or remove-equalizing delay with suitable software; this lets you run at a constant clock frequency. This can be very easy to do, but is very system specific. The details are left up to you.

Your Turn:
Line lock your interlaced, double-stuffed, transparent, counter method Scan program.

Other sources for our 60-Hz field interrupt are the second half of the counter of Fig. 5-10, or one of the new television vertical-counter sync chips such as a *National* LM1880. If we are sneaky, we can eliminate the need for a separate timer to compensate the interrupt jitter. For instance, if the first few stages of your divide-by-H counter are available, these can be directly read to get a measurement of the jitter. Once again, the details are system specific.

The crucial question is "How much throughput does an interrupt-driven cheap video Scan leave us?" The quick answer is "Much more than you would guess."

Chart 5-1 shows the available throughput *remaining* for many popular display formats. Short displays will have an almost negligible effect on throughput. We see that we can get a double-stuffed 12 × 80 display and still have almost two thirds of the usual throughput available for normal computer use.

The throughput is calculated by seeing how many total lines you have, and subtracting three more than the number you need for your live Scan. The result is expressed as a percentage. The extra three lines take care of your sync and setup. If you are careful, these lines can also be used for your companion Cursor and keyboard scanning.

Double stuffing will always help us much on throughput. The most dramatic example is in the 256 × 256 graphics, where the

Chart 5-1. Full Transparency Throughput Versus Display Format

Aphanumerics	Computer Time Remaining
1 × 32 or 1 × 40, double stuffed	97%
1 × 32 or 1 × 40	95%
16 × 32 or 16 × 40, double stuffed	68%
12 × 80, double stuffed	62%
16 × 64, double stuffed	58%
16 × 80, double stuffed	50%
32 × 32 or 32 × 40, double stuffed	38%
16 × 32 or 16 × 40	38%
12 × 80	25%
24 × 80, double stuffed	25%
16 × 64	17%
32 × 64, double stuffed	17%
Graphics	
128 × 128, double stuffed	74%
128 × 128	50%
256 × 256, double stuffed	50%
256 × 256	2%

throughput is 2% for a regular display and 50% for a double-stuffed display. To maximize your throughput, keep your display as short and compact as possible, use double stuffing, and minimize the number of lines between character rows.

One surprise in Chart 5-1 is that 64-character lines are less efficient than 80-character lines when it comes to throughput. For a given number of characters on the screen, the number of lines you are usually willing to eliminate going to 80 characters exceeds the percentage change involved in lengthening each line from 64 to 80 characters, explaining the discrepancy.

USE A SLEDGEHAMMER

Sometimes your display and its Cursor may be so sophisticated or complex that it needs nearly the full attention of your microprocessor. Or other programs in your computer system may need all the throughput they can get. There may be limits on your other programs that prevent *any* interruptions at all. One situation in which this happens is when timer loops, real-time clocks, or other timing activities are an important part of the program. Other times, you might want to run your display remotely from your computer in the traditional terminal fashion.

What can you do to get full transparency in these special cases? The answer is obvious. You throw in your own microprocessor and

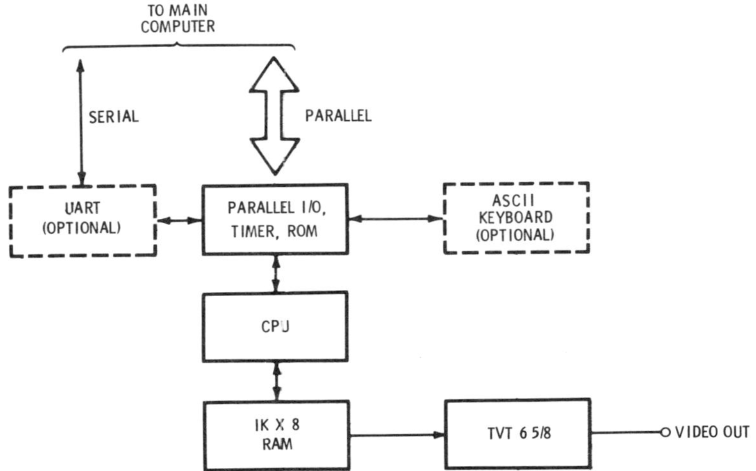

Fig. 5-11. Adding dedicated microprocessor chip is sledgehammer (but still cost-effective) approach to transparent cheap video.

display memory ahead of your TVT 6⅝ and dedicate these new parts to exclusive display and support use.

Fig. 5-11 shows the block diagram of a typical system. We use a CPU that works with a 1K display memory RAM and a 1K or so program ROM ahead of the tvt circuitry. One IC would be needed for the microprocessor; two for the memory (using 4K static chips); one for the upstream tap; one for a parallel interface and PROM program combination; and possibly a UART/bit rate generator chip for a serial interface. A total of six or seven extra ICs would be involved, fewer if we pick one of the new "single chip" μp systems. The same circuit could support a scanning ASCII keyboard, a cassette interface, and so on, along with serial and parallel interfaces to the main computer system.

> *Your Turn:*
>
> Show a stand-alone cheap video terminal system using less than 15 integrated circuits. Have it provide all the features of a traditional deluxe video terminal and then some.

The use of a "whole new computer" may sound like a last resort sledgehammer. And, in fact, it is very rarely needed. But microprocessors and their support chips are rapidly dropping in price. Even with these added chips, the cheap video approach of an upstream tap and a Scan microinstruction dramatically slashes system complexity so much that it often provides the simplest and best route to video display.

NOW WHAT?

You have seen just what cheap video can do for you. Now you should be able to design your own cheap video software and hardware. You can see just how easy it is to let ordinary speed microcomputers do all the timing needed for video display, while still staying within the limited bandwidth of a largely stock tv set. You should be able to use the cheap video tricks-of-the-trade on your own, picking up double stuffing, full interlace, memory repacking, and whatever degree of transparency you need for your use.

What is next? Where do you go from here? Here are several cheap video concepts that need your attention and you can be an important part in helping to find their solution:

* Design an **8080 Adaptor** that goes between the TVT 6⅝ and an 8080 microcomputer system. Use two 74LS174 latches on the high address and the upstream tap lines to get around the 8080's floating address times. Connect your display memory address line A9 to a source of 500 kHz during a Scan to double the apparent memory-access speed to once each microsecond.
* Provide a cheap video system to pick up **Benton Harbor and S-100 bus compatibility.** The best way to do this initially is as a simple tvt add-on to an existing memory card. Patch or otherwise modify your Extended BASIC or other software to work directly into display memory space.
* Can you use a single microprocessor and a pair of 4K static RAMs ahead of your tvt to **do a complete, transparent, stand-alone terminal?** Can you do the entire terminal, including keyboard, with fewer than 15 integrated circuits and costing less than $50 at hobbyist retail?
* Do **long line-length alphanumeric Scans at normal horizontal speeds.** Approaches to this on a 6500 or 6800 would include brute force Scan programs, address line A9 switching (*a la* 8080), or speeding up the CPU, either all the time or else only during a Scan Microinstruction.
* Build a **HEX-ASCII adaptor** that lets you directly display machine op-code. This makes your cheap video system into a super front-panel debugging aide. One workable approach appeared in the October, 1977, *Popular Electronics*. A better route would

be a much smaller card that fits between the tvt and the character-generator module.

* Create an **end-of-line bell ringer** that uses one of those dollar "Japanese Sonalerts" to signal end of line and other entry or Cursor errors.
* Use some refinements on software controlled vertical position to produce a **gentle scrolling cursor** that slowly moves up (crawls) rather than jumps disconcertingly as do almost all present Cursor systems.
* Show **Scan and Cursor coding for a 6800 base system.** What about other systems like COSMAC, the IM6100, and so on?
* Use a LM1889 to build **a modulator that gives you one of four colors** for color displays. Add circuitry as needed to get Channel 3 and 4 rf output as well as full sound capability.

So, where does cheap video go from here? It is all up to you!

APPENDIX **A**

The ASCII Computer Code

Table 1-1. The Standard ASCII Code

BIT NUMBERS															
→ (b7)								0	0	0	0	1	1	1	1
→ (b6)								0	0	1	1	0	0	1	1
→ (b5)								0	1	0	1	0	1	0	1
b_7 ↓	b_6 ↓	b_5 ↓	b_4 ↓	b_3 ↓	b_2 ↓	b_1 ↓	COLUMN → / ROW ↓	0	1	2	3	4	5	6	7
			0	0	0	0	0	NUL	DLE	SP	0	@	P	`	p
			0	0	0	1	1	SOH	DC1	!	1	A	Q	a	q
			0	0	1	0	2	STX	DC2	‖	2	B	R	b	r
			0	0	1	1	3	ETX	DC3	#	3	C	S	c	s
			0	1	0	0	4	EOT	DC4	$	4	D	T	d	t
			0	1	0	1	5	ENQ	NAK	%	5	E	U	e	u
			0	1	1	0	6	ACK	SYN	&	6	F	V	f	v
			0	1	1	1	7	BEL	ETB	'	7	G	W	g	w
			1	0	0	0	8	BS	CAN	(	8	H	X	h	x
			1	0	0	1	9	HT	EM	)	9	I	Y	i	y
			1	0	1	0	A	LF	SUB	*	:	J	Z	j	z
			1	0	1	1	b	VT	ESC	+	;	K	[	k	{
			1	1	0	0	C	FF	FS	,	<	L	\	l	¦
			1	1	0	1	d	CR	GS	—	=	M	]	m	}
			1	1	1	0	E	SO	RS	.	>	N	^	n	~
			1	1	1	1	F	SI	US	/	?	O	—	o	DEL

In the TVT 6 5/8, ASCII bit 8 is reserved as a cursor or an entry flag.

A "1" displays the cursor; A "0" does not.

A "1" prevents entry; A "C" allows entry.

Examples: The numeral "3" is an ASCII Hex 33 or Binary 00110011 ASCII Coding
"6b" is a lower case "k."

APPENDIX **B**

Hex-Octal-Decimal Conversion Chart

UPPER HEX DIGIT	LOWER HEX DIGIT															
	0	**1**	**2**	**3**	**4**	**5**	**6**	**7**	**8**	**9**	**A**	**B**	**C**	**D**	**E**	**F**
0	0 *000*	1 *001*	2 *002*	3 *003*	4 *004*	5 *005*	6 *006*	7 *007*	8 *010*	9 *011*	10 *012*	11 *013*	12 *014*	13 *015*	14 *016*	15 *017*
1	16 *020*	17 *021*	18 *022*	19 *023*	20 *024*	21 *025*	22 *026*	23 *027*	24 *030*	25 *031*	26 *032*	27 *033*	28 *034*	29 *035*	30 *036*	31 *037*
2	32 *040*	33 *041*	34 *042*	35 *043*	36 *044*	37 *045*	38 *046*	39 *047*	40 *050*	41 *051*	42 *052*	43 *053*	44 *054*	45 *055*	46 *056*	47 *057*
3	48 *060*	49 *061*	50 *062*	51 *063*	52 *064*	53 *065*	54 *066*	55 *067*	56 *070*	57 *071*	58 *072*	59 *073*	60 *074*	61 *075*	62 *076*	63 *077*
4	64 *100*	65 *101*	66 *102*	67 *103*	68 *104*	69 *105*	70 *106*	71 *107*	72 *110*	73 *111*	74 *112*	75 *113*	76 *114*	77 *115*	78 *116*	79 *117*
5	80 *120*	81 *121*	82 *122*	83 *123*	84 *124*	85 *125*	86 *126*	87 *127*	88 *130*	89 *131*	90 *132*	91 *133*	92 *134*	93 *135*	94 *136*	95 *137*
6	96 *140*	97 *141*	98 *142*	99 *143*	100 *144*	101 *145*	102 *146*	103 *147*	104 *150*	105 *151*	106 *152*	107 *153*	108 *154*	109 *155*	110 *156*	111 *157*
7	112 *160*	113 *161*	114 *162*	115 *163*	116 *164*	117 *165*	118 *166*	119 *167*	120 *170*	121 *171*	122 *172*	123 *173*	124 *174*	125 *175*	126 *176*	127 *177*
8	128 *200*	129 *201*	130 *202*	131 *203*	132 *204*	133 *205*	134 *206*	135 *207*	136 *210*	137 *211*	138 *212*	139 *213*	140 *214*	141 *215*	142 *216*	143 *217*
9	144 *220*	145 *221*	146 *222*	147 *223*	148 *224*	149 *225*	150 *226*	151 *227*	152 *230*	153 *231*	154 *232*	155 *233*	156 *234*	157 *235*	158 *236*	159 *237*
A	160 *240*	161 *241*	162 *242*	163 *243*	164 *244*	165 *245*	166 *246*	167 *247*	168 *250*	169 *251*	170 *252*	171 *253*	172 *254*	173 *255*	174 *256*	175 *257*
B	176 *260*	177 *261*	178 *262*	179 *263*	180 *264*	181 *265*	182 *266*	183 *267*	184 *270*	185 *271*	186 *272*	187 *273*	188 *274*	189 *275*	190 *276*	191 *277*
C	192 *300*	193 *301*	194 *302*	195 *303*	196 *304*	197 *305*	198 *306*	199 *307*	200 *310*	201 *311*	202 *312*	203 *313*	204 *314*	205 *315*	206 *316*	207 *317*
D	208 *320*	209 *321*	210 *322*	211 *323*	212 *324*	213 *325*	214 *326*	215 *327*	126 *330*	127 *331*	128 *332*	129 *333*	220 *334*	221 *335*	222 *336*	223 *337*
E	224 *340*	225 *341*	226 *342*	227 *343*	228 *344*	229 *345*	230 *346*	231 *347*	232 *350*	233 *351*	234 *352*	235 *353*	236 *354*	236 *355*	238 *356*	239 *357*
F	240 *360*	241 *361*	242 *362*	243 *363*	244 *364*	245 *365*	246 *366*	247 *367*	248 *370*	249 *371*	250 *372*	251 *373*	252 *374*	253 *375*	254 *376*	255 *377*

Octal Values are shown *in italics;* e.g., *377*

Examples:

Hexadecimal 6D is Octal *155* or Decimal 109.

Octal *154* is Decimal 108 or Hexadecimal 6C.

Decimal 195 is Octal *303* or Hexadecimal C3.

APPENDIX C

Pinouts of Selected Integrated Circuits and Other Components

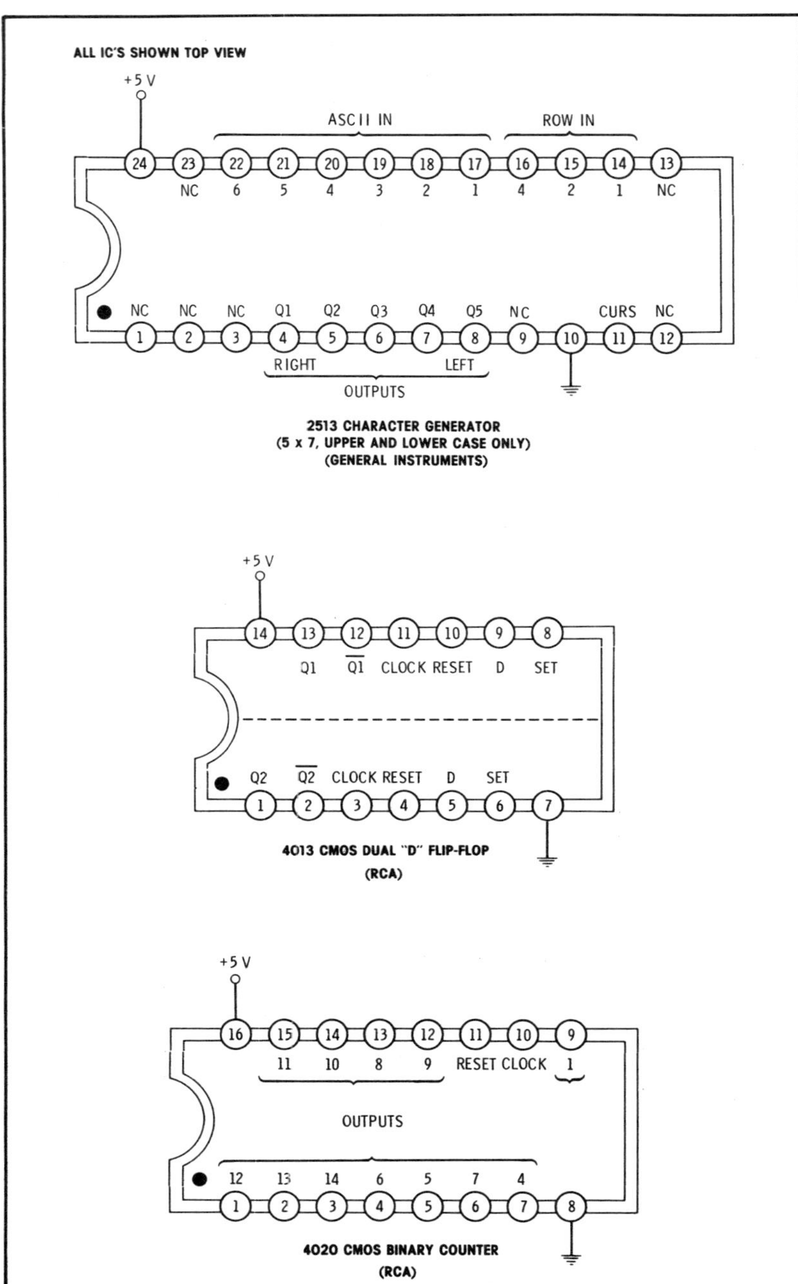
ALL IC'S SHOWN TOP VIEW
+5 V
ASCII IN
ROW IN
24 23 22 21 20 19 18 17 16 15 14 13
NC 6 5 4 3 2 1 4 2 1 NC
NC NC NC Q1 Q2 Q3 Q4 Q5 NC CURS NC
1 2 3 4 5 6 7 8 9 10 11 12
RIGHT LEFT
OUTPUTS
2513 CHARACTER GENERATOR
(5 x 7, UPPER AND LOWER CASE ONLY)
(GENERAL INSTRUMENTS)
+5 V
14 13 12 11 10 9 8
Q1 Q1 CLOCK RESET D SET
Q2 Q2 CLOCK RESET D SET
1 2 3 4 5 6 7
4013 CMOS DUAL "D" FLIP-FLOP
(RCA)
+5 V
16 15 14 13 12 11 10 9
11 10 8 9 RESET CLOCK 1
OUTPUTS
12 13 14 6 5 7 4
1 2 3 4 5 6 7 8
4020 CMOS BINARY COUNTER
(RCA)

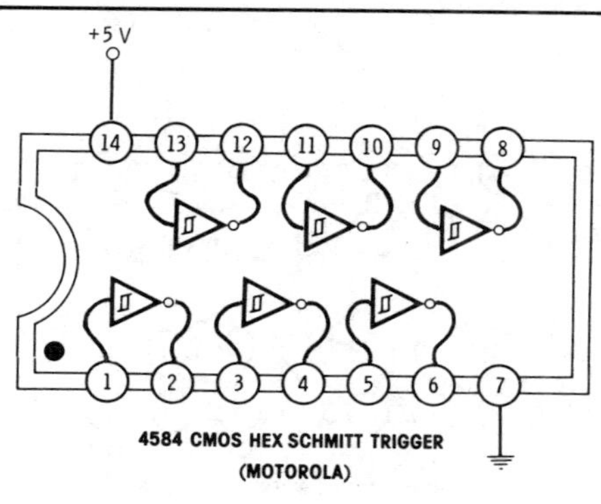

4584 CMOS HEX SCHMITT TRIGGER
(MOTOROLA)

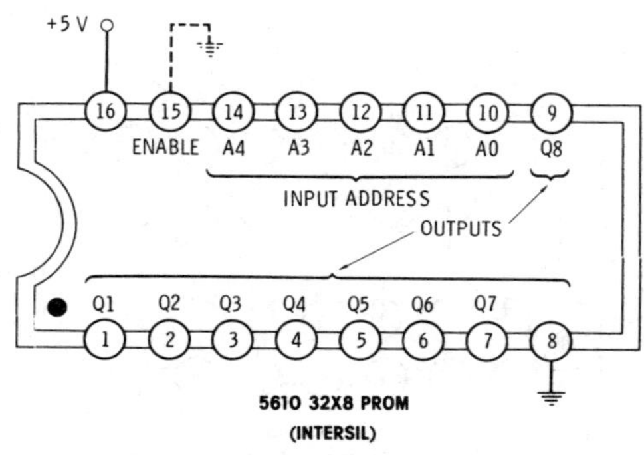

5610 32X8 PROM
(INTERSIL)

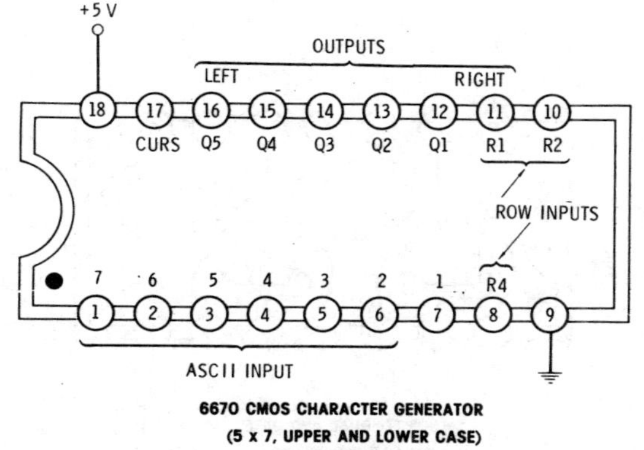

6670 CMOS CHARACTER GENERATOR
(5 x 7, UPPER AND LOWER CASE)
(MOTOROLA)

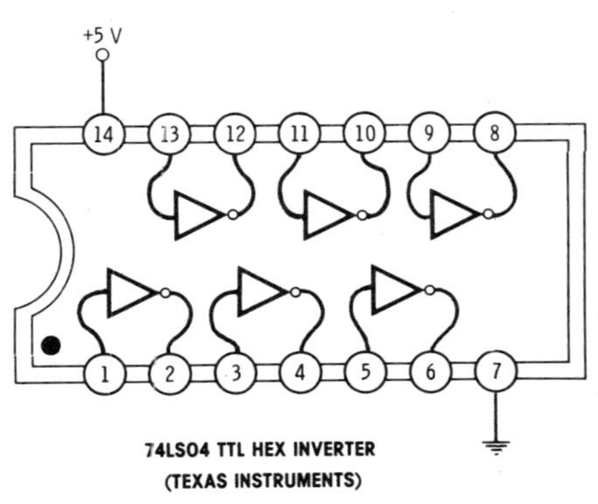

74LS04 TTL HEX INVERTER
(TEXAS INSTRUMENTS)

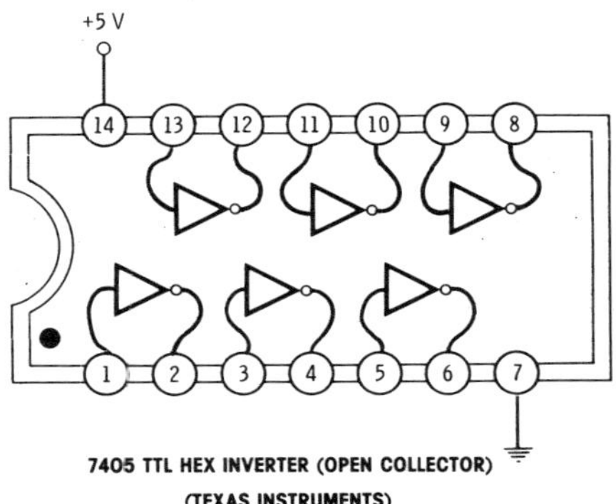

7405 TTL HEX INVERTER (OPEN COLLECTOR)
(TEXAS INSTRUMENTS)

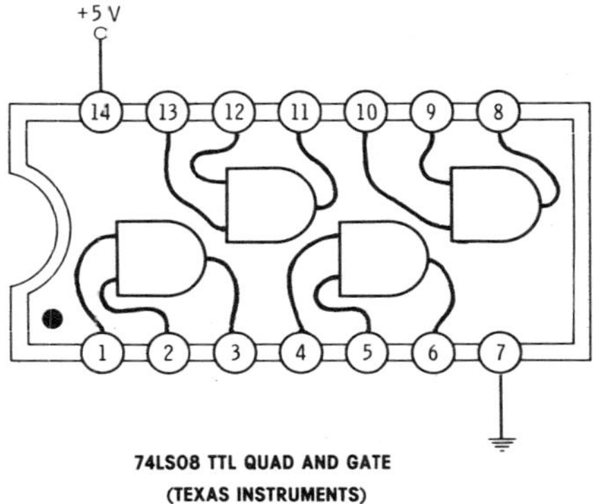

74LS08 TTL QUAD AND GATE
(TEXAS INSTRUMENTS)

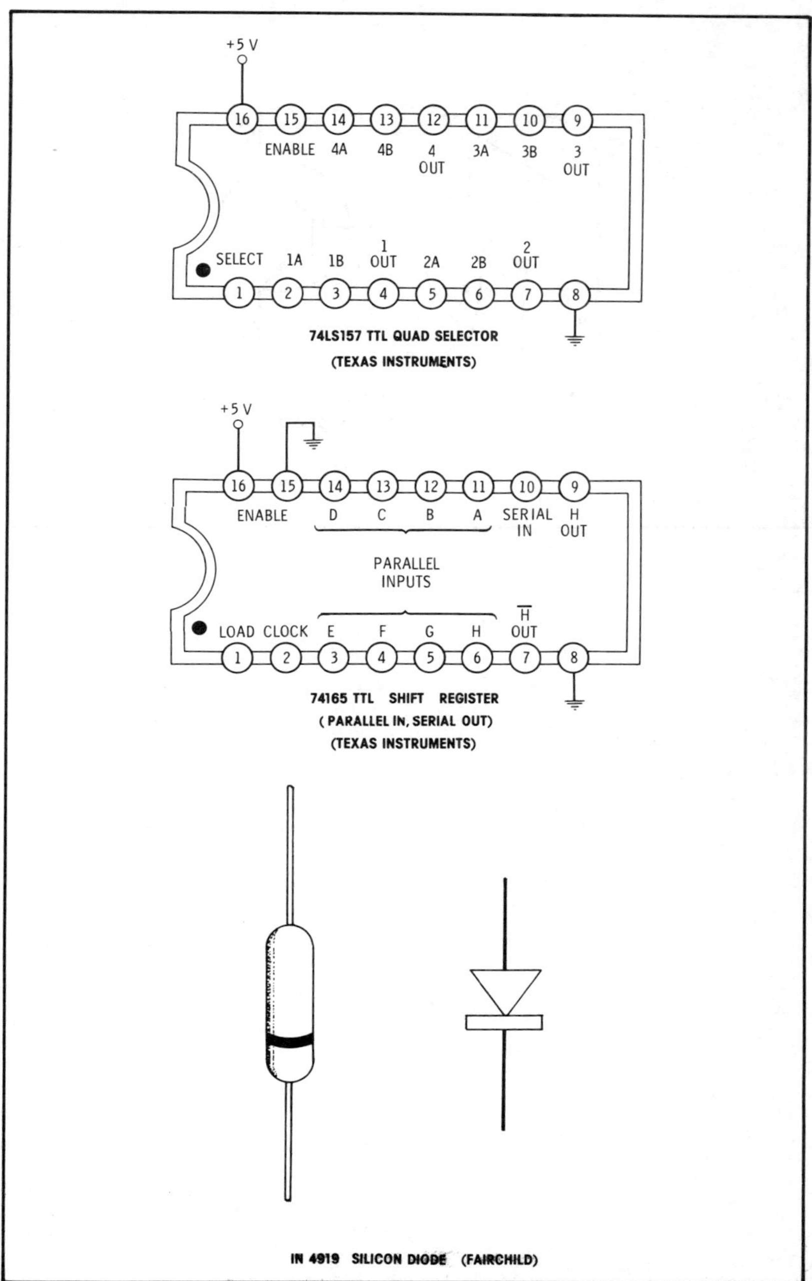

IN 4919 SILICON DIODE (FAIRCHILD)

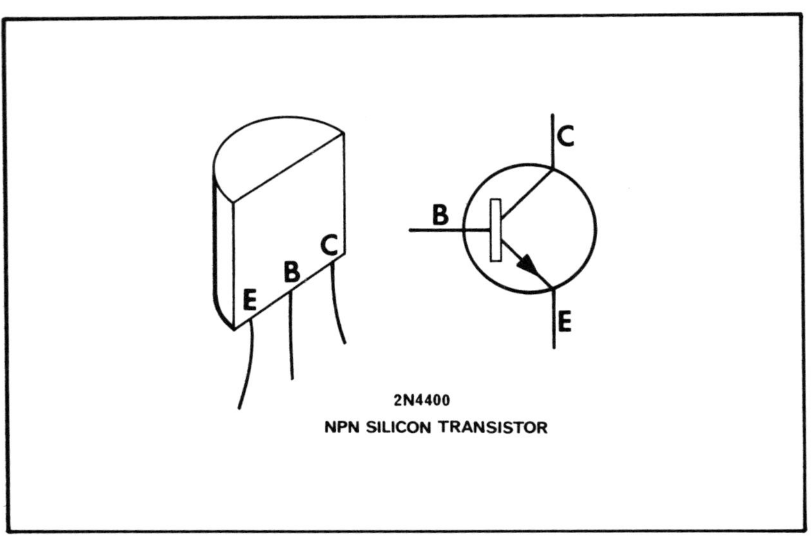
E
B
C
B
C
E
2N4400
NPN SILICON TRANSISTOR

APPENDIX D

Printed-Circuit Patterns

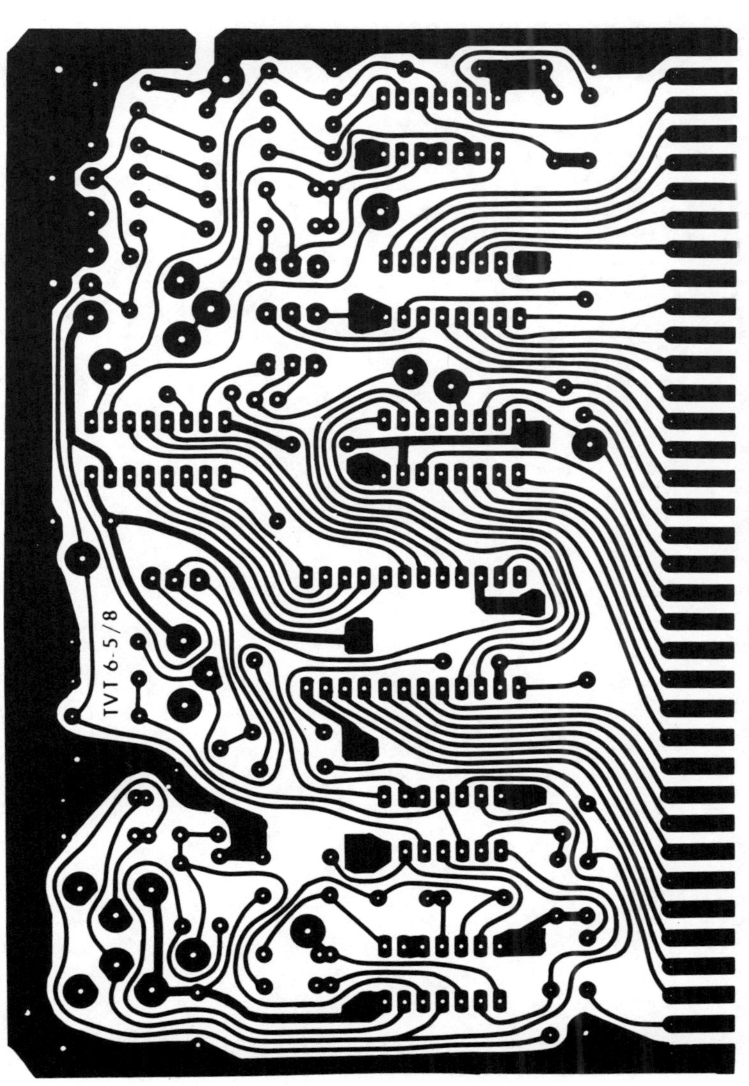

Full size pc board pattern for TVT 6 5/8.

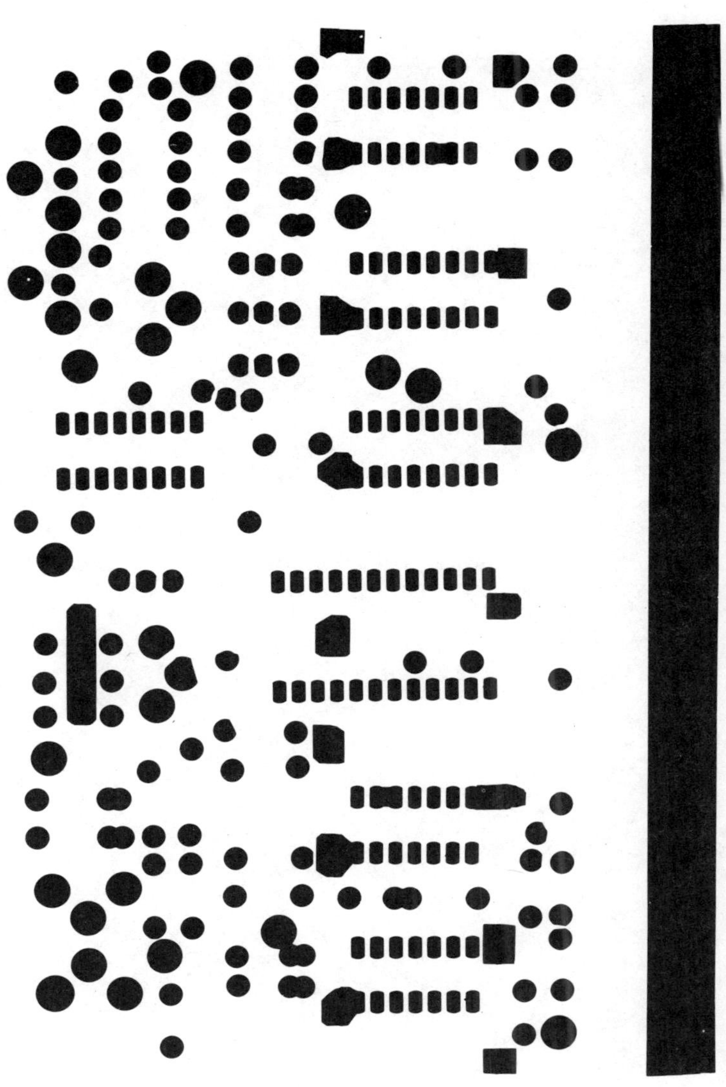

Solder mask for TVT 6 5/8 (full size).

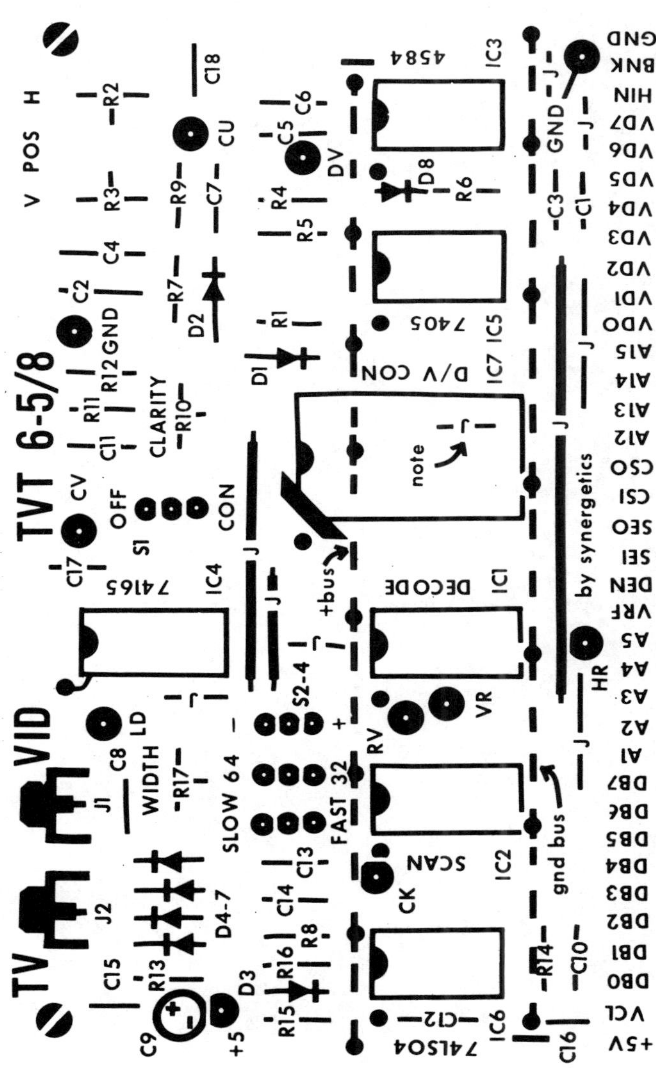

Component locator for TVT 6 5/8.

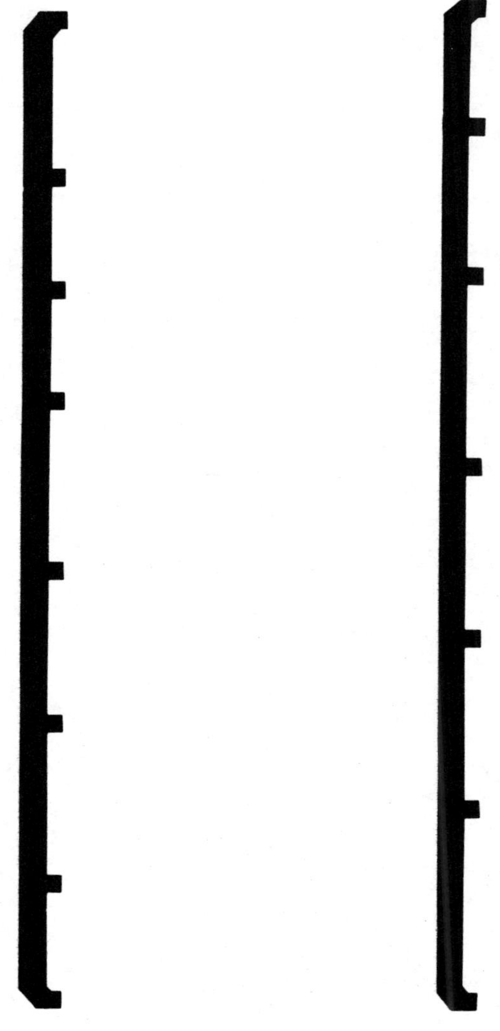

(A) + bus. (B) Ground bus.

Full size bus strip patterns.

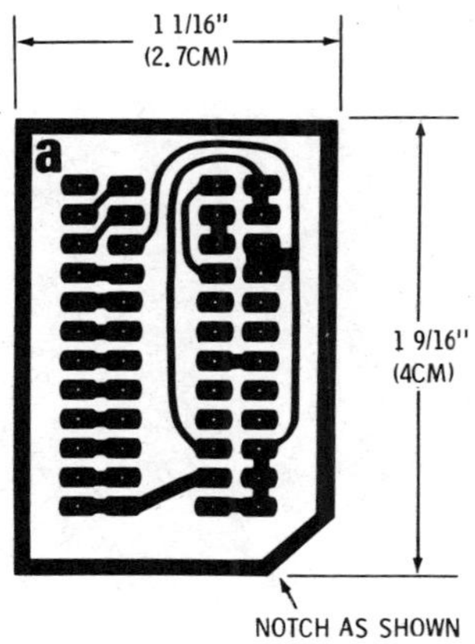

Module A foil pattern.

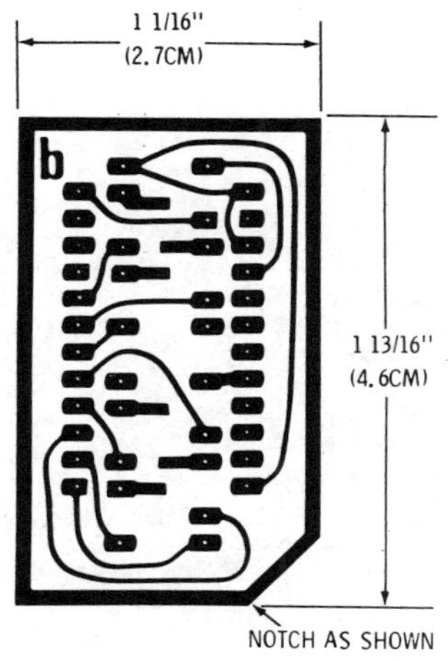

Module B foil pattern.

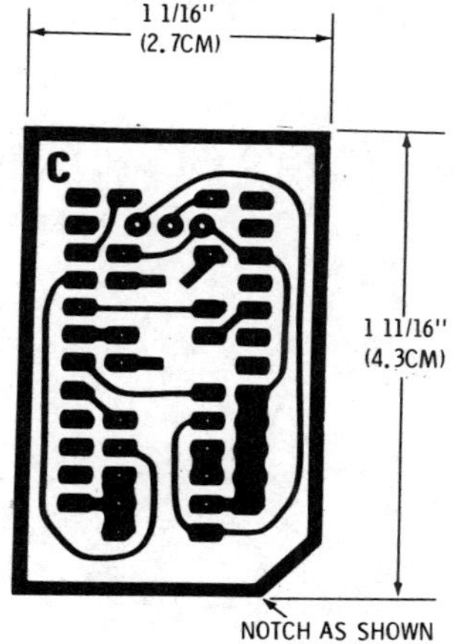

Module C foil pattern.

Index